Jungle-Wallah
to
International Businessman

A Memoir

John G Macnaughtan

For my children,
Alistair, Timothy and Amalie

and my grandchildren,
Tod and Mia

Preface

When I consider how my life's been spent in this amazing world and wide, I acknowledge that I've been buffeted by the slings and arrows of fortune, then raised to the heights by chance and opportunity. Some of the resulting adventures I share with you below.

As I set out from the East it was still the norm to travel by ship and do so via Suez and Gibraltar. My first flights were on Flying Boats. The world has shrunk so fast since 1955 and I am amazed at how well-travelled so many are today. I am also amazed at how little some see. Will this all change after the COVID-19 pandemic time in which I write? Also communication has altered beyond belief, with results not always positive, changing the experience of travel and relationships.

What have I to offer? The trouble is that the older I become the less there is to say and the less I know. It has all been said before and much better than by me. So why write and just add to the world's mountain of print? Original thought is rare; agreement on 'facts' is diminishing; interpretation is everything and that abounds. Truth, integrity, loyalty and understanding – virtues I was taught – are now mere soundbites, and it seems one man's truth is another man's interpretation.

Well, my adopted sister Ninoo (informally adopted by my parents after her family's generous hospitality to us in India) published in December 2019 her book on her own 'life's journey'. This charming work, which she called *The Journey of My Life,* may not reach a large audience, but she's achieved it. Her tale is of being a £3 immigrant into the U.K. Her 'journey' is astonishing and is worth a nod of one's time. I closed the book and thought how engaging her style and how clever to maintain such harmony where no offence was given, despite having to navigate her life as a single Parsi lady who left India for the first time at the age of twenty-four. Having turned down three would-be Indian suitors, she had viewed her prospective life as an unmarried woman in India, where she was loved and cherished, but knew she would become smothered as an individual into being a family Aunty. She took her chance in a country she held in esteem and has made a full and worthwhile life for herself, been an inspiration to others and a valued friend to many. Along the way she has tried to educate her masters and she tells her, often harsh, story with charm and love. She gives me inspiration to proceed.

Ninoo Bhagwagar

Now as I said, Ninoo is a Parsi. She superbly underplays any hint of racism but one little reference to this tribe of Zoroastrian fire worshippers who migrated to the coast of Gujerat over 1,200 years ago, escaping the aggression of the Moslem hordes occupying Persia, is worthy of recall. It was the Parsi who emulated the British when they arrived in India at the time of Clive of India (mid 18th century) and the East India Company. It was they who helped build the great trading post of Bombay and the reason why today that city has so many Parsees therein. In one area they recognised the chance to prove their prowess, and that is in the sport of cricket. Cricket had been espoused as 'the unifying force of a great nation come to civilise the less fortunate world of the oppressed and bring with it the gentlemanly attributes of fair play and sportsmanship'. Not only did the gallant Parsi bring their first Parsi Indian team to the UK, only to get thrashed in the 1880's, they had the pluck to regroup at home and in 1890 they took on the British amateur gentlemen on the 'maidan' in Bombay and beat them. The significance of this was not lost on either side and had consequences every bit as important as the mutiny of 1857. It even spurred on S. S. Bengalee, the man who had presented the match prizes, to write that it was 'the community's greatest hour since the battle of Navahand (in the 17th century) between the Zoroastrians and the Arabs'. Ninoo has that pluck when provoked!

I was brought up to be very aware of my Scottish ancestry. In the hall of every house in which I have ever lived I have hung the framed picture illustrating the long genealogy of the Macnaughtan Clan, all the way back to 1215 – see Appendix One. The clan had five castles in the West of Scotland, hailing as they do, from the Loch Fyne region on the coast. Only Dunderave remains and that was lost to the clan in the 17th century when a member fell in love with a girl of the Campbell Clan and sought to marry her, only to find that on the wedding day when he arrived home that he had been cheated and his 'wife' was the elder sister. He promptly absconded with the younger sister to Ireland and in so doing forfeited Dunderave to the Campbells. Then lands in and around Dunderave were taken after the Battle of Killicrankie in 1689. 'Never trust a Campbell' my Uncle Gordon warned me some 400 years later!

Dunderavè Castle
Loch Fyne

The Macnaughtans were not a warrior clan as their dress tartan attests. The Scots are a proud race, and Scots do not lose their accent. Also it could be argued that until the Bevan Act of 1945 reformed the English education system, Scotland enjoyed a higher level of education. Scotland too boasts of a classless society (not really true, but certainly different from the Sassenachs down South) and with its brand of Presbyterianism brings a strict moral code and work ethic. Still today I take my kilt with me when I travel, not for any 'show off' reasons but purely because it is so practical when invited to events, be they weddings or funerals, when I am not sure what to wear. A kilt always looks 'dressed'. We read out the Rabbie Burns poems, as good Scots do, especially on the 25th January and try to emulate the accent needed so to do. The records that Dad played while relaxing in a bath after work would be of the Harry Lauder type – 'Roaming in the gloaming', 'I love a lassie' et al., and I know the words of his songs. I still play my Dad's 78' record collection on his valve driven record player!

The Scots were a force in Burma, not so much in the Government but in the trading sphere of the famous 'Steel Bros' of Glasgow (trading in rice, teak and oil), the Bombay Burmah Company who developed the teak business, started by the Wallace family in the 19th century and the Irrawaddy Flotilla Company, the largest inland water business in the history of the world from 1865. On returning to the UK our family were active in the various Scottish Associations that still prevail in the bigger UK cities and we would go to Scotland each and every holiday to different golfing hotels accompanied by Dad's mum 'granny Mac' and to catch up with my cousins.

'Where are you from' is a much-asked question these days in the U.K. I hear that it is often taken as an offence by those 'of colour' (a peculiar and unnecessary expression) who can answer 'from Brixton' or such, and with an unspoken 'and I've as much right as you to be here'. What is really being asked is, 'You clearly don't come originally from here, so who are you and where were your roots?' I do not know how to answer such a question, and so usually reply with one of my current addresses because I am so apparently plainly British, as my colour and accent attest. But I love being asked because I can honestly tailor my reply to the circumstances, having been born in the Far East and brought up in Burma, lived in six African countries then three years in Australia and I have been kicked out of more countries than the proverbial Jew. It's like Ninoo being told what wonderful English she speaks; what other language should she speak? She's a daughter of the world's proudest Empire and has taken the trouble to value education.

I too am from that place.

Out of Burma

Why was I born in Calcutta; to be a forever Bengali Babu? Why was it that I spent my very early years on a tea plantation in India, to become, in my father's words a 'Jungle-Wallah'? A long story, so let me begin.

Between the two world wars, both sides of my family had settled in Burma where my grandad, Captain Godfrey ran the docks on the Rangoon River as a Harbour Master and my Dad, John Meiklejohn Macnaughtan, worked with the Irrawaddy Flotilla Company (I.F.C). Grandad Godfrey first arrived in Burma in 1926 and brought out his family in 1934 when Mum left school aged fourteen. Mum and Dad met in Rangoon and they married in May 1941.

To be stationed in Burma in 1939 was considered a lucky option. It was referred to as 'this Idyll; this safest of places'. The biggest fear was perhaps from within. The Brits knew that the indigenous Burmese resented them, but their greater loathing was reserved for the Chinese who monopolised their trade, and for the thousands of Indians imported by the Brits to build the railways. The Burmese, in turn, were hated by the tribes peoples, notably the Karens, Chins, Kachins, whom they had persecuted and still do today. When Brigadier Aung San took his 'Burmese army' of 'freedom fighters' to Japan in 1940, it was not taken too seriously. After all the country is surrounded on three sides by mountain ranges and they are covered by thick jungle. Of the four great rivers, the Irrawaddy, together with its tributary, the Chindwin, was well controlled by the British and the Salween and the Sittang in the West is considered unnavigable. There were no railways and the roads scarce. As a result, any defence of Burma was the responsibility of a Commander in Chief in Singapore. Indeed, Japan was only considered a threat from early December in 1941 when they bombed Pearl Harbour.

Deeper thought, and certainly hindsight, makes the need to prepare for an invasion eminently clear. Japan had few natural resources and Burma was rich in oil. Also, in its struggle with China, by holding Burma the Japanese would cut the land route by which China could be supplied – along the famous Burma Road. All of this seemed fanciful in Rangoon or even in the Maymo Hill Station where British troops were stationed. No doubt Christmas celebrations could proceed in 1941. The surprise Christmas present from Japan was duly delivered on the very day of the 25th of December 1941 when the Japanese Zeros bombed the harbour in Rangoon.

Who would have thought that the ensuing war in Burma would become the largest land campaign fought by the British on land during the Second World War? (This is well described in Louis Allen's book in 1984 *Burma, The Longest War, 1941 - 45*). Yet still today those British combatants and the escapades of the 14th Army are barely known. Those troops dubbed themselves 'the forgotten army', and the term was later adopted by historians. Rt Hon The Viscount Slim wrote, 'The 14th Army, the largest Allied army of WWII was built of many races and religions'. The speed with which the Japanese moved surprised everybody. The biggest shock of all was the fall of Singapore on 15th February 1942, but before then, at the end of 1941, the Southern tip of Burma at Victoria Point was occupied. British families throughout Burma made haste to leave with Rangoon being occupied by the Japanese in March 1942. Thailand had remained neutral, allowing the Japanese army a speedy, unexpected and unchecked land route into South-East Asia.

There are many published records of the British and Indian exodus from Burma. Indeed, the Indian population was less worried by the Japanese arrival than that of the Burmese themselves as they were only too aware of the Burman's negative attitude towards them. The hardship that followed is always an individual tale. Joy is quickly spoken.

Both sides of my family were to lose everything to the Japanese – all of their possessions and in the case of Mum and Dad, losing all of their wedding gifts as well. Not to mention their health. Grandad Godfrey managed to secure a place on one of the last troop ships leaving from Rangoon to Calcutta for my gran and their young son, Ralph. Mum's ‘passage to India’ was a little faster as the Irrawaddy Flotilla Company had the franchise for Imperial Airways in Burma, and the company found a place for her on one of their Short Sunderland Flying boats and flew to Calcutta.

Grandad himself waited till the Japanese were almost entering into North of Rangoon before he commandeered a flat-bottomed River Boat, boarded up the sides and took the last of the women and children who had refused to leave until the last minute. With 100 Indian crew, a huge number of wives and children aboard, including Lady June Hobson, all got out and after a week at sea went into shore at Akyab, which the Brits still held at that time in 1942. The boat was commandeered by the Army but only after Grandad had secured in return the safe passage for all his passengers and Indian crew to Calcutta. This short paragraph does no justice to the brave and harrowing journey he made with an untrained crew.

Dad’s Long March

John Morton, the Manager of the Irrawaddy Flotilla Company, wrote regular reports. These include memorable phrases like: ‘There are over two hundred of our fleet sunk at Mandalay. Imagine how I felt drilling holes into their bottoms with a Bren gun’. His final entry on the 4th May 1941 read ‘This morning we re-assembled at 4 a.m. having worked all night sinking ships and paying wages. We go to bed for one hour before our trek to Manipur’. Ahead of the Japanese invasion, Dad and the rest of the Company's remaining employees, led by John Morton, went upriver to destroy all their beloved Clyde-built paddle steamers to prevent them falling into enemy hands.

This episode is well-documented, revealing and many faceted, involving great hardship and bravery. While it is worthy of repetition this is not the place. The story is long and gruelling and reads like a *Boys Own* magazine adventure, but it was for real. When Dad finally arrived at the Chindwin River he found most of the British army trying to escape across this mighty river. It was at Kalewa, in North-West Burma, that Dad was decorated for his part in getting the last of the British troops across the Chindwin to escape into India. He himself was

The Scuttling of the Irrawaddy Flotilla Company Fleet
An Act of Denial to the Japanese Invader
From Irrawaddy Flotilla *by Alister McCrae and Alan Prentice, 1978*

one of the last to leave and made his way on foot eventually into Calcutta. Like all those who walked out of Burma and across the mountains of Assam and East Bengal he was lucky to survive. Sickness, starvation and exhaustion saw hundreds consumed by the forest, never to be heard of or their fate recorded. Barely recognisable and riddled with dysentery, Dad met up with Mum again, in Calcutta. He had covered over 1,400 miles since last seeing his wife nearly a year earlier in Rangoon – like walking from London to Morocco, but through much jungle.

When Mum arrived safely in Calcutta (January 1942) she managed to obtain a job working for British Intelligence. When Dad arrived, in mid-September 1942, he joined the Burma Navy (consisting of four Corvettes but their number fast-growing from 1942; see Government Publication *Burma's Navy* in which Dad is much featured) vowing he wouldn't walk another step after his cross-country adventure. Incidentally when Dad did arrive in Calcutta my Mum promptly showed him some of the War Office plans for the reoccupation of Burma saying to Dad that 'surely this can't be right'. When Dad saw that the plans involved going through now firmly occupied areas he hit the roof saying that whoever had recommended such a route was ignorant of the situation. Mum was able to query this and get the plans changed. Wingate's Chindit operation using guerrilla tactics was the only way to fight the Japanese and hold them down until a greater force could be deployed, which Britain couldn't entertain, considering the war in the Far East to be secondary to that in Europe. Charles Orde Wingate created the Chindits and was an exponent of unconventional military thinking. He was later killed in an air crash in India in 1944. The final battles of Kohima and Imphal in 1945, preceded by the incredible battle of the Admin Box in the Arakan, which was the one that really broke the tough spirit of the Japanese, were certainly the turning points of the war in the East and maybe rank amongst the most significant battles of Second World War.

When Dad reported for duty on arrival in Calcutta the doctor declared him unfit and too ill for service. (Indeed I still have his naval uniform. Dad was a well-built man but his uniform beautifully fitted my 13 year-old son, so emaciated was the poor man after his tough journey). In particular he needed to clear his dysentery, and the doctor in Calcutta advised that, as the 'new' Pasteur Institution had established themselves in the healthy hill station in the Nilgrili Hills in the South, he should go there and to Coonoor in particular to be cured and to convalesce. This happy advice led to Mum and Dad being housed by the Bhagwagar family on the Adar Tea Estate – in Peshotan Hall – where they stayed for over three months until Dad was declared fit to return to Calcutta where he then 'rejoined' the Burma Navy, and Mum resumed her 'Intelligence' office job.

It must have been some eight months after my parents returned from Coonoor that I was born in Calcutta in August 1943. It was quickly decided that Calcutta was no place for a new-born child from a near penniless, homeless British family. Happily, Mum and Dad had the very solution and some 12 months after leaving Mum arrived back with me to Coonoor to stay at the Bhagwagars, where we remained for the duration on the War and while Dad was at sea. I was brought up as a member of this happy Indian family as a fourth child. I was much mothered I am told.

I have no direct memory of Coonor or Peshotan Hall where my Mum took me by train from Calcutta. However, the Bhagwagar family, who took us in, have remained faithful friends and even family, so close have we since become. I am reminded of these days by Ninoo and by the many photos Mum took to share with Dad who was of course away, serving in the Navy. (Much, much later I and eldest son Alistair, at different times, were to stay with Ninoo's mum, by then living in Bangalore, and also to visit Ninoo's elder sister, Nergez, where she lives with her ex-IAF husband Roy). We then returned to Rangoon in 1946.

Briefly Back to Burma

From India back to Rangoon provided a few early memories starting with my third birthday held on the tennis court of 'Belmont' one of the Irrawaddy Flotilla Company houses, into which my parents and I moved in 1946. I remember donkey rides organised by my parents, but above all my birthday cake in the shape of a shoe (the one old Mother Hubbard lived in). That was an awakening moment for me, and probably for my parents and their friends setting out to make a life after devastation – for Burma was devastated: first by the 'Brits' hastily destroying anything of military value as they retreated, and then by the 'Japs' who seemed to have no regard for their surroundings, and to whom war was an excuse for their savage cruelty. I attended the local Convent kindergarten.

Mum told me of the relief they felt on returning to Burma, which was shared by all those who had left some five years earlier. The atmosphere was palpable, old friendships were quickly remade, but it wasn't the same. Following the country's devastation, hot-head politicians, led by Brigadier Aung San, (a brave and clever man who was assassinated by one of his own Cabinet ministers thinking him too liberal and inclusive of the minor tribes) were determined to replace colonial government with indecent speed and little rigorous thought, by their own, apparent, undeniable right. Little thought seemed to be given to the Karens and the many loyal hill tribes, amongst whom were also the Chins, Kachins and Shans and an ungovernable territory was passed

Mum, Dad and Me in 1946

on to bright, but not yet wise and worldly, young Burmese. Those who could predict the consequences were ignored, and anyway Britain was bankrupt and couldn't afford to fund the restoration of the colonies. Granting Independence to ungovernable territories was easier than addressing the problems that made them ungovernable in the first place, other than by an 'alien' force.

The 'what ifs' of history need writing. I have a letter written to my Dad in Christmas 1962, the year that military government officially took over in Burma and the country effectively cut itself off from the rest of the world, from U Saw Herbert, one of his employees. Written in Burmese script on the left and translated on the right he asks, 'Thakin John, enough is enough; when is the Government coming back?' It is interesting that after Independence there were many references made for the 'return of the Government'.

We were not long for Burma after Independence was granted in January 1948. My Dad though was asked to stay on while the I.F.C. was nationalised, the remaining paddle steamers sequestered and a couple of new ones ordered from Denny Brothers on the Clyde. Trade along the Irrawaddy was the commercial lifeline of Burma, and this company was still the largest inland waterway transporter in the world.

Scotland

The Henderson Line ship which took us back to Scotland. The S.S. Prome had been taken over by the Admiralty in 1940 and was fitted out as a Mine Depot Ship. It was badly bombed but returned to service after the war and was operating between the UK and Burma into the 1960s

Mum and I sailed for Scotland, where Dad's Mum (Granny Mac) had recently lost her husband (my Grandad, Joseph Macnaughtan, a lawyer) and lived with her widowed sister Tan Tan, and her eldest son, Uncle Gordon, in Devon Lodge in Helensburgh. This was also my father's family home so it was good for Mum and me to feel close to him in his absence so far away. Then along with my new-found cousins, Gordon, Dougal and Ann, the children of Uncle Duncan, off I went to the local school, 'The Hermitage'. Life was strange in Helensburgh, the stone house was cold, and the one open fire was dominated by Granny Mac with Tan Tan treated very strangely. Mum seemed to be resented, but, being a warm, humorous and lively soul, she brought in laughter and harmony where none had existed. For Mum to see how Granny Mac treated her maid, Mary, let alone sister Tan Tan, was hard, Presbyterian and solemn.

London

The contrast a year later, when we went to live in Grandad Godfrey's little terraced house at 3 Overdale Road, West Ealing, was enormous. Upstairs Gran and Grandad occupied the front double room, Mum the back room. I had to share a bed in the small spare bedroom with Mum's youngest brother, the autumn fruit of the family, Uncle Ralph. Our days there were busy and fun. Grandad went to work at his newly set up café on the North Circular Road at 5.20 every morning, and didn't return till after 6.30 at night at which time dinner was served for us all. Ralph was about to join the R.A.F. and I went to the local school. Mum and Gran kept the house and looked after the chickens in the back yard, which kept us supplied with eggs plus the occasional Sunday roast. The whole place was run along military lines which was necessary if order and cleanliness were to be maintained. The front room was the 'Sunday Room' and, though rarely used even on a Sunday, it had to be kept spotless 'in case of visitors'. It also had the family piano upon which my Gran, Mum and Uncle Ralph played.

Otherwise we had only the living room-cum-dining room, behind which was the little kitchen. There was no central heating and only a gas stove with a gas boiler sitting above the bath in the small communal bathroom. The only toilet was outside at the bottom of the garden. But that house was a happy one. Laughter and love pervaded its very bricks. London's dark humour put life into perspective. Grandad Godfrey, being a qualified naval Captain, had been offered a ship to skipper by the British War office in Delhi, when he returned from Burma via Akyab and Calcutta, but refused – he had fought at Gallipoli

Gran and Grandad (Captain) Godfrey

in 1915 and told the authorities that he saw 'what a mess they'd made of running a war last time and he was going to fight this one his way'. He did. What a colourful character and one who deserves a biography of his own. He was trained on steam and sail ships having run away to sea to join up at the age of 12, but giving his age as two years older. He certainly had the most colourful of lives and his seafaring tales filled my childhood with tales of foreign parts and the most romantic and dramatic of experiences. His was a fairy tale, but tough, life. I was to learn many life skills from his hard-won survival experiences.

Outings to visit Great-grandmother and Great-grandad Sayers were always an adventure. They were lively Victorians, and delight of delight, had a horse and cart from which Grandad Sayers had started his fish business, and where, in the subsequent Ealing shop, Mum had worked as cashier until the age of fourteen alongside all the members of the Sayers family. Humour, laughter and warmth filled this typically London fraternity. I still have the announcement of the closure of the fish shop in the 1960's and I am still sad to read it for it describes what a real institution it was for over 65 years. At the time I remember thinking I belonged to something locally important, especially when I sat in the fish shop and was shown off to loyal customers by my uncles. Great-grandad Sayers could play the banjo by ear, and I would sing the Burmese and Kareni songs my nanny had taught me and he would soon strum out their tune.

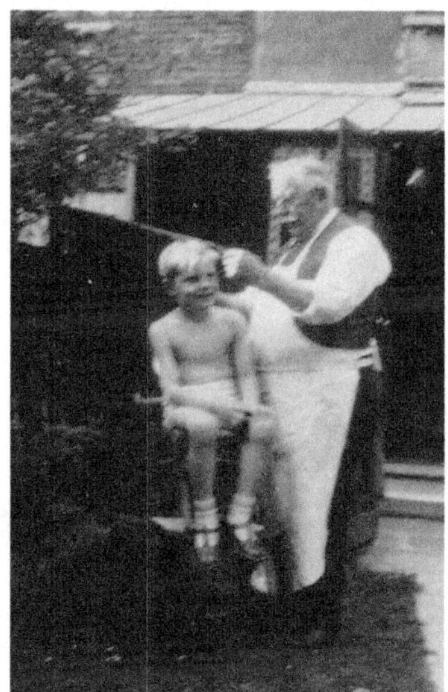

Great Grandad Sayers cutting my hair in his back yard in Ealing

The Family Reunites

When Dad arrived back in the U.K. in 1950, I didn't recognise him. I was six years old and he seemed to be an intruder in the already overcrowded terraced house in Ealing. To have a sixth person resident and now sharing Mum's little back room seemed wrong and I resented it. I was no longer the little jungle-wallah that he lovingly remembered – or so I thought until I grew up.

Dad was offered a job back in Glasgow with his old company Hendersons, but neither Glasgow nor the job was very enticing in 1950. By some chance three colleagues – and fellow Scots – from the Irrawaddy Flotilla Company, who had also just returned from Rangoon, were offered a job by a consortium of Kentish farmers, who, like my Grandad, had kept chickens during the war and now needed to make a living from it. So Stonegate Farmers was born and run by my uncles – Stuart MacDonald, Alan Prentice – and Dad. Uncle Stuart had been the first back from Burma and he worked in the Head Office in Tunbridge Wells. Dad ran the branch in Wye, and Uncle Alan the branch in Heathfield, all in Kent and East Sussex.

The four IFC boys back in the UK, from left to right, my dad, John Macnaughtan, Stuart MacDonald, Alister McCrae and Alan Prentice. Alister stayed on with Henderson's in Glasgow until his retirement and was the author of several books on Burma of which Irrawaddy Flotilla *was one, co-authored with Alan Prentice*

These three tough, highly educated, Presbyterian Scots, each with an enormous work ethic, built up this company. They were paid very little to do so by their consortium of farmers but this was during post war days of rationing. Mum and Dad started life in Wye, Kent, living in the 'Kings Head' pub – 'no place for a child' declared Dad who promptly went to see his bank manager and sent me off to the best boarding, prep school in Great Chart, near Ashford – 'Friars School'.

This was my preparation for later scholastic life at the fee-paying Public School, Sutton Valence School near Maidstone, Kent. There my first two terms included 'fagging' for a House Prefect. This taught me how to iron shirts, press trousers, and clean shoes – including the insteps – clean out the fireplace every morning in the study, lay and light an open fire, not to mention the weekly chore of 'Duraglitting' the brass buckles on my fag-master's C.C.F. (Combined Cadet Force) battle dress uniform once a week.

While we boys had to write a letter home once a week, the letter I always looked forward to receiving was from my Grandad Godfrey. It was never a long letter but it was always well received like the one that read 'Dear John, please find enclosed 10/-, because I can't. Love Grandad'. When he heard that I had to do not just my own ironing but that of my fag master too, he quickly wrote to me that the way to turn a chore into a pleasure is by beating the system and getting the result in a fast efficient way. i.e., 'When ironing a shirt, you do first the collar, then the breast, damn and blast all the rest'. For the trousers simply, 'put them under your mattress and next day you'll find them pressed'. He had many such short cuts for coping with the chores of life.

Fagging and caning were part of life, C.C.F. a must; 'societies' and after-hours hobbies hugely encouraged. From 7.15 a.m. till 10.00 p.m. the day was filled with 'stuff'. For my last two years I was a House then School Prefect, and it was helpful for the boys' well-being that through my various fags I and the other Prefects could keep in touch with how new boys were settling in and quietly have a word with matron if necessary, or, at the other extreme, keep an eye on any bullying. This system must have been effective in the days of Empire, but still applies today where leadership is vital, and it often appears that to be a good master you need first to have been a good servant. This must be a difficult concept to get your head around today when so much of schooling is curriculum based and so competitive. The days of the 'fag' and 'cane' are gone and most agree that the world's a better place for it. Maybe, but I'm not sure that we have replaced it with anything better. I look at how we punish and see over-crowded jails with inmates doomed to reoffend, but with corporate corruption going on unchecked or largely covered up, especially when it is international and of a size to embarrass or depress world markets, I doubt the punishment fits the crime any better today than in yesteryear. It's not that we've become too soft, that may be, but that we delude ourselves to thinking we have become 'better'.

I caned miscreants for the most minor offences, like talking after 'lights out', and punished them with tougher chores, like picking the stones out of the new rugby pitches at 'Upper' for real misdemeanours with a plethora of punishments in between, usually involving cleaning or running around the block several times. Giving boys 'lines' or sending them to 'detention' was up to the Masters to deliver and administer. Major offences like bullying or stealing were passed on to the Housemaster to deal with.

My school cane; shocking all with its notches. Each one represents a victim

We had visitors from all walks of life to supplement our daily routines and time passed too quickly. My Indian 'family' came over to see me, and how proud I was to see them and show them around. My school years, boarding from age six till 18, were happy ones. As Head Boy and going up to London to address the Clothworkers' Company was a huge experience and a great privilege.

As I've often recounted to my family, my happy school days seemed little to do with academia. School days, lessons and prep were to be suffered; I gave up doing Latin and Greek – the first after nine years and the latter after three – knowing little Latin and less Greek. But I was in all the top teams for my age in Cricket, Rugby and Hockey, and was the School's High Jumping Champion. The only trouble came when my parents were summoned to Sutton Valence School when I was 16 to learn that I had only passed one mock 'O' level – English Language. To move on to the Sixth Form required at least six passes out of the nine subjects I was taking. I remember my father giving Roger Douglas, my Housemaster, a roasting for my performance; holding him and not me responsible. Easter 1959 was the first holiday throughout which I worked. I scraped through seven 'O' levels and then two and a half years later had to re-take French, which I had failed, as I needed a language to get into university. Representing the school in the Debating Society, gaining my colours in the major sports and ending up as Head of House, then Head of School were the climax of very happy days. Not to mention obtaining the 'A' levels necessary to be accepted into 'Little Balliol by the Sea' – Sussex University.

University was a contrast. I never thought of my life as a privileged one. Others do and have. My Dad worked six days a week and we went to Church on the Sunday. He toiled at his allotment at weekends, and the odd evening, to provide enough food for the three of us; his salary was consumed by repaying the Bank for the loan on my school fees, and when that was repaid it was transferred to repaying a mortgage on a house. Our needs were modest and born out of years of rationing. We had also known the good life overseas, of having servants, including a cook, a chauffeur and a nanny for me. Our holidays were prescribed by Dad's two weeks, taken in visiting the Scottish relatives and particularly having Granny Mac staying with us. C.C.F. camps during the summer holidays; picking hops (smelly) or apples gave me modest pin money during the summer months, but particularly working with Norman Huckell, the Pro at Neville Golf Club in Tunbridge Wells, with my handicap down to 11 by the age of 14 – it's never been in sight of that since.

Sussex University, 1962 - 1965

'Tucked away in a wooded valley of the South Downs lies one of Britain's supreme contemporary status symbols. To have a child at the University of Sussex is beyond question the most absolutely OK thing in Britain now. To have a former pupil at Sussex is a matter of boasting for headmasters and headmistresses around the country. Only in 1961 did the first fifty brand-new students enter the muddy building-site of Sir Basil Spence's leviathan: a place among them now has become almost as much sought after as a Fellowship of All Souls. Which is absurd, but which is also symptomatic of something very deep-seated – and really very healthy – about present attitudes to the whole business of education here in Britain. We do not know just how we want young people to be educated; but we want something other than what we have got. A new book, from the teachers and creators of Sussex themselves, describes what they feel they are about. It is heartily welcome as precept. It may yet be valuable as a warning too.'

From a review of *The Idea Of A New University*,
edited by David Daiches, 1964

Sussex University was the first of the 'new universities'. I said I was good at sports and indeed was chosen to represent Kent in the Kent Schools Boys Hockey team. Sutton Valence School had one of its old boys, Mike Elmitt as Captain of Oxford University's Hockey team. I'd heard that he was keen for me to go for Oxford for that reason, and St Edmund Hall suggested I apply to read Geography, which was seen as a more social option than my chosen subject of history. I was appalled and hit upon Sussex not for the right reason – its amazing Faculty – but rather because its newness and ideals appealed to me. I was a fish well out of water.

Sussex was a product of the swinging 60's, created by a Faculty with a dream about a new way forward for education; created to break barriers and boundaries. I arrived to find societies like the

Trotsky society, one of the biggest – 'Change for the sake of change' – a world where CND activists beleaguered me to walk the streets. A beautiful girl enticed me into a socialist lecture where I heard words that had never entered my vocabulary or mind, like 'Dialectical Materialism'. I truly felt inferior and unfit. I ceased all sport; I read *Das Kapital* from end to end and didn't understand it, preferring the Webbs and their brand of egalitarianism. History was different too with days of *Religion and the Rise of Capitalism* by R.H.Tawney replacing the battle I had fought between Namier and Butterfield, Christopher Hill and E.P. Thomson. Marxist and social historians replaced the Whig historians Macaulay and Trevelyan. It was baffling, exciting and very frightening. My new friends took some keeping pace with, especially the girls. Cokie's (Caroline's) Dad became a socialist peer, Lord Delacourt-Smith. 'Peppy', another ex-India child became a very dear and lifelong friend, a free thinker and indeed playwright, and Dick Vernon remained true to himself as an independent minded and very bright misfit and free thinker. I was alone and buffeted in a new sea, by the sea.

'Sussex' would say 'that's what education is all about'. Maybe that's right. I remember Thabo Mbeke, from South Africa, arriving at the University. His father, Govan Mbeke, was a leader of the South African Communist Party and later the African National Congress. Thabo was destined to become President. He was late into his first term and had nowhere to stay. We had a spare room and of course he was welcomed. I remember him as a Communist Party Member in the fullest sense, a huge chip on his shoulder, and with a seething sulky attitude. No blame there. It led me to think about apartheid, not from any theoretical view – that was a no brainer – but from a personal view. How could 'a bright cookie' like Thabo ever be denied the best education regardless of colour or creed? But 'communism' and the creed of disruption it engendered – was that any solution? Thabo soon found his own circle, but I remember when the Rivonia trials were taking place in South Africa and Thabo appeared on BBC television and helped to whip up opinion against the Apartheid/Nationalist government – aiming primarily to stop his father, Govan Mbeke with others, from being given a capital sentence. Thabo organised a march from London to Brighton to draw attention to this trial and I was very humbled when he came up to me to say it would mean something to him if I would join the march. I had never marched for any political dogma or CND protest, but I remember saying to Thabo that I would march beside him because it was for his father and because capital punishment was not right, but I told him I still condemned his crime of blowing up Johannesburg station with loss of life.

My Headmaster at Sutton Valence, Ronnie Evers, must have written a glowing reference about me to Sussex. Certainly my interview didn't go well – they discovered I'd never heard of Edward Gibbon's *Rise and Fall of the Roman Empire* let alone read it. But as not just a Public School boy but also Head of School and with some sporting prowess – these things counted for nought – I got in. I majored in History at the EngAm (English and American) School only because I didn't know what else to do. The funny thing was that I soon learnt how well trained and taught I was at 'my' Sutton Valence. I had superb notes from Charles Porter and Roger Douglas particularly at 'O' level.

I was told that I was lucky to have a scholar like Asa Briggs, who was to become Vice-Chancellor or Sussex, and David Daiches as mentors. Indeed, it was only in my third year that I came to appreciate this – depending more on my regular tutors Maurice Hutt and J.P. Corbett. It was not uncommon to have to submit at least three essays a week at Uni, and on top of that show notes and reviews of selected issues at intense tutorials and seminars. In the first term we majored on the theme of *Religion and the Rise of Capitalism*. R.H. Tawney and Max Weber were the main textbooks for this. I soon learnt that though I was far from the brightest pupil I had a technique. First, I 'knew my dates', an approach drummed into me by Roger Douglas's superb 'O' level notes. Then in the Sixth Form I'd learnt to quote from sources and to form opinions after reading the opinions of others. Majoring on Napoleon for a term I'd absorbed an excellent book on the historiography of Napoleon, Peter Geyl's *Napoleon: For and Against*.

So, I had a technique and structure upon which 'history' could build. Dates and chronology are like the scaffolding in building a house. If you have these firmly grounded, you could erect a house quite rapidly; but after erecting the shape of the house you must quickly pull down the scaffolding and let the house talk to you to define its purpose and best use.

To do your essays each week it was necessary to read at least ten books on each subject each week. Again I'd learnt how to read at school. I would collect a number of 'known' books from the library and simply absorb the index and chapters and structure of the book and get a view of its approach, then move to the next book until I had half a dozen views from which I could quote. Then I'd choose a couple of books to represent 'my views' – but would never quote from these chosen books. I'd learnt too that it was historians that were marking history essays and these historians like to see familiar names of known historians referred to, so it was always good to quote a university historian like a Macaulay or Trevelyan on a 'political subject', and then an E.P. Thompson on a social topic or a Christopher Hill for a Marxist view, and then to drop in the names of Butterfield or Namier for some controversy. These names always grabbed the attention of the 'marker' and he would fill in the gaps with his own prejudices concerning their credibility. Meanwhile one would answer questions by quoting and using an 'unknown' source or authority and never admitting or directly employing plagiarism. This technique has helped me through life. If you are opening at least thirty books a week while maybe reading only half a dozen it's surprising what names and even ideas stick. As a result, despite my fundamentally non-academic mentality, I have found a love for history which has enriched and lasted throughout my life. It gives meaning to life which I revise and rethink ceaselessly and I thank academia for this gift.

In my first week at Sussex I would always call my dons/professors 'Sir', thereby setting myself apart from other students and unknowingly winning their opprobrium by giving away my 'posh' background. I found that three or four of the girls – at Sussex strictly 50/50 of each gender were selected in 1962 – were much more even-minded, and I was lucky to have the likes of Peppy Barlow, Caroline Smith and Jackie Russell as good chums. We were all very conscious of the Sussex experiment. The idea of a new university was never absent in our outlook. We were conscious that we were different, but we had no experience of other institutions of learning, so we didn't know different from what. Thus, it was the 'Faculty' that were the real revolutionaries rather than the students, but in a way 'We' were their vehicle. So, we became quickly politicised at Sussex and campaigning against nuclear bombs or against apartheid or just against the Establishment was expected behaviour. (I called it the 'Jay twins factor' as both they and Margaret Brooke were at Sussex but in a year after mine and Sussex was sometimes referred to at the time as the 'Uni for politicians' daughters'). These political overtones were difficult for me. For example, the aggression with which the Kemp Town seat was targeted to become the first labour seat in Sussex, the County, was a new and disagreeable experience to me but a source of great pride to my fellow students. I had been taught to appreciate what I'd been given and to be thankful for it, and to show contempt for or disgust at authority was both rude and disrespectful. But if a beautiful girl like Cokie, who came from a left-wing family and persuasion, wanted me to be different, it was not difficult to oblige. Such was the earnestness of those days, and they were earnest rather than happy for me.

I had the good fortune to make a small circle of friends and indeed in our third year we all opted to live in the on-site Halls of Residences at the University where we at least had no excuse not to concentrate on work. It was a contrast to the previous year, in the Hove

Sussex University's unique architecture was designed by Basil Spence

flat, where David Sheers, Keith Dunnell and myself led a hectic social life. Keith's dad had a garage just outside Maidstone and his love of cars was soon translated into his purchase of a TR1. The original ‘passion wagon’ with a bench seat on the front and all controls on the right-hand side of the steering column and outside ‘dickie seats’ opening out in the rear. I opted for a 1931 Aston Martin complete with Wilson gearbox but not with much else except the same ‘dickie seat’ arrangement. This cost me all of £15.00 and you can see why. It consumed water and oil as well as petrol, but both cars created a stir on our trips to Brands Hatch where Keith was ‘well-in’. Both cars always performed spectacularly at the ‘uphill sprints’ at Brands Hatch, especially when Cokie or Peppy sat on the dickie seats to hold down the rear axle giving the car more traction as well as diverting the attention of competitors.

At the end of my first year at Sussex I had the fortune to go on a cruise along the Dardanelles with Mum and Dad. On board were Clement Attlee and Asa Briggs, who later was to become the Vice Chancellor of Sussex University. The former spent the whole cruise with his nose in a book(s), but Asa seemed delighted to see me, and my most enduring memory was that while cruising along the strip of water up to Istanbul I was the only one with a pair of binoculars which were strung around my neck. Asa asked me if he could borrow them. He never took them off my neck because in his excitement to spot the landing places of the 1915 expedition he simply put them to his eyes. With my neck craned to allow him access to the binoculars he never stopped talking, and although this was his first visit to this area, he seemed to know every part of the coast. I had the benefit of an insightful lecture on the expedition. What he didn’t know was that my grandfather (Captain Godfrey) was in one of the ships delivering 2,000 Australian troops into that debacle. In one day’s fighting at Gallipoli all but 400 of those Australian boys were lost. This is an episode in Grandad’s life from which he never got over nor from which he really recovered. In his last years it haunted him.

Asa was one of a kind. I went a few times to his house in Lewes, met Susan – his ‘dishy wife’ – and was at the same table as him

Cokie and I by the TR1, and then with Keith and Peppy in the Aston

on several occasions. I never felt I knew him in the sense of 'knowing his views'. But what I did see was his joy from living. He loved wining and dining. He had students to his house and seemed to have all the time in the world. At the University he was a whirlwind of activity and was nicknamed the 'Galloping Professor'. If a unit of time was an Asa, then to work at half an Asa would be prodigious. I saw him socially though, and would think that he had all the time in the world to enjoy himself and realised that the in-between times, i.e., going from one place to another, was the gap he would fill with writing. It was as though he was in a huge rush to do everything so that he could enjoy his parties or a dinner.

I would love to know what his later thoughts were on the experiment of being a key player in academia generally, history particularly, and creating the 'new learning' at the new University. He used to say, 'I wonder who will be the first Sussex student to publish a book while at Uni'. Well, it's taken me a further sixty years to produce my offering. Asa would not be impressed. But like Asa I was to be no slouch in getting things done, realising early on, thankfully, that, in the words of an old teacher's report, 'time lost cannot be retrieved'. It is a maxim which has served me well. Another is 'Explanations are no Excuses'. I had this quote on the door of my school study (we called them 'shows') so that when a young recalcitrant came in to be punished he might think twice before explaining that either it wasn't him or he had the best reason for it.

I suppose the one idea I could take away from a University of Sussex experience is the value of 'cross fertilisation'. I cannot imagine now studying history without having done some philosophy. I cannot think of how to choose a non-academic career without those 'odd' lectures by Asa Briggs, David Daiches and others on Industry and Academia.

University for me, and some might find it surprising, was an upsetting experience. Surrounded by Trotskyites and dominated by socialist thinking and finding that dogma and rigidity were prevalent amongst 'convinced' students. Ban the Bomb sit-ins were common in the Sussex of my days as were marches on the streets of Brighton. These issues were not huge for me. I was always grateful for what I'd got, even if it was less than others, and I knew it was up to me to work harder if I wanted more. So many of these rebels seemed angry and upset with society, life, and in themselves. I felt guilty at being happy and content. Why should I be discontent and complaining about what I did not know? My training was that life is a relay race and my job was to pass on the baton leaving the world if possible in a better state than I'd received it. It was not everybody else's fault.

I remember one anti-*apartheid* University talk when the motion was debated, and passed, that no South African products should be sold at the University. I found no-one to explain to me why the obviously silly concept of 'separate development' should have been conceived, let alone implemented, in the first place. What was it about South African Afrikaans society that allowed *apartheid* to become 'Law'? If we could understand this, then perhaps we'd understand how things could be done better and even maybe avoided. The usual answer in a democracy is 'let the people choose', but of the then 20 million South Africans 75% were black and not educated or at least differently educated. If 'globalisation' was going to dominate the twentieth century, then a meritocracy would not favour a democracy in South Africa. Could we wait for democracy failure and huge famines and pain to be the way for 75% of a population, or should we just have law and order imposed until this number reduced and then rebelled. At the same time, surely it would be better to build up the Civil Service at least for three generations so that hothead politicians would have the checks and balances of proven law to act as restraints upon their tribal corruption.

Now no-one wants to be a Civil Servant in Africa, but wants to gain from the exploitation of colonial masters' contracts or resources, which often as not came as 'foreign aid'. The high-sounding words of the 'moral leadership' from the UK need redefining. However worthy, this 'aid' hasn't worked as effectively as it could, and has assisted the temptation towards corruption as it all too often came to be seen as a source of free income. It requires a rethink, especially given the activities of modern day China, which has a programme of tied loans that amounts, effectively, to colonisation. Also, who knows how many Chinese have no other home than in Africa. Not that this is anything to be happy about; but ignore the awakened giant at your peril, as Churchill said. Make no mistake China is no friend to democracy and its (CCP) authoritarian regime is both unattractive and frightening in its threat to a civilised world. Xi Jinping oversees an ambitious State using its wealth and size to exploit the West's self criticism and to bribe its industry, education and governments to be 'friends of China'. There is no compromise, as the protestors in Hong Kong, the Uyghurs and the Taiwanese will agree. It's a very Cold War, being cleverly won by China with not a shot fired.

Democracies of the world 'beware' for while you self destruct in self-righteous talk of 'morals and rights' there is an amoral elephant in the room with no regard for 'our' values and intent on a path of self promotion of the Chinese Communist Party. Beware those who rewrite history to justify all that's gone before as the prelude to their own messianic ambition. China's present leader Xi Jinping is engaged in this rewrite now and it and he are dangerous. He is not listening but acting very fast in all pervasive directions, which 'we' chose to rationalise (as it lets us rest in peace for another short period), whereas it needs confronting by both 'good example' and 'an equal and opposite intolerance'. Listen to what the Chinese Hong Kongers who quit Hong Kong tell us. You could not talk to a Hitler or a Stalin; Xi Jinping is of that ilk but of a dimension that makes minnows of the rest of the world.

But I never heard such views expressed at liberal, radical, Sussex. I would welcome the chance to sit cross legged with today's students and to hear whether perceptions are changing and confirm or deny what I've seen 'in the field'.

Starting Work, 1965

The Foreign Office seemed to offer a career I could take up with enthusiasm, and I duly applied and took part in a selection procedure that exposed one of my weak points. Traditionally, if not so much now, the language of diplomacy was French, and I, who had once failed French at 'O' Level, had claimed some facility in the language. They found me out when during the residential weekend I was called to the phone. A voice at the other end had something urgent to convey to me in French, but I was quite lost. If at Sussex my ignorance at interview of Gibbon's great work had been outweighed by a fulsome headmaster's reference, there was now no such counterweight favouring me, and my end of the see-saw crashed.

Failure to get into the Foreign Office was a blow. What now? I decided to join a company offering a Graduate Trainee Scheme. 'Personnel departments' were all the rage in the '60's, often making an attempt to bridge the gulf between academia and commercial 'real life'. This at least seemed to delay too irrevocable a decision on what to do with my life. I even flirted with doing a PhD at Sussex on the Civil War period before going up to London for several 'business' interviews. It boiled down to two companies – B.P. and Tube Investments – the former seemed more international and 'up my street', the latter was based in the Midlands *(where do they begin and end?)* and engineering biased *(what does that mean?).* My only work experience apart from hop or apple picking in Kent and working at the Neville golf club shop was working during university summer holidays as the Festival Organiser for Dorian Williams in Pendley Manor, Tring, putting on his open-air Shakespeare plays – bliss.

B.P. turned me down after a thorough three-day grilling in London – rather like the Foreign Office, which included much drink and socialising, probably to ensure I didn't eat my peas off my knife; but Tube Investments said 'Yes'. It was like going to another country venturing up to Birmingham. We were well ensconced in Tunbridge Wells and Mum and Dad had a high social life there. Dad was the President of the Tunbridge Wells Scottish Association and the MD of Stonegate Farmers. We were members of the kirk, lived between the Pantiles and the Neville Golf course, Mum loved cooking and her dinner parties brought together many local characters. In leaving Kent and the South East I also lost all my school and family contacts.

I didn't appreciate how much my perspective on life was shaped by my being a 'Man of Kent' until after I had left the South East, and by then I was too intent on trying to make a success of my move to question its wisdom. (I raised this many years later in my speech to the Chamber of Commerce; see Appendix 3.) Politicians these days talk of addressing the economic imbalances within our island. Would it not be wiser to encourage the UK's unique regional differences and through diversity grow? Over the past 80 years the engines of manufacturing have left the Midlands in favour of the sweat-shops of the East; ship building has left Scotland for Korea. This is now a time for re-creation rather than spreading existing wealth. Just as our farmers are having to rethink their use of land and livestock in the absence of EU grants we all need to find new ways in these more transient times. If I have contributed anything to the rich East and West Midlands it is in many ways thanks to my formative experiences in Kent.

Mum and Dad at the old home, 37 Birling Road, Tunbridge Wells

Tube Investments (T.I.) and Raleigh

The Midlands was an area one travelled through as fast as possible to get to Scotland. It rejoiced in dark names like 'The Black Country', it smelt of industry and coal mining. 115 of us 'graduates' set off from different corners of the UK for Birmingham in August 1965. I think I was the only one coming from Kent. We attended an engineering course at 'Chance Technical College' in Smethwick, and went on lectures at Woodbourne Grange in Edgbaston. It was easy to make friends with fellow graduates. I think I was the only historian, and there were a minority of arts graduates amongst the metallurgists and engineers, and a number of accountants. I found myself lodgings in Handsworth whilst working in Smethwick – my landlord was a plumber with a lovely family, who took me at face value, despite my Southern Public School accent and it wasn't long before I was invited to join him on his weekend work, as a plumber's mate. On Tuesday nights I even got an evening job teaching history to mature students for one hour at the local Handsworth Tech. Frightening. But it gave me a huge appreciation of the author Tom Sharpe because I had classes full of 'fitters and joiners, welders and electricians'. They taught me more than I taught them – but I did learn more about history: it's no good talking about 'What caused the English Civil War', but a lot of good talking about 'How to make a revolution'.

Being a part of a motley collection of graduate trainees, I soon made friends with folk like Dai James, Rob Pruden and Chetty of the Muragappa family, one of India's leading business conglomerates founded in 1900. Chetty was a 'Chettiar' from Madras (also famous money lenders and bankers in Burma) who owned T.I. India – also, pre-Independence, living in Moulmein on the South-West coast of Burma. I was unaware of their Burmese connection up until I started my venture in that country. Sir Harcourt Brown, a Government Administrator in India, wrote in the 1900's 'The Burman today is a much wealthier man than he was 25 years ago and for this state of affairs the Chettiar deserves his share of thanks'. This organisation and family, and in particular Algy, Chetty's cousin, would later become important to me and a source of great friendship. We still have an annual reunion with some of the accountants in our T.I. group.

Left to Right: Algy Alagappan, Tony Brook, John Yetman, Marion Yetman, Milana Chamberlain, Jeremy Gilliard, Vee Gilliard, Self, Marion Jakes, Clifford Jakes, Jane Main, Richard Chamberlain, Anthony Main, Alagu Murugappa, Margaret Brook

My colleague Algy cuts quite the commanding figure on the far left of the photo above, which was taken at the 2013 reunion of the team I joined at Tube Investments. To me, however, he will forever be the lithe youth, pictured scaling the heights of Snowdon to the right. He was taking part in an expedition organised by the company through an adventure school in Plas as part of 'management preparation'. It was considered at the time to be good for character-development and leadership.

Chetty himself was the most relaxed, calm, lovely individual I'd ever met. To illustrate this, I tell here the tale of when he fell fast asleep standing up over his lathe, at Chance Technical College in Smethwick, as the cutter went about its job and then cutting into the chuck and so writing off a £30K+ lathe entirely. T.I. India quickly supplied a new machine and no more was heard of the incident, and Chetty continued on our course with his usual calm and endearing smile.

We then went around the 60-100 odd T.I. Companies in the Midlands, from Accles and Pollock to British Steel and British Aluminium, to Creda cookers and Raleigh bicycles. They were all 'an experience', a term I use in the spirit of Oscar Wilde to mean a name given to mistakes. I remember Howard Knight (a later MD of Raleigh) turning to one of the Directors of one T.I. Company and asking, 'does one have to be a Free Mason to get into this Company?' – and in fairness he was given a stiff response. I decided that T.I. Export at Five Ways Edgebaston was the company for me: selling steel, steel tubes, aluminium and representing the many T.I. companies overseas. The Personnel Manager had other ideas and said that T.I. Export was only recruiting metallurgists and engineers, so I should go into the T.I. consumer companies – Creda cookers or Raleigh bicycles. 'No way' I quietly thought about the cookers; nor was I much of a cyclist!

My first impressions of Raleigh were not great: showing Taher Aghill, a customer from Libya, around the factory, and passing by the oppressive toilets between Factory 1 and Factory 2 he murmured to me 'very good place for quick fuck I think'. He was perhaps expecting me to coerce one of the native Nottingham girls to oblige. From there to the production line of Second World War wounded young men without limbs, or otherwise injured, whom companies were obliged to employ. They welded pieces of metal using an attachment that protruded from a truncated limb, and then from there we went along the 'Golden Mile' to some despot's office where a sympathetic secretary would bring us tea in thin porcelain cups, with custard creams. It made me realise that this was not for me. Yet I was to spend another 45 years working at the company, and I am still in some sense attached. The Golden Mile has gone, the owners of the dismembered limbs are all laid to rest, and there are no machine girls, let alone seedy toilets, available for a 'quickie'. What happened?

My Dad gave me a good talking to about even thinking of quitting before I'd completed my T.I. traineeship leading to a 'Diploma of Management' at Aston Technical College, and then, when the time came, I went along to Raleigh for my interview after doing some six months 'hands on' work first in the 'tube' shop on the shop floor then as a sales rep in East Anglia, and then at a desk in the Export Department. I carefully wrote out my resignation before the formal job interview.

I walked up into the Export Director's, Jimmy Cumming's, office along the 'Golden Mile', in the Head Office at Triumph Road, Nottingham, with my resignation letter to comfort me in my pocket, to meet this ascetic character. Almost talking to himself he said 'I don't know what to do with you people; if you're any good at all you'll leave after a few months of wasting people's time, and if you're no good you'll probably stay even longer wasting both yours and the Company's time. We are being forced by the new-fangled personnel chappies to take on 15 trainees, but to do what and how? I suppose I have no choice, but not here, wasting my people's time, so tell me, what do you prefer: Madras, India or Springs in the Transvaal?' That floored me and even made me forget the letter of resignation in my pocket which would have solved his problem. I said I had no preference, whereupon he called his secretary, Ann Atkins, and dictated identical letters to both T.I. India and Raleigh South Africa, asking them to train me for six months, to work me hard in all sections of the Company and report back to him after six months whether I was any good or not. 'As for you, young man, you'll get to see how a small company works and how money flows, and whether you feel you want to be part of it. Now get going and don't come near this place until a week's time and then you'll report in each day to see when we have a reply.' Ten days later I was on a flight to Johannesburg, and 55 years later I am still travelling.

Southern Africa, 1967

As my Raleigh mentor had predicted, I learnt more in South Africa than ever could be imagined. Mick Keller, the Sales Director, met me off the aircraft and drove me to Springs in the Transvaal, and along the way gave me a lesson on South Africa, followed by a reading list of seven books including most memorably *Goodbye Dolly Grey*. 'Don't talk to me about South Africa till you've read these books; furthermore, don't talk politics, and don't mess with the Bantu, it's illegal, and remember, you're here to learn.' I did read the books. *Goodbye Dolly Grey* made a big impression on me. I did not voice my opinions but met several who did. Jack Catlin, the Raleigh South Africa (RSA) Managing Director told me two things – 'not to get involved with politics and not to bring any U.K. prejudices with me to South Africa.' He didn't stop there. 'Our job is to make good bicycles which the customer wants,' he went on. 'The customers are our Jewish wholesalers, and their customers are the, mainly Indian, retailers. Their job is to sell bicycles and keep the factory full with their requirements. We will not go down the U.K. path of selling direct to retailers – that's the wholesaler's job. Oh, and by the way, don't mess with the black girls here – it's illegal, and after three months you'll find they become whiter; but it's still illegal.' Jack Catlin lead by example. He cycled to work, slowly, never breaking into a sweat, on his black Raleigh Roadster and just as he never permitted members of commercial team to wear brown shoes, or any other 'modern' footwear, he always wore immaculately polished black leather shoes.

Now my training programme gave me six weeks in each of the RSA Sales areas of the Cape region: Natal, which included the Orange Free State, and then of course the Transvaal. As I learnt from *Goodbye Dolly Grey*, South African society had not changed much in the 50 years prior to my arrival – on the contrary becoming more entrenched. Following the rather sad Boer War and, despite the heroic actions of the likes of Baden Powell and the egotistical Winston Churchill, the tough Boers were a heroic surprise, and their fighting prowess impressive. Indeed they, the tough Boers, heroically fighting the power of Britain, caught the imagination of much of the world, including, inevitably, the French – see the poster from the town of Chartres trying to raise money for the Boer women and children, which picture I took in a museum in Pretoria. Remember it was the Brits during the Boer War who first established concentration camps. It's tough at the top; you are there to be toppled.

1902 poster raising money for the Boer Women and Children

The amazing thing was that sixty years and two world wars later the structure of South African society was remarkably similar, i.e., the Afrikaners owned the land and the politics; the British controlled industry and commerce, and the Jews controlled and had a firm grip on trade – all of the wholesalers through whom Raleigh South Africa worked were Jewish, for example L.K. Hurwitz in the Transvaal, Akals in Durban, Reliable Cycles in Pretoria, or Cape Cycles in the Cape.

So, my days were spent on long car drives to retailers in remote areas – known as 'trading stations'. What impressed me was the close rapport between wholesaler companies, their sales reps and the owners of the retail trading stations. When we arrived at a place in say 'Queens Mercy' in Natal, the Rep would open his 'merchandiser' – some 6' plus thick. This contained all the basic provisions to supply a remote trading station serving a huge area, whether it was Raleigh bikes, toys, pots and pans, or tools, both commercial and domestic, or simply nails and cosmetics. So, the length of a call consumed most of one day. After travelling with different wholesalers' reps I noted that each had his patch, and when I suggested that they compete – as I saw prices varied for the same product – I was told that 'I didn't understand the business, just watch and learn.' Then the cleverness emerged as I came to realise that many of these 'retailers' were not always businessmen but rather 'service providers'. So, while their turnover would be impressive, their control of costs and finances was often lacking, and when some major funding was required – for example for their children's school or university fees, he would talk to his friend, the wholesaler's sales rep, who totally knew his business. Credit would be arranged, the security being the property along with a promise to buy all requirements from that wholesaler and no other. Prices could then be manipulated so that over time loans were paid for by overpriced products. A monopoly of course; but the strength of these Jewish traders was enormous and widespread. Devious, but impressive – how could a British or other manufacturer break into this?

Then in Cape Town, the area Doug Clarke and his wife controlled, I made a silly *faux pas*. I noted that his wife always baked a huge number of delicious cakes for us when we returned from a trip. As they had no children, I felt I knew them well enough to tell them that Freud would suggest the cakes were a psychological need for children. Floodgates opened with Mrs Clarke bursting into tears. The Clarkes were idealists: they had come to South Africa after being keen members of the Socialist Party of Great Britain (SPGB) after the War and had decided that the world was a sad mess and that to bring children into this world would be selfish and wrong. So, they had no children; how they reconciled their ideals in conservative South Africa I do not know. But they were good, loving, helpful people, and I had upset them. I did so doubly: I decided that while in Cape Town I would get a ferry over to Robin Island and see Govan Mbeke, Thabo's Dad. I went to a police station and was told the procedure. I applied and awaited permission. After some weeks in the Cape I received a phone call from Raleigh South Africa's Managing Director, Jack Catlin 'I told you not to meddle in politics, what the hell do you think you're doing? I've had the Security Police on the phone wanting to know all about you.' I had to think twice before I realised that it must have been my application to visit Robin Island that had given rise to this phone call. Before this realisation I protested that I had never become involved in politics and felt that this must all be a mistake. Mr Catlin told me that 'these people may be wrong, but don't make mistakes'. When I figured out that it was my request to visit Govan Mbeke Jack Catlin exploded and told me that if he received another phone call, I'd be put on the next plane back to the U.K. I was shaken; it was the first time that I'd had to exercise my conscience about doing what was 'right' and 'thoughtful'. I decided to maintain my request to go to Robin Island – and I was furious when I only obtained my pass the week after leaving the Cape. This experience made me feel a coward, but now with a conscience, I determined to learn more about the society into which I was thrown, as opposed to being a non-committed, loyal, trainee.

I left South Africa with a very different attitude from the one with which I'd arrived. I had found the Afrikaners more straightforward and better friends than the Brits. Maybe their Dutch origin accounts for their directness of speech. Indeed, in Namaqualand my Jewish wholesaler would only agree to take me in to see his retailers if I could greet them in Afrikaans. I learnt off by heart such phrases as '*goode morge meneer, ik es jammer mar ik canny Afrikaans good verstanie*'. In many of the hotels in the Northern Cape no alcohol would be served until the children of the owners had gone to bed – guests often had to listen to their offspring playing the piano or other instrument after dinner and before they went to their rooms always with a curtsey or a bow to each guest, all very charming. In retrospect I feel that the inevitable Africa that the Afrikaners foresaw was that of a Zuma or a Mugabe, and they lost their world because they got a Mandela.

I had a useful contact, through my father, with the famous Anglo-American Company, indeed its CEO, Herbert Oppenheimer. I read a lot of this impressive man's views and how he reconciled running a huge business with apartheid in South Africa showing respect to employees irrespective of colour. My dad was invited to the wedding of his daughter, Mary, as the groom, Gordon Waddell, was the son of a close Glasgow (stockbroker) friend of the Macnaughtan family and with whom I still deal. I was allowed to visit a couple of gold mines and thoroughly enjoyed seeing the open diamond mine of Kimberley (now a museum having closed in circa 1915) and its famous 'big hole' in the Orange Free State (OFS).

'The Big Hole' Kimberley Mine

A new world opened up to me and I found I was welcomed into this world by such as Bert Seales (the Raleigh Manager in Durban) and his lovely wife Helen, who took me up-country 'to educate me', going off-piste to show me views and areas which otherwise no visitor would ever see, such as Richards Bay which has become a 'des res' area, beautiful and now very expensive, but at that time it was nature's paradise with sea views to die for.

I have no idea how the M.D., Jack Catlin, regarded me or what he reported back to Head Office. All I did know is that I didn't lose my

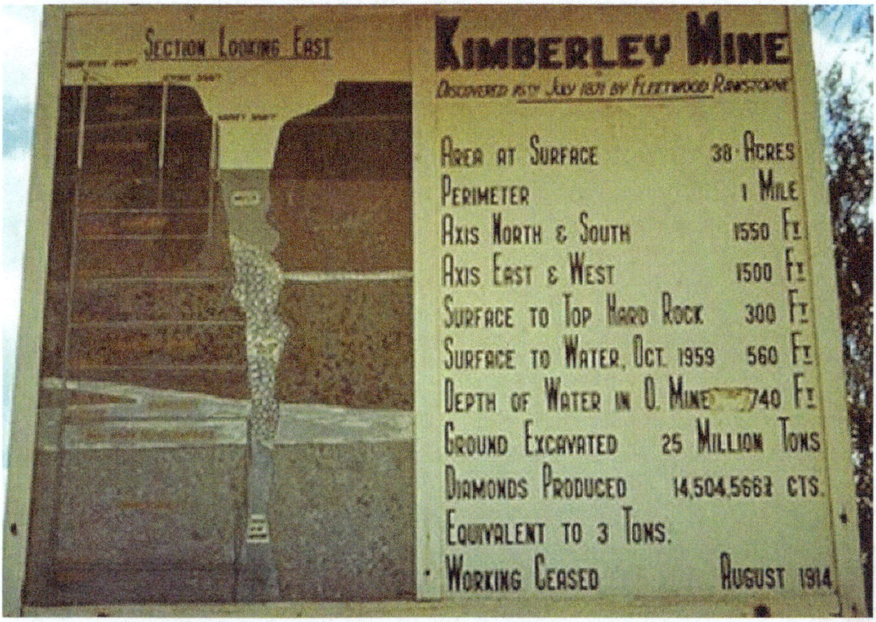

Cross-section of the largest South-African diamond mine

job. The fact was that when my six months 'training' was nearly over, and Head Office found that there were jobs to be done and someone should do them? Young Macnaughtan was becoming available. Jimmy Cumming decided to send me home from South Africa via Rhodesia, Malawi and Zambia as there was a job that needed doing in each country. He would meet me at the end in Lusaka, Zambia to see for himself how I'd fared and possibly to see if I was up to solving the next problem. It was a delight to go to Bulawayo and then Salisbury from Springs in the Transvaal. I'd even discovered I had Macnaughtan relatives working in both cities, the one a farmer in Biera in Mozambique, the other the Barclays bank manager in Salisbury. I met the former by chance, in my Durban hotel and the latter had me around to his house for dinner. I have lost contact with both, sadly.

I found Rhodesia to be a happy if tense country. There was no yoke of apartheid and the whole country felt warm and relaxed. Relations between the two major tribes, the Shona and the Matabele, seemed balanced, perhaps because political leaders like Joshua Nkomo were educated, moderate and sensible, and clearly the obvious and reasonable choice upon Independence. But first they got the Unilateral Declaration of Independence (UDI), made by a very brave but misguided man Ian Smith; then the saddest cut of all was the arrival of the wicked but cunning and politically clever Mugabe (which should have been no surprise with his Shona tribe being more populous than 'Good old Josh's Matabele').

A cartoon book I brought at the time, showing Harold Wilson looking in on Ian Smith

My first visit was there just before UDI but I was there again not too long afterwards when I had the fortune to meet dedicated white, black, Indian and other businessmen, including Tiny Rowland of Lonrho and the Liebermann family, and I was able to get my business done without too much difficulty. I bought a copy of the *Rhodesia Herald* newspaper on the day of my arrival, March 5th 1968. It was interesting but more for the news stories that had been pulled out by the very active censors than for anything that was there to read. The top stories on the front page were all missing, the space they filled simply left blank, and there were other empty spaces throughout the rest of the paper, where items of news had fallen victim to the censors. I kept hold of the paper and now, over fifty years later, it is quite a historical artefact.

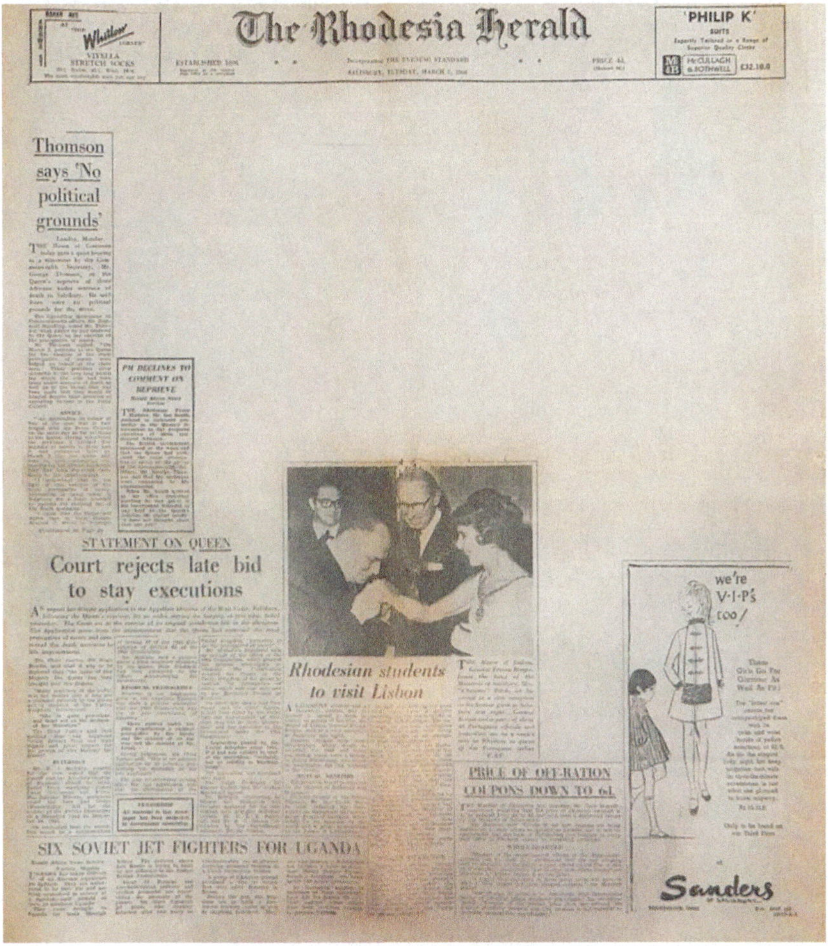

The Rhodesia Herald

'PHILIP K'

Thomson says 'No political grounds'

PM DECLINES TO COMMENT ON REPRIEVE

STATEMENT ON QUEEN

Court rejects late bid to stay executions

Rhodesian students to visit Lisbon

PRICE OF OFF-RATION COUPONS DOWN TO 6d.

SIX SOVIET JET FIGHTERS FOR UGANDA

we're V-I-P's too!

Sanders

Rhodesia was a beautiful country and I was lucky to be shown around by Mick Keller's friends who lived in Bulawayo. I visited the Rhodes monument there and also Lake McIlwaine with its nearby and rarely seen cave paintings. I have yet to find out anything to explain why they were there, who drew them or what story they tell.

From a magic time in Rhodesia I went to lovely Malawi – a poor country, but nonetheless a strong one, lead by its President, the benevolent kamuzu (teacher) Dr. Banda. It was a semi-paradise, I thought, as I took in the delights of Lake Nyasa and the Queen's View in its capital Zomba. Raleigh Industries was represented here by two Indian families, those of I.O. Adams and C.S. Patel. I was to spend an

Fishing on Lake McIlwaine, Mother and Child

Cave paintings near Lake McIlwaine

Cecil Rhodes Monument, Bulawayo

evening with each. Most members of the two families were teetotal, but one of them joined me for a drink. Naively and in a state of happy serenity I got through a few too many beers and, to the amusement of all, the elected Indian 'drinker' not only matched me (I'm not a big drinker) but with that Indian smile still on his face he actually slid, quite drunk, underneath the table. I felt stupidly proud to have drunk someone under the table and know now that it is not just a saying.

From Lilongwe and Zomba in Malawi I went on to Fort Jameson (Chipata) in the 'Copper belt' of Northern Rhodesia, now Zambia. This is a rich area with a good bike market serving the relatively well-paid miners (as in South Africa much of the workforce came from Malawi).

I was kindly asked by Raleigh's Greek agent in the Copper Belt of the newly formed Zambia if I would like to attend the Ndola Rotary Club luncheon. It was explained to me, with some devilment, that up until independence no Africans had been allowed to join the Club but a solution had been found whereby a local African Chief was asked if he would not only join the Club but be its President. (By this stratagem it would be an African that would not be allowing other African members to join.) It turned out that the President was a formidable personality of handsome proportions and a twinkle in his eyes. He clearly adored the honour of his position and the robe of office along with the chain of prestige around his ample neck.

With the luncheon over, the President rose and in ringing tones said that before he introduced the guest speaker, he wanted to acknowledge the three guests. He had noted their names – a Mr Stuart, a Mr McDonald and a Mr Macnaughtan. 'You know,' he declared 'you bloody Scots get everywhere; but I'd like you to know that I've got Scots blood in me. Oh yes', he went on, 'my great grandfather ate the first Scottish missionary sent to Northern Rhodesia!'

I was taken to the Nchanga 'open' copper mine which was one of one of the vastest excavations on the surface of the earth. Standing at the edge of the 'field', I stared around and for as far as I could see in each direction the ground had been opened up beneath me, and what looked like dinky toys were huge bulldozers operating at every level. I had never seen the like.

The Nchanga Copper Mine. See the trucks for a sense of the scale

That evening my Greek Raleigh friend suggested that if I wanted to hold the memory of this 'shocking' experience I should buy equity in Nchanga. I did – I had £100 of cash on me and duly bought shares in the Nchanga Copper Mines as a souvenir of my visit. I tell the tale as the investment paid dividends at a rate of 25% per annum. At the end of the fourth year the Zambian Government nationalised the mine paying back the face value of the investment. In my case I'd made £100 worth of dividends over four years and received back my £100 original investment. These were the first company shares I had ever bought, and I was rather proud of myself, the significance of it for me is that I have not stopped gambling since!

I was to fly down to Lusaka from Kitwe to meet up with the UK Raleigh boys – one being the Export Director. My scheduled flight was cancelled because of bad weather, but I managed to hitch-hike on the Lonrho Kingair and to everyone's amazement, I arrived in Lusaka with Jeff Scher, Raleigh's agent in Zambia, Jimmy Cumming and Bob O'Donovan in time for dinner, wearing my safari suit – long socks, shorts and cut jacket – and looking quite the old colonial to the astonishment of my dapper U.K. dressed colleagues. I learnt afterwards that this transformation was all the proof Jimmy Cumming needed: I'd passed my induction test.

Perhaps the biggest shock of my first overseas business visits, though, was the frequent response I'd had from people, especially those at Head Office, and those who had been 'trained' and so knew everything. I found time and again that to do my job successfully I had to transmit the doing of it, or rather the explanation of how I'd do it into the language of the reader back at base. I had learnt this from a silly example back in South Africa where I was told by those at Raleigh Nottingham that the reason the Raleigh Bailey Super Pump sold so well was because it was 'Made in England', had Sir Walter embossed on the pump itself, was black and heavy and commanded a commensurate price. This was why it outsold the light, more efficient Italian pumps at half the price. Of course, the reality was otherwise. The Bailey Super did outsell its half-priced Italian equivalents, but it had nothing to do with being black, or Sir Walter, or even because it was Made in England. It was simply because the grip at the top of the pump had around it three serrated washers. These gave the user a firm grip, but in fact just one such washer could do the job, the other two were highly prized as a jewelled extension of the ear lobe hole so eagerly required by young ladies in beautifying themselves. It was not just a pump: It was a jewel!

I found that when these educated and trained businessmen and accountants in particular, who knew the wily ways of business and mankind, were introduced to the truth I had discovered, I was being discussed 'as emotional and over excited'. When I tried to transmit this fun of life that so many customers enjoyed and reveal their real motivation for buying from the U.K. it was considered irrelevant.

Moving on 10 years, as an aside which is worth including here, I was delighted to read Jimmy Cumming's report after his trip in 1980 which showed how things in Southern Africa had only worsened, and the Western stomach for investment not only declined but it could be said in hindsight that it allowed the Chinese to secure a firmer hold in Africa. It expresses the sentiments widely held at the time and endorsed by my findings a decade earlier.

Excerpt from JC's Report on visit to Malawi, Zimbabwe and South Africa, 22nd March 1980 - 4th April 1980

'Informal conversations with persons of many of the developed nations in all walks of life, whom one is bound to encounter on a peripatetic journey through Eastern, Central and Southern Africa, revealed growing disillusionment and disenchantment with the capabilities of the Black African States to manage their own affairs. There were clear signs of 'aid weariness' and serious doubt about the efficacy of perpetual local dependence on the begging bowl. The increase in the numbers of hungry and poverty stricken and their nigh hopeless conditions is superficially belied by those Africans who can afford to enjoy the meretricious gaudiness of newly built hotels and European style restaurants simply because they have been fortunate to have been selected to work in spacious air-conditioned government offices with banks of telephones on the desks (which more often than not do not work) and chauffeur-driven Mercedes at their beck and call.

'The quite extraordinary bitterness felt by many Americans and Europeans at the waste of their aid and investments on abortive projects – especially those emissaries on site – was a clear indication of their frustrations. As an American put it, 'it's time we closed down the soup kitchen'.

'Somewhat exaggeratedly it is often said that the only skill that Africans possess is that of playing at their own game of politics. Those who attain positions of power have the avowed, covert, intention to enrich themselves on the proceeds of office for as long as they can be made to last. They are happy to rely on aid projects and foreign investment always provided there is 'something in it' for them. This 'something in it' permeates down the chain of command; and, in certain of the beggar states, it has become the accepted lifestyle of all and sundry.

'The Rhodesians are having their first taste of it, because they are presently being canvassed (coerced) for subscriptions ('or else') to fund the forthcoming Independence Day festivities. Not having had any previous experience of what is regarded as the norm outside their borders, they are not taking too kindly to it, and expletives about gooks, coons and mutts are commonplace.

'There is no gainsaying the fact that certain of the beggar states are fast becoming total economic disasters (for example, Tanzania), despite all the aid that has been poured into them since their attainment of independence. Nevertheless, this does not prevent their leaders from continuing to bite the hands that feed them. It is, therefore, no wonder that the opinion seems to be growing that if they want any more hard currency, free of charge or in low interest loans, they should get it from the bandits of OPEC whom they applaud, or from their Eastern European and Chinese comrades with whom they vote in the United Nations.

'The poor of these countries are not starving because Europe and America are eating too much. The major cause of malnutrition is the system of agriculture adopted by them along the lines of Eastern Europe. Were they not now wedded to this system, countries such as Zambia would be regular exporters of grain instead of having to rely heavily on imports from South Africa.

'If, therefore, there is not a change of attitude in the present policies being followed by certain African states, there is a danger that they will find themselves sitting in the mud eating anti-capitalist rhetoric in the years ahead.'

Nonetheless Africa 'gets in your blood'. I was hugely sad to be flying back to London after nearly a year (1967) in Southern and Central Africa, but on my return there was an incident which happily brought me back to reality. My Mum had left her Triumph Herald near Heathrow for me to pick up on arrival, with the keys concealed in the rear exhaust. I made my way from Heathrow to my home in Tunbridge Wells to be with my parents and driving along a route I knew well. It was a dull grey day, not knowing whether to rain or just remain dull. The little semi-detached houses and old roads looked small and grey.

England appeared dirty and sad, and while day-dreaming I nearly missed a right-hand turn in South London and screeched the lively Triumph round, the tyres squealing. I made the turn to find a London 'bobby' on the corner. He yelled 'pull over'. I wound down the window and all I could see was a big Afrikaans *oke* ready to sort me out with a hefty fine which he would pocket. I waited for the 'bobby' to come over, and he put his head to the window and said, 'You got shares in Dunlop mate? Drive carefully and get on your way.' I was back. The little houses and untidy streets became warm and inviting. It was a quick and lucky incident, and a lesson which made me happy to be home in this unique island with its tolerance and lively wit.

My stand at the Tripoli trade show, 1968; displaying all the key brand names; Sturmey Archer, Humber, Rudge, Raleigh, Phillips, Hercules, BSA

35,000 Lost Bikes, Libya 1968

Back at Head Office I had a good grounding in exporting by working for Gavin Duncan (an ex-Kenya hand) and with John Rowberry responsible for sales into the Africa Continent. Their training stood me in good stead for my next experiences. It was also great to get into life both at Raleigh and in the UK and indeed playing cricket for Erronzed (the Herons Head being the headcrest logo of the Raleigh brand).

It wasn't long before I was given my first real project. During the Six Day Israeli war in June 1967 American and British goods were subjected to destruction or offloading at any European port. In Raleigh's case there were 35,000 bicycles 'lost' around the Mediterranean ports – the largest number known to be in Libya. My job was to locate these bicycles, take possession of them and sell them in the country in which they resided and remit the proceeds to Nottingham. Simple. Also simple was the fact that the Government Export Credit Guarantee Department (ECGD) had paid out around 75% of the value of these bicycles. This had to be returned upon payment of an eventual sale and only the balance retained, so my challenge was also to sell them at full price. In May 1968 I left Nottingham with the Bills of Lading for all the 'lost' bikes, and so on finding their whereabouts the products would be legally mine. I had funds to clear the goods from any port, and authority to sell the bicycles and remit the proceeds – amazing power and trust.

The Libya to which I ventured was a monarchy under King Idris – at the time, a refugee in Turkey. It was, and still is, three countries: The Fezzan in the South, Tripolitania, and Cyrenaica. Each area is quite different. I was to spend several months mainly in Tripoli, but also Benghazi, to locate the 35,000 bicycles, which is the subject for a business report rather than for this book. But find them I did, and sold them, with the exception of 500 bicycles which I later discovered were still at the Suez Canal and only released when it reopened in 1973. It was my good fortune, or so I thought, that most of the bikes were still in the docks at Tripoli and Benghazi. To sell these to the original consignee was to make my job much easier as it avoided the prospect of having to run around the ports of the Mediterranean however appealing that may have sounded. To give a flavour of the job: 25 bicycles were packed altogether in Completely Knocked Down (CKD) form in two soft wood boxes – a frame box and a wheel box. Each was about 5' x 4' x 4'. It was easy to identify matching sets. It was not easy to see where my bikes were in the docks as they had been hastily off-loaded and their whereabouts not recorded. The usual route for disposal would have been by auction. I had located about six retail customers, in most cases the original customers who had ordered the bikes, and in these cases I was simply able to put the customer in touch with his consignment. Upon payment I could handover the relevant Bill of Lading for him to clear his goods. Maybe I sold 16 – 17,000 bikes taking this 'easy' route. I then had to dispose of others where the customers were not even in Libya. To sell these was a challenge and in short when I thought I'd identified a customer I went about hiring a donkey and cart, putting lots of 50 bikes in four cases on the cart from the port and, after paying the clearing and port charges, walking the donkey and cart to the prospective customer through the streets of Tripoli. This must have been a strange sight for the locals but relatively easy, if time consuming and conspicuous. The next job was getting the customer to pay for his order of 25 bikes (minimum), in cash, then walking with the donkey and now empty cart along to the bank in downtown Tripoli and organising payment into 'my account' and from there to the U.K. Not so easy! Each journey from port to dealer to bank was individual, nerve wracking, sweaty, and a story in itself.

Our biggest customer in Tripoli was in fact our Phillips-branded distributor Mohammed Gheiadi. Mohammed was 'out' when I arrived, but he had ordered some 3,000 bikes, so I visited his shop every day and by chance struck up a friendship with his son Ibrahim. He even took me out in the walled city of Tripoli and we went to see a famous Egyptian Arabic singer, Umm Kulthum, who was world-renowned – she was about 80 years old. Ibrahim and I became chums. He told me after a couple of weeks that his Dad would be returning from 'Africa' and that it would be 'next week'. I had lots of time as my daily call to Ibrahim was either a very short affair during the day to check on his Dad's progress or a chance to sit with him in the evening.

During this interlude, the actual anniversary of the Six Day war, June 1968, occurred. At this same time I received an invitation along with the many other visiting Brits to a party at the Embassy, and was asked to bring a sleeping bag. We all arrived at the Embassy suitably prepared and were ushered into the cellars and told we would be staying there for a couple of nights. The Ambassador addressed us in the evening of the anniversary and I recall he related to us that he had received a call from his American counterpart who wanted to declare a State of Emergency so that American citizens could be flown out. The British Embassy had declared in a speech to the effect of 'Crisis What Crisis?' and Britain refused. We felt proud to be Brits; but I now wonder. After three days and much good food and drink I sadly left and went back to my hotel.

All was quiet in Tripoli and I resumed my wait for my 'saviour' Mohammed Gheiadi. I had been through all the Phillips-branded bicycles at the Port that had been 'lost', dividing them from the Hercules and Raleigh ones. About a quarter were Phillips-branded. I intended offering them to him at a higher mark-up than for Hercules and Raleigh. If he would also take some of the Hercules and Raleigh I was going to offer a 'buy one Phillips and have one Raleigh free' deal. I had worked out all sorts of permutations in the time between meeting with Ibrahim and his Dad's arrival so that when we met the deal could be closed and I could go home.

It took two weeks for Mohammed to return. He had travelled from Chad. Word preceded his arrival with much 'buzz' in the Soukh. Ibrahim and I went along in advance to meet and greet Mohammed. I thought of him by now as an old friend, although we'd never met. He did arrive, but not alone. On the outskirts of Tripoli, a veritable cloud of dust and sand heralded his coming as a cohort of camels came along behind which some two dozen black and dirty individuals trailed, bound one to the other. Mohammed was a slaver! He had gone to Chad to buy some slaves destined for Saudi Arabia. I can't remember the details between my comprehension of the situation and the next events. The last thing on Mohammed's mind was Phillips-branded bicycles. He had crossed the Sahara on a camel and was only thinking of exchanging his human goods, for much gold and silver to his Arab brothers. In the market place his 'goods' were quickly put on display, I remember the excitement and noise, I kept close to Ibrahim who seemed to want to distance himself from me, and our friendship cooled. 'Would I like to inspect the boys?' I declined, but in this unreal world I did manage to acquire a couple of the manacles which bound the boys together, I have them at home with me now.

I still have these slaves' manacles

I did feel very dirty and disturbed; what should I have done? But I did sell him all the Phillips bicycles, without any discount or inclusion of the other brands.

Another personally embarrassing story concerned the Raleigh Distributor. I shall never forget Taher Aghil, an awful man, who after I had previously taken him around Raleigh showed me overwhelming friendship and kept me in his office for hours on many days while he harangued his customers. I believe he was trying to impress me with his power. On one occasion he invited me for a night out. I remember going to my hotel, having a shower and putting on my one suit for the occasion. Taher arrived, hardly looked at me with white shirt, tie and jacket, but came out of his office in the smelly clothes he'd worn all day and walked me into the maze of streets inside the walled city of Tripoli. A maze from which I would never find my way out unaccompanied. We stopped in one 'hole in the wall' arched 'shop' where there were two chairs in front of a curtain, upon which we sat and waited until a young lady emerged through the curtains which revealed a bed and not much else. 'You go first,' said Taher 'and I'll follow', I won't relate my response but suffice to say that Taher went in while I sat, and waited, and heard, and then he came out angry, and in silence he led me out of the labyrinth. I never had dinner that evening.

Two days later with business still outstanding with Taher, I ventured into his office. As usual, six or eight people were waiting for him on chairs, with his desk at one end. I waited patiently until I thought it would be too subservient and counter-productive to wait longer and went up to him and suggested we finished our business – he had 'bought' the Raleigh branded bikes but not given me the cash. He started shouting at me and since I felt I had little to lose I gave him back in kind. After some minutes of this I suddenly became aware of a large gentleman beside me drawing a gun and putting it into my ribs. Ali Aghil, Taher's brother, was the Chief of Police in Tripoli! 'No one spoke to Taher like I was doing, and I should apologise and leave,' he told me firmly in Arabic. I did eventually complete my business with Taher – but not on that day.

Yet another incident occurred when I was with the Brothers Trading Company, who had returned from Aden (they were Libyan) and started trading in Libya. One of the three brothers was married to an impossibly gorgeous Danish girl. The brothers had bought many of my 'lost' bicycles and clearly made a good profit and I was the recipient of their gratitude. Weekends of parties in the Fezzan under huge tents, and out hunting during the day were the order of many a day. I never did know what we were hunting for except that we always returned to huge feasts cooked in our absence. But on one such trip I met an Irish girl married to a Libyan. She looked sullen, miserable and lost. I must have told her my hotel in Tripoli, for a week later she appeared. She was running away from her husband who she said beat and abused her; she showed me the most horrendous cigarette burns on her body and told me awful stories. I fell for all this and as a good 'white knight' approached the British Embassy and to cut a long story short, managed to get a passport and her out of the country and back to Ireland. (Remember I had gotten to know the Ambassador because of the Anniversary of the Six Day Israeli War.) Three months later, when I was back in Tripoli, I learnt she had returned to her husband.

Nor did my job finish there, between Mohammed Gheiadi, Taher Aghil and the Brothers Trading Company I had sold the Tripoli bikes all at a profit, but it had taken a toll on me. I was physically and mentally exhausted. I proceeded on to Benghazi, where another lot of the 'lost' bikes were supposed to be. Benghazi was and is very different from Tripoli, with nicer people somehow, and a slower, cultured pace of life. My hotel in Benghazi was not the haven I had had in Tripoli. It was memorable for its toilet, its cockroaches and its filth. I had spent six weeks in Tripoli and it was a relief to arrive in Benghazi despite my poor hotel. Also, I found a real business ally in Benghazi in my Clearing Agent who knew and delivered to my customers – an Englishman, John Haworth with his Maltese wife, Maria, who deserve a nice 'remembrance' from me. Better times are always hastily skirted over, and I experienced none of the painful experiences that had beset me in Tripoli. With the Haworth's kindness I traced another batch of my bikes and could resume working on clearing my stock with much sweat but little pain. Together with those sold in Tripoli they amounted to some 25,000 bikes and by now I was intent on ending my assignment and returning home despite the unsold and still missing 10,000. These I would sell on my next trip to Tripoli a couple of months later with a few going to Malta.

I used to escape from Libya from time to time to Malta. What a delight to see Malta which in those days was very British and the harbour with all its naval history so nostalgic to see. In Malta it was the Muscat family who had a bicycle wholesale business, who looked after me and even bought some of the Libyan stock. The Muscat brothers, Louis and Joseph, were not only gentlemen but took me to their home for meals and seeing my physical condition mothered me and even insisted I went over to the adjoining island of Gozo to swim and dive. Then I went, in another interlude from Libya, to Athens where Taki Gounoropoulos and his wife Dora made a fuss of me, and where many plates were broken and much dancing to bazooki bands took place – it was the days of the Generals and the 'real' Greece! But this was a step too far, as I'd arrived exhausted from Benghazi and was returning from Athens to Tripoli, where I fell ill with a huge abdominal pain and bursting head. I had to call a doctor. He arrived at my hotel in Tripoli, spoke no English and had long fingernails. He plunged these talon fingers into various parts of my stomach, and I yelled with each plunge and in every area. He prescribed me some medicine, which he happened to have with him, and which I vowed not to take. Three days later after a diet of only boiled water I was restored.

I found the Tripolitanians a difficult mix and remember thinking they suffered from combining the worst of the Italian traits with the worst of the Arabs – I leave the reader to interpret this as they will. Benghazi was quite different and so much easier – more relaxed, more Egyptian, in their Arabness.

Enough of Libya which, for much of 1968, had become my home, where I enjoyed many more adventures, such as digging for Roman coins over a weekend, while happily finding and selling most of my bikes. It also had brought me close to Malta – before the misguided but clever and complex Dom Mintoff's anti-British rule from 1971, but also to Greece under the Colonels from 1967 – happy interludes for me. And my reputation was secured as an overseas trouble shooter and fixer.

In December 1968 I got married to Susanna, a Dutch girl whom I had met on holiday in 1966 and kept in touch with between my trips. I enjoyed her gregarious personality. She had lived in Brazil and France and was living in Belgium. I discovered she had no mother tongue but was adept at picking up languages, an interesting talent. We initially communicated only in French until her command of English surpassed mine of French. She enjoyed travel which was as well, as before I could get my feet under the desk at base I was sent out to Kenya where I found a lovely flat in Westlands, Nairobi. Happily, Sue loved it.

The Kenya National Trading Company, 1968 - 69

My Westlands Apartment in Nairobi, Kenya, front and rear view

Africa then called in another guise and of quite a different cut – East Africa to be precise – where the programmes of 'localisation' (the term used for replacing predominately Asian businessmen with African ones) were in full swing. Raleigh enjoyed a dominant market share (maybe some 80%) in this region. CKD (completely knocked down) bikes, offered for sale in only two colours and three frame sizes of basically one bike, were good business for a mass production company. Once lost, this market of some 60,000 bikes p.a. (all only available in Black or Raleigh Green) would be difficult to replace and create problems for the Nottingham factory. So, I was sent to Kenya to work as an 'Adviser' to the newly formed Kenya National Trading Company (KNTC).

My brief, officially, was to help the Chairman of the KNTC, Peter Kinyanjui, in his quest to bring up African businessmen to take over that part of the economy dominated by the 'Asians', as the Indians were called. Peter Kinyanjui had visited Raleigh in Nottingham on my return from South Africa at the end of 1967 and struck up a good relationship with my boss Jimmy Cumming, which was natural, of course, given the latter's command of the Kikuyu language. I met Peter in Kenya, and he made me understand the political nature of his mission, in trying to 'Africanise' his country. All of Raleigh's customers were of pre-partition Indian origin.

Initially, and after returning from Libya towards the end of 1968, I went on a six-week introductory trip around Kenya with the Raleigh Distributors – Gailey & Roberts (G&R) (United Africa Company, i.e., Unilever) – to learn the Raleigh business. My Raleigh brief was to hold the existing market for at least one more year, and then slow the decline of U.K. sales so that the factory could respond by switching production over to the USA race bikes for which demand was increasing. I was lucky to go around the market with a guy from the Mkamba tribe. This tribe had been loyal to the 'Brits' in colonial times and was favoured accordingly. It was easy to see why: they were not Kikuyus, but they were closer to them than the second tribe in Kenya, the Luos in the West. Machakos was the capital town of the Mkamba where I was invited to meet my colleague's family and was spoilt with much African feasting, which was testing.

When I took up my secondment in Kenya in early 1969 I found that I was the only non-African member of the KNTC, which employed some 200 people in Nairobi. My boss was a Luo, Caleb Yaya. I employed an ex-G&R Raleigh man, Parminus Karanja, a Kikuyu. I set about listing all the likely African businessmen who had applied for a Trading Licence, and I was one of three signatories to the granting of a Trading Licence. This put me in an apparently powerful position. The Indian businessmen viewed me with huge suspicion but as I had met them with my Mkamba man I made one or two friends, the most notable was a highly educated Ismaili family, Ismail Kassam of Kassam Kanji. He quickly told me that the Asians' grip of trade was at best going to be compromised and at worst it would be ended.

In order to obtain a Trading Licence, the Indian *duka wallahs* sometimes simply appointed one of their African staff to be the front man, re-form the company under his name, and, putting only a little capital into the re-formed company, they obtained the Licence, and then continued as before. The KNTC could save face and declare for example that Kenya Cycle Mart was now 'Karioki Cycle Company'. Ismail Kassam refused such 'hanky panky' – fought the whole system after applying for a Trading Licence – and lost. He and his family of two daughters became close friends and even advisers. How does one ever replace the experience of generations of Gujarati traders whose work ethic and experience has been passed on from one generation to the next?

However, if those mainly Indian traders were soon going to lose their trading licences, then surely a Kenyan African could fill the void? I covered the length and breadth of Kenya from Mombasa to Kisumu and from Moshi near Kilimanjaro to Nanyuki and Mount Kenya and held evening seminars in each of the towns along this route. I don't keep a diary but I do sometimes scribble down meeting notes and occasionally my itinerary. I am out of breath just reading the itinerary of a tour of Tanzania a couple of years later, in March 1971, which will serve to illustrate the nature of these trips (See map at end of chapter for a sense of the geography).

8th March	Dar es Salaam – Tanga
9th March	Tanga – Moshi
10th March	Moshi – Arusha
11th March	Arusha
12th March	Arusha – Singida
13/14th March	Singida – Nzega – Tabora
15th March	Tabora – Shinyanga
17th March	Shinyanga – Mwanza
18th March	Mwanza – Bukoba by steamer
19th March	Mwanza – Musoma by steamer
20th March	Musoma – Mwanza by steamer
21st March	Mwanza
22nd March	Mwanza – Dodoma
23rd March	Dodoma – Morogoro
24th March	Morogoro – Dar es Salaam

In the bush, and proudly showing the African and Lion poster

From my desk in Nairobi, it swiftly became clear that the Trading Licences that I was authorising on behalf of the KNTC were indeed for Kenyan companies, but they nearly all belonged to one tribe – the Kikuyu. This was fine in the Central and North area where Kikuyus were dominant, but not so elsewhere. I quizzed my Luo boss about this, who took me out of the office to explain that 'British colonisation was being replaced by Kikuyu colonisation'.

It was a dangerous time at the end of the '60s: the charismatic leader of the Luo – Oginga Odinga – very effectively highlighted the pranks of the Kikuyu. Then Tom Mboya, a young and charismatic Luo leader, was shot and killed in Nairobi. Caleb Yaya took me to his house and explained about the Kikuyu, and when he saw that I was sceptical, he invited me to attend an 'oathing ceremony' where, in the Kikuyu heartlands of North Nairobi up to Nanyuki, boys at about the age of puberty danced into a frenzy. Under the blood of a cow, whose jugular was cut, they drank, swearing allegiance to their Kikuyu tribe. We actually drove to the vicinity of one such ceremony, but I felt too frightened to be 'blacked up' and have my blond hair cut and dyed.

I got to know many budding businessmen from nearly every Kenyan tribe. After a short time, I could distinguish the tribes by their name; often I could distinguish them by their behaviour. I wrote a pamphlet on how to import and sell products from overseas to give out to prospective new businessmen at my upcountry seminars. My good friend Ken Dancey was the Manager of the National & Grindlays Bank, and when he warned me that my efforts were at best in vain and at worst personally dangerous, I answered, 'Possibly, but I have to try'. When he saw the success of my township seminars – success being measured by the numbers who attended – he asked that if I gave him the list of those names and addresses of attendees who expressed interest in starting their own business, he would do a credit check on them – very confidentially. I can't remember now, but if over the course of three months I'd given him a hundred names he was unable to help with over 50%. Of the balance he was able to warn me off at least 15%, and of the remaining 35% he would point out that they were mainly all from one tribe trading in another tribe's area but able to obtain grants/money to do so. He warned me of the consequences. I did the same task in Uganda, and Ken's colleague at the bank there also gave me credit references on my short list. This gave me a huge advantage over my KNTC colleagues in doing my work with some apparent success.

However, I can say, without any pride, that after a year of devoted effort I had started up a handful of new business traders in Kenya where there had previously been only one. His name was Omol Obambo and he operated out of River Road, Nairobi. At the end of my first year there was still only one left trading, Omol Obambo, but I had the luck to meet, help and work with another and charming businessman, Laurence Kariuki, who did go on to be a very prominent Kenyan businessman until he died, I heard, in 2020.

My success rate in Uganda, where I undertook similar work, was higher, and I put this down to introductions given me by the Gailey & Roberts (G&R) team to some of the movers and shakers in that country, chief among them the wife of the President, Milton Obote. Through this I was able to replace G&R with an indigenous organisation owned by the Mayor of Kampala, Gurdial Singh, an Asian and his business mate, another Asian. But the smoothest and most charming of all in this team was Jackson Ssentongo, (known as 'Double S'), a leading Bugandan businessman and a big friend of Madam Obote – the President's wife. When Idi Amin replaced President Obote my little indigenous coterie continued to do well during the first few months under a Sandhurst-disciplined leader who seemed to be equipped with a huge sense of fun, even humour. I thought my future in Uganda to be secure.

Back in Nairobi it was less so. None of the lovely students in my seminars seemed to follow up after my tuition. When I returned to my desk in Nairobi I saw that most those to whom trading licences were awarded were from one tribe – the Kikuyu. Meanwhile I had long been friendly with many of the traditional 'Asian' retailers. All treated me with wariness, but all were welcoming. Sardar Singh Vohra was the most successful trader in River Road. He did huge business and then informed me that it was he who made sure Omol Ombambo stayed in business down the road, but that he would never succeed. Sardar Singh Vohra told me that he would be leaving Nairobi as soon as he could get his money out of Kenya and would set up a hotel in London. He did, and I met his brother, Onouph, at his home in North London. He proudly showed me his impressive chain of London hotels, including The Rembrandt Hotel. It was not unusual amongst Indian families to cover their bets at Independence with one member of the family taking out a British passport and citizenship another to take an Indian one and a third to take the nationality of the country they were in. In this way they had options to join their family.

Cycle Mart & Exchange was another large Nairobi retailer, whose owner asked me to recommend the list of names of those Africans I had tried to train, with my assessment of their abilities, which I did. Within a year they had an African frontman for their shop. I noted it was the most 'relaxed' Africans amongst my recommendations that were chosen. Kassam Kanji in Nairobi was my favourite retailer, and different from the others. Ismail Kassam, his wife and two daughters were a delight. Their Ismaili educated and worldly background made them easy and real friends. His introduction to the Nairobi Jockey Club, and to business clubs in Nairobi, made me feel relevant and connected. Meanwhile I was compiling my hopeless list of upcoming African businesses, spotting the tribal bias, and also seeing how I was being manipulated. I then decided to unload to the High Commissioner, Patrick Laver. His dinners were a home from home; he was bright, helpful and positive. He listened to my stories, asked me questions and invited me back.

But work does tend to dominate life, and during the day I sat in an office with four Kenyan Africans, and with another hundred in the KNTC offices in Kenyatta Avenue. Parminus Karanja my ex-United Africa Company (UAC) employee, knew his job from UAC days, and went about it with a confidence that made me feel ignorant. He was also very focussed on the KNTC mission of 'localisation'. He was, happily for me initially, a Kikuyu living in a modest *shamba* which he didn't want to take me to see. He treated me with suspicion, and I felt even dislike. He was at times unnerving to sit alongside.

My position as 'Adviser' was also unclear, and of course I didn't know who I was advising and how to do any particular job. It was my boss, the hugely confident, very bright, Caleb Yaya, who really befriended me. From him I was to learn a little of the KNTC's *raison d'être*. Caleb was a Christian. He asked me to join his family at church services, and he invited me to be his son's godfather. Back at the office Parminus Karanja, my efficient and well-trained (by G&R/UAC) Kikuyu sidekick coolly told me that my friendship with Caleb Yaya had been noticed and that 'I should be careful'. I thanked him and asked him to help me. I pointed out to him the names of traders whose request for trading licences passed my desk for signature every day were all from one tribe. He advised me to sign all those with the Kikuyu name from a Kikuyu area and pass the others to Caleb Yaya's equivalent manager and let him sign those.

What I also didn't appreciate was that my 'whiteness' of course stood out. Nobody knew who I was or why I was there, but I stood out and then worst of all I had immediately warmed to a Luo – Caleb Yaya. Suspicion would turn to dark thoughts, to all of which I was initially oblivious. Try as I might with Parminus I never got deeper than the content of his work – he hated Luos – and I was now becoming a lost cause. The next bad thing I did was to go to the Accounts Department and ask to see 'the books'! I was shown volumes of entries and workings and saw each scribe's function in recording the inputs and outputs. But of a Balance Sheet or Profit and Loss account there was no sign, and whenever I asked, I was referred to another volume of figures. Accounts were not my forte – I was there to bring Kenyan African businessmen into business and to keep up sales of Raleigh bicycles.

Africans generally I found to be collegiate and to love chat, music and laughter. What is more, one is drawn into this world of 'family'. Then the continuous *'Jambo habari' 'Mzuri tu' habari ya gani, nzuri tu, habari ya Watoto'*, the question and replies were always the same, and as a ritual you found it either irritatingly leading nowhere or inclusive and warm and engaging. By the time you had got through the greetings you had finished your first bottle of Tusker, and when a '*lette pombe ngine qua Msungu*' (meaning: 'bring more beer for the European') arrived at speed you soon went with the flow. Talk of politics was endless, and while I expected talk of the British influence in Kenya, or the sins of the past, I received none. I did hear though of a united expectation to emulate what the 'Britishers' have or had. Otherwise, I felt that my prejudices and South African experiences had no place in my KNTC world. A year later, and having become a lot 'blacker', I could go so far as to say that for all its faults the Africa route along which I was travelling was the only route that would survive and succeed. It was corrupt, it was unfair, but it was African and done in an African way. I was a *Msungu*, a European, and expected to behave like one. In fact, when I tried to be more African, whether in my dress or even my behaviour, this was not appreciated, but a good laugh. I had to re-learn. To survive in my job, I found the route to respect was to be the 'perfect white man', to show respect, to teach and to lead from the front. They could misbehave and expected to be punished when I caught them out, but then we should move forward. Tribe and spirituality were strong, and man was fallible and to be forgiven, but above all – move on. Punish, correct and laugh, but I'm not sure if I was allowed to be 'wrong' or 'weak'. I could be 'silly', I could play games, I could make a fool of myself on the dance floor or within a group, but the secret was laughter.

The best illustration of this was an incident on my way from Nairobi to Kampala, driving in my Ford Cortina car (not a 4x4). I was to be in Kampala to meet the Gailey & Roberts (ex UAC) sales force. My usual routine was to leave Nairobi dressed scruffily, as I would collect all the dust and dirt from the *murrum* (mud) roads in the car. Then there was a little club/bar – Chez Suzanna's – just on the outskirts of Kampala, where I would wash, change, polish my black leather shoes, put on my tie and be ready to play my part as though the dust of the road had never touched me. As I was about to turn into Suzanna's I saw an army lorry pulling in ahead of me. 'Gosh I must get in before that gang,' I thought, and quickly parked my car and rushed to the bar. I was about to order a beer when one huge bloke in very grand military attire shouted at the barman, 'Twenty-one beers please'. 'Excuse me,' I said, 'I was here first and just ordering.' He gave me a pitying look and simply said 'Twenty-two beers barman'. Idi Amin had just bought me a beer.

Murchison Falls in North-West Uganda

As an aside, it was just after this particular trip to lovely Uganda that I did a safari up to the North and East of the country to both the towns of Arua and then Aru in the Congo (no border control and Indian traders in both towns sharing the changing tariff regulations in each country) I managed to squeeze in an unplanned visit to Murchison Falls (some 160 miles from Kampala). It was spectacular and made more so by the surprise visit to a place where the Nile is forced through a narrow cleft in the Rift Valley producing a dramatic waterfall. Even more dramatic was the night spent under canvas when the rhinos ventured out of the water and literally surrounded my tent. I stayed awake ready to run. The game we saw was better than anything I'd seen in Kenya or even in the Serengeti and more frightening.

Hippos scampering away from my boat

To continue along my 'African' theme, when I came to leave East Africa after being in the area for some three years, and was seriously considering making a life there, I wondered what conclusions I could draw. Colonialism had brought together false boundaries, making ungovernable territories into a political entity. Missionaries had been a shining light in outposts feeding and adding to the natural need for superstition and belief in age old customs. Societies and differentiation had not really broken down but had often been replaced by 'laws' which had to be bent to fit the local practice.

I never saw in East Africa any starvation; I rarely saw Africans unclothed. I saw women in traditional women's roles of course, but many young women were starting in commercial life; I saw uneducated men solemnly meting out local justice and being obeyed. I had observed educated sick men in Nairobi going first to their witch doctor for a cure before turning to Western medicine. I had noticed the aid agencies trying to fit local society into their preconceived pattern. Local society was happy to oblige, but didn't change. I felt imposed aid or visits by rock stars or princesses were a pageant and bit of fun but not so helpful. I could help only by being a white man, and since it was black men ruling their country, only black men would bring about change and education. The trick was to find a Mandela rather than a Kenyatta, or a President Arap Moi, let alone an Idi Amin or a Mugabe. But that generalisation could be true of the world.

Around my time, elections were held. Peter Kinyanjui was standing for Starehe State – a Nairobi suburb. He asked me to write some speeches for him. I felt so important. In between all of this I was visiting African businessmen from Mombasa to Kisumu. In the evenings I held seminars in each little town on running a business and keeping accounts. I became involved with many local tribes, thinking I would be their gateway to wealth, and soon this drew suspicion within certain of the KNTC management. I had confidence in my friendship with the Chairman Peter Kinyanjui to 'rise above all this petty office politics'. I also found out that many officers of the KNTC were receiving bribes from Asians, and others were setting up their own families in business and so on. I quietly kept notes, and when, naively, I felt more confident decided that I would spill the beans to my mate Peter Kinyanjui. Big mistake. As I cockily reported to him from my notes about the intrigues of his staff and their 'goings on' I saw his face becoming set and angry. Thankfully, I had the sense to stop my denunciations, and with good African body language I burst out laughing and said 'I hoped, he, Peter Kinyanjui would forgive me, but I needed his advice and wanted to be open and conscientious towards him. What should I do Mr Kinyanjui?' His relief matched mine and he too burst out laughing also with relief. 'You be getting to know Africa.

Welcome.' We laughed, but I knew my days were numbered in Kenya. From then on I felt a fraud. I was leading a double life: one with my masters in Nottingham, the other within the KNTC; keeping in with Peter Kinyanjui on the one hand, and on the other promoting the wrongs of the KNTC's practices, and finally betraying the Asian friends upon whom my sales actually relied.

Peter Kinyanjui did see that my presence was a potential embarrassment at best, and a time bomb at worst, and so it was that when my contract came to an end it was not renewed, and we all saved face. When Peter Kinyanjui calmed down after our meeting, he took me out of the office to his Club. Here he told me of his political ambitions and why, by getting into politics he could really deal with the task to which he was called. The KNTC was merely a parastatal organisation to replace the old colonial trading companies like UAC and John Holt – there was bound to be favouritism and some corruption, but in the grand scale of things this was nothing to the bright future that lay ahead.

I had saved my job; I had recovered from my damning report which fortunately I had not delivered in full and where the most damning parts had not been revealed. Peter Kinyanjui then took me under his wing and asked me covertly to help him get into Parliament! 'Write my speeches,' he said. 'Give me suggestions on how to answer questions in Parliament.' I kept my nose clean and wrote suggested speeches for Peter Kinyanjui to deliver, and though I don't know if he did, I do know he didn't get elected. I kept Patrick Laver at the Embassy informed.

The tensions of working within the parastatal organisation of KNTC got to me. After work one Saturday Sue and I went to a golf range where I shot off 100 balls; I felt no better. However, on the way home we drove past Wilson Airport and Sue suggested we drop in. Two hours later she had signed up for a free flight taster, so I did too.

Sue loved flying and was a natural. She chased turbulence and thrilled at G forces. Her pilot that day was Jim Spall, one of the Aero Club's best stunt pilots. Seeing how she reacted to stall turns Jim put the Cessna 150 into a spin, and such was Sue's delight he promised to take her up in the Club's Chipmunk and really fling her about the skies. My pilot, who became my trainer, was Peter Shepherd (The M.D. of Renault in East Africa). He took me for a picturesque trip over the Ngong hills, over the craters of the Great Rift Valley, and I returned entranced with the huge geography that is Africa – and now KNTC tensions seemed a trifle.

We threw ourselves into a course of flying, leading to a Private Pilot's Licence; rarely missing a weekend at Wilson and never missing the monthly air rallies of forced landings, figures of eight, cutting the toilet paper the most times before a roll thrown out at over 5,000 feet hit the earth. Sue even won the forced landings event one weekend, and the pewter cigarette ashtray prize was at once one of her proudest possessions. Meanwhile, after the necessary forty hours of flying, with circuits and bumps and solo cross country, I gained my Private Pilots Licence (PPL).

My weekly life of travel around the country to visit and educate new dealers and traders, followed up by office work in the evenings and, even after flying at weekends, continued to take its toll – until I hit upon the idea of flying to see my customers. I could do daily trips, save on hotel bills and actually cover more ground and dealers than on endless car journeys. I wrote to Raleigh requesting permission and received the superb Jimmy Cumming's reply that my insurance would not cover any flying accident, but I should put in expenses for my 'normal' journey; which would include hotel, petrol and meals/entertainment. I worked out how to do this at a profit and save a day a week of time at work. What was more, the dealers loved it. I would fly to Nakuru, circle over the Cycle Mart and Exchange shop, open and close the throttle to attract Mr Shah's attention, who promptly chucked any customers out of his shop declaring 'his Raleigh' man was here. Then he would drive to the newly grassed landing strip to collect me, and proudly reopen his shop – often with treble the number of customers waiting to see who this man from the skies in his '*machine ndege*' was – and in those days my hair was long and blonde – so I didn't disappoint. An hour later I was on to Kisii and then Saroti or Kericho and home for dinner. I hasten to confirm that this happy procedure didn't last long enough to be too impressive, but the Raleigh man became known, and my flying skills improved!

I do recall an embarrassing flying story: I entered a map reading exercise at the Aero Club. We were given coordinates to fly in a triangle from Wilson airport towards Thika in the Aberdares and then turn west on another leg of the triangle to another coordinate and turn back to Wilson. I was accompanied by one of the two judges on the competition for this 40 minute 'game'. I had a couple of hours fuel in the tank and off I set having done my ground flight plan. I had noticed that at the first reference point there was a small bridge, I also noted that I had a tail wind for this leg. The first leg I calculated to take some 6 – 7 minutes but after 10 minutes or so there was no sign of the little bridge. I thought I had overestimated the tail wind so decided to make my westerly turn. This was the long leg of the journey and on I proceeded to what should have been a clear junction on the topography of the land. After a further 30 minutes along my compass bearing, I had no alternative but to confess to the judge that I was lost. He said he would take control. Ten minutes later he too said that he was lost! We had been going for nearly an hour and had an hour's fuel left. Fortunately, my fellow pilot knew the Aberdares and we followed a track which led to the famous Tree Tops Game Lodge. We happily located the Lodge, but

Cessna 150 at Magadi Airstrip, on my first cross-country flight with my instructor, Peter Shephard getting off the plane

after several more minutes. From Tree Tops it was a 20-minute journey back to Wilson. He explained to me my initial error of underestimating the tail wind at the height at which I was flying on the first leg of the journey. I not only reached the area of the little bridge in less time than I had expected but the wind had also blown me off course by enough to make a ground sighting unreliable. The judge was aware of what I had done and chose to let me get into trouble and thereby learn. However just as I had misjudged the tail wind speed, this now had an adverse effect on flying against the wind back to Wilson with fuel running out faster than calculated and with a head wind. As you can see, we made it and I didn't do well in the competition. I lost a lot of confidence after this little debacle. Flying South-East to Mombasa was easy, as below me was both a road and a railway; flying North West to Kisumu the same. But to fly in a straight line strictly on a pre worked compass heading with bush land beneath was another matter. This was in the days when your so-called flight 'computer' was strapped to your knee and there were no radio beacons. I had had a good lesson.

When the time came I did not want to leave Kenya. Thanks to my Private Pilot's Licence, I had partied on uncharted beach islands off the Mombasa coast, camped in game reserves and visited much of Kenya. I felt at home, loved the country, made many friends but was inwardly very insecure in my daily work. In less secure moments I felt I could call upon the British Consul, Patrick Laver. He too was on his own and his dinners were good. When my work permit expired – and not renewed – he told me that he had been concerned for my safety and was prepared to get me out of the country. I was thankfully too naïve to see it and anyway, by the time I left I had maintained my duplicity and felt I had won a kind of confidence with my KNTC peers – no face was lost except perhaps mine. It was difficult not to love the East Africa of the remnants of the colonial times in which I partly lived.

We talk of 'Africa'. It is a huge continent: the whole of the U.S.A., China and India could fit into it with space for Western Europe too. It is profitable too to look at a tribal map of Africa showing all the major tribes and their whereabouts and then overlay the political boundaries and ponder the consequences.

I reflected on this when I arrived in South Africa. I had known it through the press, for its *apartheid* and Boerish governments, I had heard it through my history lessons: the 'Stand at Rorke's Drift' and the Boer war and the exploits of Baden Powell and Winston Churchill, the Great Trek of the Boers, Chaka and his Zulus and Miriam Makebe's Zhosa Click songs. The books Mick Keller gave me to read were all of the Macaulay and Trevelyan variety of 'Whig' history. But they made sense in the context of the South Africa that I visited. The story fitted with my perception and helped me feel a part of it all.

In Kenya I started in the same way. Back home I'd learned how the East African regiments fought with the British in the Second World War (My Uncle, Bill Godfrey, had been shot down in his Hurricane in Uganda and was posted 'missing', only to turn up many months later, being looked after by local Africans.) I'd followed all the news about the *Mau Mau* campaign while at School in the 1950s. Now, preparing to visit the country, I read the likes of Isak Dinesen's *Out of Africa,* a tale of the hardship of farming and settling, and Robert Ruark's books, especially *Uhuru*, which these days is not considered 'PC'.

When I arrived, the grand architecture of Nairobi, the lovely suburbs of Karen or Westlands, the dual carriageway roads with beautiful bougainvillea along the centre section made me realise this was a colony not to be given away. (Independence they say is never granted but always taken.) The parks where Indian families seem to mill around so colourfully on days off, all added to a picture of bliss, charm and peace. The difference was that in South Africa I went to work for an established British Company with British folk diligently doing the job they had learnt in the U.K. There I met Jewish traders who once again fitted in with my preconceived ideas, and the Boers who, once I had them explained to me, also fitted into the world as I conceived it. What was different in coming to Kenya was that I was the only white man in a black organisation in a newly Independent Country. I obtained a first-hand insight of the future too. When I left the office, I occasionally visited the various British Clubs or even hotels or the Long Bar at the New Stanley Hotel, and it was easy to go back to and to appreciate the colonial times and behaviour.

A poem that has always resonated with me is Rudyard Kipling's '*Pagett, MP*'. I have had many Pagetts visit me overseas, and they are always a trial. One such – he will remain nameless but let's call him Mr P – was a main board director who came to check on my initiatives in Uganda. All at Raleigh UK had had a say on Kenya and Tanzania, but for some reason had not discussed Uganda. I knew that this Mr P would be impressed with the Unilever bosses of United Africa Company, from whom I had wrested the Raleigh business, passing it to a local operation. This had not just UAC's blessing but their help with the transition. Of course, to an old school Brit the comparison with my local new men like 'Double S', and Gurdhial Singh, the Mayor of Kampala, was stark. The UAC boss in Kampala was a Swiss, Kurt Waller, who was also the Swiss Consul for Uganda and politically savvy. My Mr P loved him and discussed all sorts of grand subjects including his suspicions on my initiatives. Kurt did not pick up on this English duplicity. When the time came for Mr P's departure I drove him out to Entebbe airport and suggested we had dinner at the fine Entebbe Hotel before catching his midnight flight. What I had forgotten was that this was the week of the Lake Victoria flies. Around Lake Vic the air is a black cloud of these tiny creatures that have a 24-hour life. Into the Hotel we went, waving aside the clouds of insects, and indeed the hotel was relatively fly-free. However, when the soup arrived one such flea hit the light above our table and, instantly killed; fell into Mr P's soup. I hadn't realised the effect these harmless creatures were having on Mr P, as that fly in his soup was for him the last straw in a week that he had found stressful. He totally 'lost it', slammed down his spoon telling me that 'if I couldn't get rid of these mosquitoes I should take him straight to the airport and go'. I didn't need telling twice, I'd had enough of his pomposity and dropped him early for his flight and went back to dinner at the hotel before the long drive to Nairobi. It was here at Entebbe that I met Richard Dowden a newly-arrived teacher, who was living nearby. Some years later he became a journalist, and reading his articles, I found that his views on Africa coincided with many of my own. I recommend his book *Africa: Altered States, Ordinary Miracles*. He gave me a signed copy when I met him, much later on in Bath in 2018.

PAGETT, M.P.

Pagett, M.P., was a liar, and a fluent liar therewith, –
He spoke of the heat of India as 'The Asian Solar Myth'
'Came on a four months' visit, to 'study the East' in November
And I got him to make an agreement vowing to stay till September.

March came in with the *koil*. Pagett was cool and gay,
Called me a 'bloated Brahmin', talked of my 'princely pay'.
March went out with the roses. 'Where is your heat?' said he.
'Coming', said I to Pagett. 'Skittles !' said Pagett, M.P.

April began with the punkah, coolies, and prickly-heat, –
Pagett was dear to mosquitoes, sandflies found him a treat.
He grew speckled and lumpy – hammered, I grieve to say,
Aryan brothers who fanned him, in an illiberal way.

May set in with a dust-storm, – Pagett went down with the sun.
All the delights of the season tickled him one by one.
Imprimis – ten days' 'liver – due to his drinking beer;
Later, a dose of fever – slight, but he called it severe.

Dysent'ry touched him in June, after the *Chota Bursat* –
Lowered his portly person – made him yearn to depart.
He didn't call me a 'Brahmin', or 'bloated', or 'over-paid',
But seemed to think it a wonder that any one ever stayed.

July was a trifle unhealthy, – Pagett was ill with fear,
Called it the 'Cholera Morbus', hinted that life was dear.
He babbled of 'Eastern exile', and mentioned his home with tears;
But I hadn't seen my children for close upon seven years.

We reached a hundred and twenty once in the Court at noon,
(I've mentioned Pagett was portly) Pagett went off in a swoon.
That was an end to the business. Pagett, the perjured, fled
With a practical, working knowledge of 'Solar Myths' in his head.

And I laughed as I drove from the station, but the mirth died out on my lips
As I thought of the fools like Pagett who write of their 'Eastern Trips',
And the sneers of the travelled idiots who duly misgovern the land,
And I prayed to the Lord to deliver another one into my hand.

Rudyard Kipling

Kampala was a joy to visit nestled around its six hills and not far from the Nile's source – Lake Victoria. I would buy cheroots from a local Bugandan who sold them from a huge sack at five shillings a handfull. The trick when smoking them was to throw away any that wouldn't easily draw. Africanisation under President Obote seemed to have a more relaxed face than in Kenya and when indeed Obote was replaced by Idi Amin many thought better times lay ahead. I did. I also knew well all the wahindi traders, not just in Kampala, but in many of the large towns which I had visited with my salesman Jackson Mbuga. One of the kindest of these Indian traders was Rajabali Valimohammed. When it was his turn to leave, he asked me for help. I rang the Managing Director of Raleigh Canada, Dennis Hensby, who gladly offered him and his clever son Farid a job. Farid Vaiya later went on to be appointed the CEO of Raleigh Canada! Kampala too was the home of an old United Africa Company friend of mine, Ted Mackay and his wife Joan. His house backed onto the gardens of the President's Palace. You don't mess with Idi; one day Ted was shooing-off some of Idi Amin's chickens that had crossed into his garden and was eating the seeds just planted by Joan. He was promptly kicked out of the country and came to stay with me in Dar es Salaam until he could return to the UK.

But 'hurrah', no sooner did my contract with the KNTC end than I was sent to Dar es Salaam to begin the implementation of a new East Africa Raleigh bicycle factory. In good Raleigh style between Kenya and going down to Tanzania I was asked to return home to the UK via Sudan as a 'situation' had arisen there that needed resolution.

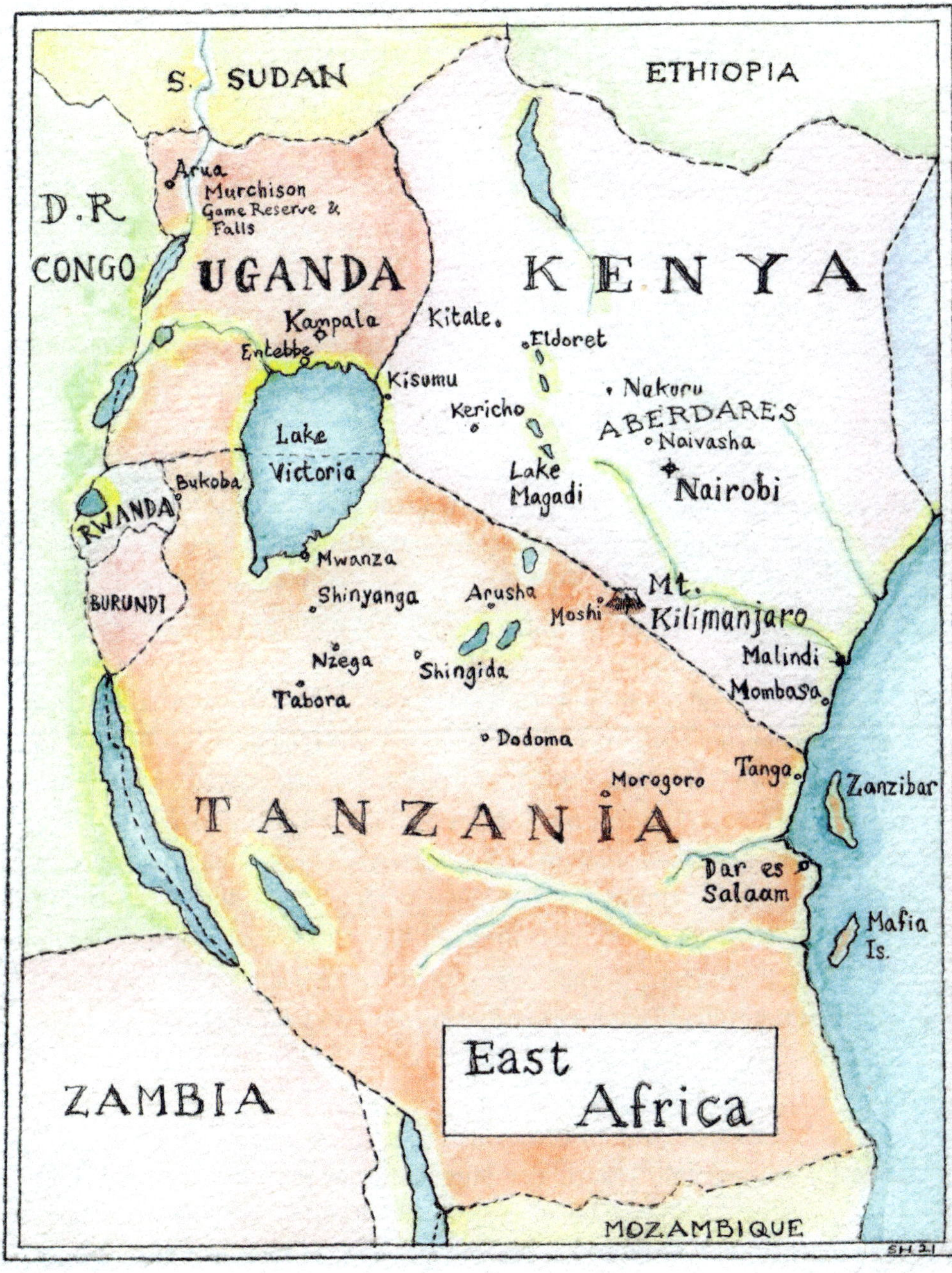
S. SUDAN
ETHIOPIA
D.R.
CONGO
Arua
Murchison
Game Reserve &
Falls
UGANDA
KENYA
Kampala
Entebbe
Kitale
Eldoret
Kisumu
Nakuru
Kericho
ABERDARES
Naivasha
Lake
Victoria
Lake
Magadi
Nairobi
Bukoba
RWANDA
Mwanza
BURUNDI
Shinyanga
Arusha
Moshi
Mt.
Kilimanjaro
Malindi
Nzega
Shingida
Mombasa
Tabora
Dodoma
Tanga
Morogoro
Zanzibar
TANZANIA
Dar es
Salaam
Mafia
Is.
East
Africa
ZAMBIA
MOZAMBIQUE
SH 21

The Sudanese Interlude, 1969

First a bit of background: Raleigh Industries Ltd, like so many old U.K. companies, was by the 1960's the product of takeovers and mergers. When I joined, it was in the *Guinness Book of Records* as the largest cycle manufacturer in the world. Raleigh could boast making and selling over four million bikes a year in 144 countries. With all the brand names that it accumulated – some 160 names I was told by Stan Beard in the export department – Raleigh's heritage was emerging as a must for anyone interested in the history of transport. However, one of the difficulties in such a history was the warring of the distributors in many of the 144 countries where Raleigh was competing against Phillips, Hercules or BSA. But by 1964 they were all Raleigh Industries owned. Suddenly the Phillips agent, who had been the enemy, and the Raleigh man were supposedly on the same side.

The amalgamation at Raleigh's Head Office created difficulties in individual markets. In 1971 I was to go to Afghanistan – we'll get to this later – with the unenviable task of deciding who would be Raleigh's representative in the local market; the Afghan company owned by Shiv Nandan, or the part-British owned Anglo/Afghan Agencies Ltd. In Iran too there were similar difficulties, where Tabarrok, representing Hercules, Tavikalipoor representing Phillips and Grey Mackenzie, the old colonial company which represented Raleigh all now came under the same umbrella. These sorts of tensions were only exacerbated when Raleigh, trying to rationalise its range, cut down on the 60,000 unique models they were making.

There were similar problems in Sudan, where I arrived in 1969 with the undesirable job of deciding between the Greek-owned Taki Gounapolous Company which represented Phillips and the Armenian-owned Khatchikian which represented Raleigh. There was now no room for two distributors in the Sudanese market where we were trying to fight Indian and Japanese competitors and it was becoming ever more difficult to trade. In the end I chose the Taki Gounapolous Company to represent all of Raleigh Industries Ltd rather than the Khatchikian but a coin would have been as good a way as any to choose, and neither of the two companies was Sudanese anyway.

I went around the Sudanese market with Costas Fallaris, Taki's long-term partner, giving his company credence in the marketplace. Taki Gounapolous had put in a Sudanese frontman under which to launch the new Raleigh Company thereby giving it a more acceptable 'black face' – Rifaat Suleiman Abdullah. It was this rather cynical initiative that persuaded my choice. What a trip this proved to be. A white face that was not local, and preferably British, was important to keep the confidence of all the dealers that Raleigh was genuine throughout the change. So, Costas duly took me around his platform of some 100 dealers throughout the huge territory of Sudan. After a week in Khartoum and Omdurman we went by train from El Obeid to Wad Medani – a 24-hour journey with the train stopping every three hours or less. At each station Costas had mailed ahead to ensure that each dealer came to the station for a 10 to 15-minute meeting with us. This was through the night and all of the day. I was sharing a cabin with a lovely chap, Tony Woods, from BEREC – British Every Ready Batteries. It was a life saver to have him there, we were the only two non-residents of Sudan on that train I believe. He selling his batteries and me my bikes.

One wrote market reports in those days, and out of interest I took to counting the number of sacks full of cotton stacked up alongside the rail track – thousands of them. I was in the top bunk during the night when you could hope for a 3-hour rest without interruption. It was baking hot and stupidly we opened the windows to let in some air. After an hour sweating, unfortunately I gave up, and turned on my bed light and to my horror the cabin was full of insects. I looked down at Tony, fast asleep, with a huge ladybird type insect covering his bare foot. I said to Tony, 'Tony, wake up and don't move, you have an insect on your foot, don't panic.' Tony opened his eyes, saw his foot, and screamed. At this point we both lost it, and screaming and shouting we set about using our shoes to kill all the intruders. There was blood everywhere and when the neighbours came in to see what all the fuss was about. They saw this battleground of two nearly naked Englishmen out of control slaughtering legions of flies, insects and worse.

At last, the journey ended, which it did on a high note for me in Wad Medani where Costas informed me that one of the biggest Raleigh dealers lived in the neighbourhood. Sadly, he said this chap couldn't see us as he had a family occasion on the day of our arrival. 'How many bikes does he buy?' I asked. 'Five hundred a year,' said Costas, 'every year'. 'Indeed, his shop is made out of Raleigh packing cases.' 'Well,' I declared, 'we must go and see him'. Costas was not amused, but must have thought, 'Right, I'll show these stupid English. They have no idea of local conditions.' He then arranged for the three of us, Tony, himself and me, with two guides plus a police escort to go and see this customer. We were up before the sun and set forth. If, like me, you've ridden a camel at a zoo or during a visit to the pyramids in Egypt, you'd think this might be fun. The reality of several hours on a camel is not an experience you'd repeat. We did it. Our dealer was thrilled and had prepared a dish of camel meat for our lunch, washed down with Coca

Our fleet of camels relaxing, somewhere south of Wad Medani

Cola. He placed an order for 1,000 bicycles and showed us his resplendent shop all made from the softwood boards of Raleigh packing cases. But was it worth it? Perhaps only because it's yet another story, an experience from which my body ached for days thereafter. Unknown to me at the time, it could have ached a lot worse. I didn't understand why we had to have a police escort of some six or so soldiers armed with rifles plus the local chief of police. In total the party numbered 14 people. As we set off I had assumed that once underway our escorts would fall out. Only on the journey back did the chief of police regale us with hair raising and blood curdling stories. There were two tribes in the area, the Dinka and Nuer, that had been feuding for centuries. One of the customs of these tribes was to expel boys at their time of puberty and they could only return to claim a bride if they had castrated a number of their enemy. Apparently a white pair would count for more – how do you tell the ethnic origin of such a dismembered part, I hear you ask? I didn't wait for the reply. Other more bizarre tales soon filled the time and eased the pain from riding these rather smelly and uncomfortable beasts.

I saw the High Commissioner back in Khartoum and told him some of my experiences. He asked me for a copy of my report and some six months later I read his report in 'Africa Confidential' of the numbers of sacks of cotton rotting at the side of the railways from El Obeid to Wad Medani!

We were with a Greek in our travels, and in many of the villages we visited there was a Greek Club – with many of the British Clubs, closed down after Independence. The Greek Clubs were lively, fun and a centre for the exchange of the most unlikely of stories with characters that defied description or belief. My first visit gave me many memorable scars, and sometimes I even remember experiences which were too extreme to be repeated. I hasten to add that the Sudan and particularly Port Sudan, on the Red Sea was not a place I'd ever forget, and for positive reasons. I hope a couple of photos will tell a tale which I include to remind me of those only fit for oral transmission!

Costas Fallaris, Tony Woods and I go hunting in this Wheeley Jeep

On the balcony overlooking Port Sudan

Tanzania 1971/2

I duly returned from the Sudan to the UK before taking up my role in Tanzania with their National Development Corporation (NDC) to establish them as the local manufacturer of bicycles in East Africa. This move was potentially life changing for me with the implication that upon its successful implementation I would be called upon to remain in Tanzania and run this company. I embarked on the project with much excitement.

Raleigh Industries had decided that the only way to protect their 80% market share in the East Africa bicycle market was to set up local production with the Government issuing tariff protection from imports. This had been successfully employed very early on in South Africa in 1952 and in in Malaysia in 1968. Tanzania was the largest of the three East African states and so the logical place in which to establish a production unit. I was sent there to bring about this decision and make it a reality. I failed; but the process was a fascinating one.

By the time I was in Dar es Salam I was becoming more 'African' in outlook, and because there is no majority tribe in Tanzania it was easier to be above tribal issues than in say Kenya with the Kikuyu, or even in Uganda with the largest tribe of Buganda. The idealism of President Julius Nyerere was infectious, and although the standard of living in Tanzania was much lower than Kenya and the people poorer, there was a warmth throughout the country which was much less tribal than its neighbour with its dominant Kikuyu tribe. I set about learning Swahili at the local Goethe Institute, and practised in my (NDC) office with the girls of the typing pool who would give me and my Canadian colleague, Charlie Singer, a phrase of the day which we had to repeat to the head lady of the typing pool. We learnt many rude expressions and repeated them without really knowing what we were saying, reducing the girls to fits of laughter.

To give the flavour of living in Dar es Salaam one little story can suffice. The expat world of Dar was small. Social life revolved around the Dar Club, the Yacht Club and the gorgeous beaches. Work was all consuming, but in the constant humid heat it was also draining, and much liquid intake was necessary. Dar was, for an expat, a little village, and agreeable too. Christmas 1971 saw the production of *Goldilocks and the Three Bears* at the old colonial Little Theatre. One of the more 'colourful' Dar locals was a gregarious Lebanese lady – Erica – who was chosen to play the part of Mama Bear. When her lines came up 'and who's been sleeping in my bed?!' an old boy from the back of the theatre stood up and shouted, 'Hands up who hasn't!' Erica loved it, and the audience erupted. True pantomime participation.

In Tanzania I met Swedish Volunteers working passionately for 'volunteer services'. I bumped into them in the most unlikely of places in villages like Dodoma or Morogoro, and sometimes shared a beer. It always appeared to me that while they engaged with local people they had never mentally left Sweden, and kept their superior Swedish views unmodified. As I became inevitably involved with politics in Tanzania, and then too the building of the (white elephant) Chinese Railway from Dar to Lusaka, I felt that the influence of these well-meaning Swedes was minimal.

Julius Nyerere's socialist state in Tanzania made for a much softer society than the harsh capitalist state of the Kikuyu in Kenya. One of its many downsides was 'shortages', the shortages that come from state planning. The government meant well, but somehow expected an altruism from its people which was forthcoming verbally and on intent, but rarely translated into effective action. Witness the Ujama collectivised villages. One other case was the shortage of housing, including for the small number of expats that had been brought into Tanzania with no thought of how they were to be housed. Sue and I arrived in Dar, and after less than a week of staying at the Pan Afric hotel was offered an amazing house in Oyster Bay owned by the Commonwealth Development Corporation (CDC). Apart from a living room the size of a tennis court, it had three double bedrooms each with a bathroom attached. I had made friends with a German family the Weissflogs, who had been living in the Pan Afric for over three months in one room with their three year-old son, Sten. As it was coming up to Christmas, I suggested that the three of them move in with us over Christmas, and, if we got along, they should all stay. They did, and we could. They were a delightful family, and thanks to them I was introduced to the very powerful German colony of expats. I became friends with their Ambassador, who was a frequent dinner guest – the contrast at that time with the U.K. High Commissioner was remarkable; the latter being more 'political' and the former totally dedicated to trade.

Tanganyika had been a German colony. The Treaty of Versailles in 1919 put it under British control, and very happily the economic region of East Africa was born – Uganda, Kenya and Tanganyika. With the merger of Zanzibar and Tanganyika, it became 'Tanzania'. One episode sticks in my mind as a comment on life as it has become. Dietmar Weissflog, a civil engineer, was due to go to Tanga, up the coast from Dar es Salaam, for a couple of days. He returned with a tale to tell. He had met an old African who spoke the most beautiful old German, and had confided to Dietmar his preference for the German system over that of the British newcomers in 1919. 'You know,' he said, 'if you were caught stealing a sheep by the Germans you were beaten eighteen times in public and allowed to go. Under the British you were caught, put into prison, then tried and then sent back to prison for at least six months. How are you meant to look after your family under the British system?'

The Raleigh factory was to be located in Morogoro which is inland from Dar es Salaam. I took one look at that and hastily changed it to Moshi which is in the North, on the slopes of Kilimanjaro in the territory of the lovely Chaga tribe. There were to be three expats – a Managing Director, a Commercial Director and a Production Director. The three bungalows being built were designed in a super colonial style, and I ensured the terraces were enlarged and that one of the houses included a swimming pool. I then had to remove the squatters in the area of the factory and houses, also a learning experience largely meaning that when out of sight you became out of mind and the squatters simply would move back.

Back in Dar es Salaam I located myself in the National Development Company (NDC) offices in the Port area. I paid frequent visits to the State Trading Company (STC), since this trading company was the exclusive importer of Raleigh and other bicycles. It was thanks to my contacts here that I later discovered that while the NDC sat on the right-hand side of Nyerere the STC sat on his left-hand side. They were playing conflicting games: the NDC wanted investment and employment; the STC wanted trade. I found that the Chinese 'Tanzam' Railway, basically a political gift from Chairman Mao to socialist Nyerere, was to be paid for by 'as much Chinese produce as possible' – of course this included bicycles. To be discreet the Chinese bicycles were not imported through Dar es Salaam where I and my NDC colleagues would see them, but north of there in Tanga where the bikes were offloaded. (Funnily enough, I was friendly with the local Reuters journalist and he asked me to fly him along the Chinese Railway with the passenger door removed so that he could film, an interesting aerodynamic effect on the aircraft too, but it was educational in respect of what was really going on in far-out places, with many Chinese living in far corners never to return to China of course.) My revealing of this duplicity between NDC and STC saw the end of the Raleigh factory and of me. In fact, I telephoned my Head Office in Nottingham and later discovered that this call had been tapped, and hence my expulsion from what I thought was going to be a dream job. I loved Tanzania even more than Kenya and I was kicked out. I had even agreed to buy an old 180 tail dragger Cessna from an Arusha farmer and dreamt of flying escapades to my old Kenyan chums, and weekends on the Dar es Salaam golden beaches. In retrospect all this probably was for the best but at the time I was 'gutted'. Life ahead looked set for much struggle but in an environment which I loved, and well-housed potentially in Moshi, next to a golf course and a large mountain and selling a product for which there would be an ongoing demand. As ever, politics intervened and the country, as well as myself, were the losers.

Before I left there were two incidents worthy of recall and which stand apart as do the islands in which they took place.

In July 1971 I was asked by Mr Karachiwallah to come to Zanzibar as he wanted to place a complicated spares order – could I come the next day? (We made a lot of profit on spare parts, so I'd certainly be there.) In the tropics you have 12 hours of light and 12 hours of dark. I was only VFR-rated (for visual flight), and on single engine propeller planes. It was a three-hour flight from Dar to Zanzibar, so approximately seven hours of flying time, what with paperwork and winds, etc. After one of my many 'white nights' I got up in the dark, drove to the Aero Club where I had booked out a lovely Cessna 182, filed and submitted to the control tower my flight plan, completed my pre-flight checks, and got permission to take off just as dawn broke. Karachiwallah duly met me and drove me to his office in Stone Town. He had completed 80% of his order but the remaining 20% needed my help with specifications and prices. I never looked at the part of the completed order otherwise we would have missed the necessary special curry lunch and the essential pleasantries which were always needed to fill in the blanks about how the order was to be paid for, and who were the customers he was supplying. All was fully and acceptably explained, and at 15:00 hours I took off back to Dar with a worried eye on the crosswinds. I literally arrived at dusk and with a wink to the control tower all formalities were happily covered. That evening I had been invited to an outrageous beach party on Honeymoon Island and fired up by my day, proceeded to (un)dress for the party. We returned in our Zodiac inflatables the next morning. It was two days later before I looked at Karachiwallah's orders and totted it up – it came to over £1 million in 1971 money! My salary in 1970 was less than £3,000 p.a. I did all sorts of sums calculating that an agent should earn a 5% commission etc, etc. Nonetheless I, modestly, understatedly, submitted the order to Nottingham expecting telegrams to be sent to me and my heart pumped in anticipation. No reaction from H.O. I reflected on those 36 hours of day and night, going through each and every moment. No, I'd covered everything.

The point of my telling this story here and now at length, is that it all had a sad end. First Raleigh did not have ECCD (insurance) cover on Karachiwallah, despite my submitted local bank references showing he was good for £1 million; these were not accepted, nor were the business references I had also supplied. Karachiwallah simply did not feature on the Insurance Company's records. So, the order could only be supplied 'On Discretion' to a maximum of £25,000 per shipment. Paltry stuff in my new world order, so dear Karachiwallah paid for every £25,000 in advance before shipment and a further £25,000 on arrival. This should have meant twenty shipments over two years. I had promised the first shipment after a three-month lead time with the whole order completed over the following nine months. After three years only 25% of that order had been despatched. In the meantime, Karachiwallah's customers had to buy what they needed from India, with 'copy' Raleigh parts at much lower prices of course and quality. I could have collected myself the cash from each of the Zanzibari dealers prior to shipment and remitted these to Raleigh. I knew Karachiwallah could pay more up front on request. But no, Head Office plodded on by the book doing what Head Office does – their way and no-one getting into trouble. Anyway, it was the 1970s with a three-day week and redundancies looming – what to do? I was told by the factory that getting an order was the easy part.

Two years later in 1974 I was in Australia struggling to get an order for two bikes from dealers, totalling less than £100. It seemed always to be a story of ignorance, bad debt and much whingeing. When your goods arrive, you find his funds committed to a cheaper regular source from a rep who's now a friend.

I reflected upon the sorry pass to which the UK had descended, particularly in its manufacturing sector. Give me my Gujerati duka wallahs any time, compared to the ignorant opportunists and new breed of retail chancers. These people, the Gujeratis that is, were used to being abused by their local dealers, by government officials, and taken for granted by folk like me. They had taken their retail experience around the British Empire, providing an infrastructure and spreading wealth over areas no white man would want to venture to or live in. Goods and life's necessities reached the poorest areas and resulted in money circulation and extensive wealth creation. Still, and despite many hardships they endured, they were always polite, socially generous and engaging, giving of their time and energy, and they treated me like a lord. What business UK Ltd lost throughout the '70s without even knowing it. Where are they now? Living in Leicester, and doing very nicely.

My office in Dar es Salaam offered a splendid view of the city's very natural harbour. The view from the pilot's seat of a light aircraft was even better!

Mafia Island, 1971 and 2016

Sadly the Dar Aero Club was not of the standard of the club at Wilson, Nairobi. There were no monthly air rallies to maintain your flying skills, and little social life. However, I did become friendly with the Lufthansa pilots whose knowledge dated back to colonial days, and they told me some secrets. One of them was Mafia Island. I couldn't resist, and Dietmar's wife and son, Karin and Sten, wanted to join me for a weekend there. It was magical, but it had a nerve-tingling ending. I booked two rooms at the north end of the island near to the little grass runway strip at the only rest house. Here we met a Liverpudlian diver who was delighted to have company and to show off his knowledge of the best dives and corals. These unspoilt coral gardens were a paradise. At that time, I had not passed my Paddy diving certificate, and anyway there was no place to hire equipment. We simply put rocks in our swimming trunks to deepen and hasten our dives, and had only a snorkel for air. There were coral pillars coming up from the bottom of the sea with different fauna, flora and fish to be explored at each level. We were young and unaware of the danger of 'the bends', and only came up for air at the last moment, and very quickly, from depths of some fifteen metres. Karin and I were euphoric with our discoveries, and then on the beaches, with son Sten, we found a wealth of shells that would be difficult to see let alone find these days. We left all of them there. The weekend came to an end too quickly.

Then came the time to leave, and the nerve-tingling moment arrived. When I had come into land on the grass strip, I was aware of the shortness of the runway, but had simply side-slipped the little Cherokee onto the runway thereby losing height quickly and making for a short landing. Taking off was another matter. It wasn't just the length of the runway that was worrying; it was that the palm trees at either end that had grown of course since those Lufthansa pilots landed and took-off from there. My Liverpudlian diver friend felt I would make it if I took off all weight including jettisoning as much fuel as possible. We actually left our weekend cases and contents at the Rest House and, dressed in swimming trunks, tee shirt and flip flops boarded our plane. Karin was quite relaxed, thank heaven. I then pushed the Cherokee to the far edge of the runway, arranged for six Africans to help, with two sitting on the tailplane to hold it down, another two to man each of the chocs on the wheels and two to hold the wings while I revved up the engine till the little plane shuddered and I signalled 'chocs away'. All six simultaneously dropped to the floor and let the wheels free. The Cherokee roared away to face the oncoming palms trees, and with the stall warning screaming in my ears, I pulled back on the stick and cleared the trees with sweat and fear, and then with a sense of euphoria. This was followed by shock at my idiocy of ever attempting this feat. Maybe I exaggerate as I recall this, but this frightening experience actually made me a better and more careful pilot. Why do we need to experience such lessons in order to learn?

Such was the impression Mafia made on me that, 46 years later, I decided that I simply had to take Ane Marie and the twins there, to show them the island, along with some other places I wanted them to see in this part of the world. You will be introduced to them later on in this memoir – good things are worth waiting for. …

I arranged a full trip for my return in Christmas 2016 starting by staying in Nakuru in Kenya with my Raleigh Licensee, Sanjay Shah and his wife, Neelam and their family. I was keen for the twins to see how a successful and thoughtful Jain family lived and how they used and regarded wealth. Our day visiting the famous St Andrews School in Turi where the Shahs' eldest son, Niray, was a pupil was so worthwhile with many of the teachers knowing the twins' teachers in the UK. It was reassuring that the values of a solid UK Public School education were being maintained and appreciated in Kenya and with many past and future Presidents among its alumni. One of the Shahs' close friends was Mrs McCall, who I knew from my Aero Club days, and happily we went to her lovely colonial house shortly before she passed away.

We visited the nearby game reserves, seeing the Great Rift Valley, the famous Thomsons Falls and so much else. It was a particular surprise when Neelam and Sanjay suggested we should visit Julia McColl to find that I knew her from my Kenya days when she was Julia Rutherford and very active at the Aero Club, of all things she was to die soon after our visit, so I am glad to have this picture of us in her colonial 'shamba'. Then onto Nairobi to stay with the parents of Tim's Radley school chum, the Roests, in the lovely district of Karen where Ane Marie was intrigued to see Karen Blixen's House having seen her place in northern Sealand in Denmark. Then, against my will, we spent a couple of days in Zanzibar, which turned out to be the highlight of our trip, with a stay at the Baraza Hotel claiming to be one of the world's

With the Shah family at the Thompson Falls Lodge

Julia McCall's house in the Aberdares

best. We visited spice fields, sampling varieties of the traditional source of Zanzibar's wealth then returning to our top star hotel to enjoy a profusion of irresistible food.

The Bazara Hotel, Zanzibar

From there we went to what I intended to be the trip's highlight – Mafia. They say never go back, and 'they' are right. From an island with a population of some 2,500 souls in 1970 it now had over 60,000 inhabitants. It is now the dry fish centre supplying all of East Africa. It has a tar road running from north to south built by the Americans, no doubt for strategic reasons to be a base on the Indian Ocean. I recognised nothing; but of-course got chatting to some locals who knew where the old grass strip was and back I went to find that 'my' Rest House was being pulled down to make way for another grand hotel. At least I was able to regain my bearings. I decided to get away quickly and we went on an organised boat trip and swam with whale sharks, which were a wonder for us all, but left with sadness in my heart at the changes in my secret place.

We left on a twin-engine plane, and the French pilot let me take over flying after take-off and before landing, which was a consolation, especially as I recalled the terrain over which we flew. It did prepare me for Dar es Salaam the last leg of our journey where even my sumptuous bungalow in Oyster Bay had been pulled down and replaced with a two-storey modern hideosity. The Oyster Bay Hotel had also been turned into a bijou hotel by the son of the owner who I knew – the Bailey family. I went quietly to the cemetery near Oyster Bay where Jimmy Cummings baby son, also 'James', was buried dying in his first year; alas the grave and little tomb stone was no longer there.

It was no longer 'my world' but what a privilege to have lived in that world.

Amalie, with her hair in braids, walks Mafia Beach

The Middle East, 1972 onwards, including that 'mountainous mess of medieval mentalities' - Afghanistan

The long and winding road through the North-West Frontier

Back in Nottingham in 1972 and being called a 'Field Sales Manager' I was put in charge of a territory stretching from Afghanistan in the East to Nigeria in the West and down to Southern Africa, but not including South Africa which had been run by its own factory in Springs, Transvaal since 1952. Business trips could be of up to six weeks in duration, but if the trip lasted three months you were allowed to be accompanied by your wife! But the six-week trips were long enough for you to become really involved with where you were. After much desk work, I made my first visit to the Middle East proper with different tasks and objectives in each area. There were to be many more.

My first visit to Afghanistan saw me going from Kabul to Kandahar in the South then to Herat in the West and from there to Mazar-i-Sharif in the North and back to Kabul via Pul-i-Khumri and Kunduz. All in a Volga Russian taxi – this was before the Russians came into Afghanistan. I wasn't aware that so many cities like

Kandahar and Herat were originally named after Alexander the Great (356 – 323 B.C.), since Herat was the Arabic version. The beautiful mosques were exquisite to visit as were the places themselves with history, unpreserved, but all around, although it needed interpreting. My Afghani driver, seeing my interest, went out of his way to take me to places of significance where I saw the passage of over two and a half thousand years of travel, conquest, and trade. These diversions left me with memories of an uncharted world which I presume few have seen. I was not able to access these sights on my return as I would have liked to pass on such an experience at least pictorially. It does underline the value, and the fear, of 'following your nose' or trusting a fellow being and hoping the path is clear and without danger. It made me aware and reflective of the fascinating lives that explorers like Wilfred Thesiger or even Livingstone had indulged, and less known others who have been lost to posterity. These lonely travellers will have had thoughts and exposure to events and attitudes which made little sense but stimulated their minds and outlook as have mine. Trying to fit these into a preconceived pattern or to make sense of them from a 'taught' outlook seems to me a folly, but neither is it comfortable to be left with a conundrum.

The daily diet in Afghanistan didn't suit me well. Living off camel meat kebabs and watermelon, and with long car drives and little exercise I lost both weight and physical energy, but my mind was fed to overflowing.

It was at Pul-i-Khumri in its beautiful mosque that I had women asking if I were a doctor and thrusting their blind and sick babies at me waiting for a magic touch. At the time I saw no other Western people during my Afghan adventure and enjoyed the Moslem architecture in these cities.

My Russian Volga Taxi and Driver

The Mosque at Pul-i-Khumri

The drive from Pul-i-Khumri to Kabul via Kunduz was extraordinary as it went through the mountains on a unique road constructed by the Russians, circa 1960.

A mountainous pass

The Raleigh Distributor (whom I had little hesitation appointing as the Raleigh Industries Ltd Agent – as opposed to the Anglo-Afghan Ltd operation which had an English MD) was the young, 30 year-old devoted Hindu, Shiv Nandan. His cousin brother, Krishan Kumar, had come to Nottingham, so I knew of him before. (His attempt to buy the Raleigh Agency for Afghanistan in cash across Mr P's desk in Nottingham had failed; I was happy to appoint him freely, such was brother Shiv's calibre, but I would have driven a harder, non-cash, deal had I known before of this little charade.) Shiv was a great philosopher, and I was impressed with his morning ritual of prayer, exercise and meditation, which would last from 5.30 to 7.15 a.m. It prepared him for a working day which would last from 7.30 a.m. to 7.30 p.m. I tried to emulate him, but after a couple of weeks did not find the focus to meditate or even to be able to sit in the yoga position, let alone do the exercises and purge the body – very vocally – of all the toxins therein.

Enjoying Camel Kebabs in Kabul with M.N. Dhar and Krishan Kumar

Before leaving Kabul, I addressed all the 'new' Raleigh dealers at my hotel, a new experience for them, but it was a great success, and we did get over a year's business from them before the Russians took over the country! The Afghani dealers were some of the most astute, clever traders I ever met, and they had to be to survive in this unstable country. Some of them were incredibly wealthy too, but you would never know which ones. Krishan Kumar (Shiv Nandan's wealthy elder brother) joined us in Kabul too, so we had a full force supporting Shiv including M. N. Dhar a real burra sahib from Calcutta, and myself.

Dealer presentation in Kabul; l - r, interpreter, me and M.N. Dhar

My second visit to Afghanistan had an interesting and very export-related experience to relate. When the orders I had taken during and before and after my trip many dealers reported of various shortages from their consignments. After some six months I noticed that there was a pattern to these shortages: in one all of the saddles would be missing, in another all the pedals and yet another the pumps and so on, what is more all of the cases were reported to be intact. So, I set about doing a check prior to shipment taking a photo of the contents prior to the case being nailed down. Sure enough from one of the cases I'd photo'd shortages were reported. I set out to trace the problem. I asked them to open no more cases until I had arrived in Kabul and again sure enough there were shortages from within cases all perfectly intact. I decided to follow the trail of shipment from the UK to Karachi and then by land from there to Kabul. I needed to go no further than Karachi. There at the port I was shocked to learn that there existed a syndicate who knew exactly of what two soft wood cases of CKD bicycles comprised and exactly where each part was packed. From one case the saddles would be taken and from another the front forks and so on until they had 25 complete bicycles. Needless to say, the nails had been removed and replaced with a precision that defied trace. I was actually shown all of this by the harbour master himself – almost showing off the ingenuity of his work force. I asked what was in it for him and he openly told me that he received a pay-off for ignoring the tampering with the cases. 'How much' I asked, and he told me the modest figure. It was simple to resolve this – I paid him, from then on, a small fee higher than he was receiving from his men and sure enough the shortages ceased! Nor did my amazement end there. Employing my African techniques with laughter rather than judgement and dismay at the ingenuity shown at the port I asked to see other tricks his guys were up to. The most lucrative concerned foreign aid from the USA. He showed me a huge area of crates newly arrived from the USA and with the words US AID stencilled in black on each case. There in the corner was a little old, wizened Indian with a pile of stickers labelled 'Gift from the USSR' which he overlaid on the stencilled 'US AID' words. These were then being sent up to Afghanistan.

From Kabul my trip would usually progress to Tehran and then to Baghdad, Basrah, Kuwait, Abu Dhabi, Dubai and down through the Emirates to Oman, and from there I would fly to Beirut, Lebanon and into Athens and then home. I would do the whole of the Gulf States in five days, arriving on the early flight and taking the evening flight out and on to the next State. The trip from Kabul to Tehran was short with the three intelligent, competent, agents: Grey Mackenzie, (Raleigh), Tavikalipoor (PHC), and Tabarrok (Hercules), who were all so well organised that the Iranians' visits were always ones of courtesy and service with sophisticated traders and, like all good news, there's little to be said while much was done. From memory, and to give an idea of the size of business Raleigh Industries were doing in Iran at this time, some 60,000 bikes were being sold a year, plus supporting spares and accessories. It was to be like visiting a different country in my first visits in the days of the Shah from the, still present, Ayatollah days with only the Tabarrok family remaining in business throughout but working under very different circumstances.

However, I will pause here on the Tabarrok story, as later in my life I got to know them well. Khosro, Tabarrok's eldest uncle, had the role of grandfather and, in 1907 together with the mother and three younger brothers (the father of the family, being the city trustee was taken hostage by the Bolsheviks and died) escaped from Ishqh-abad (Turkmenistan) east of the Caspian Sea. From there they arrived in Iran at Mashad, which they decided would become their home. Their original family name was Sadeghoof, but with such a Russian sounding name and the bad Russian reputation in Iran, they decided they had better change their surname. The first names of the four brothers from elder to younger were Taghi, Bagram, Reza and Karim. So, they took the initial of each name in Farsi to create their new family name TBRK which is pronounced as Tabarrok. They are the oldest of Raleigh Industries Ltd distributors in the world, starting in the early 1930s with the Hercules brand. It was a no-brainer for me in the early 2000s, when I was heading up Raleigh International, to appoint them as the Raleigh Licensees. The continuation of the Tabarrok operation is now secured by his well-educated daughter and twin sons, who have joined in, and modernised and expanded the operation, which is still based in Tehran and where I had a happy visit.

Back to my story or rather to fast-forward to keep continuity. In 2006, Khosro Tabarrok invited me to the re-launch of Raleigh which some three hundred dealers from all over Iran attended. I shook the hands of over two hundred dealers and for two days, with no Farsi, had patiently to listen to the presentations and then meet and greet very many who, to a man, hugged me and welcomed me. Khosro said 'run with it all John, we're having a party at home tonight making all this worthwhile'.

Tehran sits at the bottom of large mountains high up upon which the old Shah had his Palace. A little lower we drove along a street and stopped outside a white wall peppered with gunshot and topped with security fencing along it, stopping at a huge iron gate which led into a sort of concrete moat where we parked and alighted. Then we ventured through a more elaborate iron door, a couple of yards from which a superb oak door opened into the Tabarrok house. I cannot describe the taste and glamour of that house, with its precious Persian caligraphy upon the walls, elegantly furnished, and then onto the roof garden overlooking all of Tehran. 'Tea?' said Khosro, and in the most exquisite silver tea set he poured out a superb and much needed dram of the best single malt.

At the party that night I was introduced to the 'old Iran' and friends of the Tabarrok family, and the most beautiful of ladies. Then along came one guy rather small and bald but with eyes and a smile that brought immediate recognition, for he was the brother of Goodarz Hakim-Nejad, my friend from school days. That evening the reminiscences of Sutton Valence brought tears to my eyes and with much drink we relived a life of 45 years before. When the time came to leave, Hakim's wife came up to her husband and in Churchillian tones exclaimed, 'Sir you are drunk,' only to get the prompt response, 'Madam, you are ugly, but I shall be sober in the morning.' Where was I? – in one of the most educated and civilised homes in the world and we are now ignorant of this place to the loss of all. I look forward to the Tabarroks inviting me on Iran's 'Picnic Day' one year.

Iraq was very different. My first trip, flying from Tehran to Baghdad in early 1969, was a nerve tingling shock.

One of the few times I thought ahead was when in Kabul, looking at the coming trip, I discovered Haji Abdul would be celebrating 50 years of selling Phillips bicycles. I asked Shiv Nandan, my Afghan agent, if he could get a framed plaque to mark Haji Abdul's half century – the logo of the Phillips bicycle is the lion, and in the most tasteful way the Afghan artist recreated this lion and matched its power with that of Haji Abdul over his fifty years of tenure.

Iraq was an exciting country for me, as a historian. There was so much to see and every one of its ancient sites serves as a reminder that this land, once called Mesopotamia, is a cradle of civilisation. One of my tours presented an opportunity that was not to be missed – a chance to visit Nineveh, where I took the photo below. It is a special place. Seeing my interest, my colleague offered to take me to Ur, which is named in the Bible as the birthplace of Father Abraham. We didn't make the trip, sadly. Ur was 700 miles away, to the South of Baghdad. A real regret.

A Princess of Hatra

The Phillips agent, whom I'd never met, this Haji Abdul Hussain Ali, not only met me at the airport but was waiting at the bottom of the aircraft steps where he wanted my luggage ticket and my passport. He passed them to his colleague who rushed away while Haji Abdul took me from one side of the airport to the other. Was I being kidnapped? He introduced me to his son Ibrahim who was standing beside a single engine Auster aeroplane. Confused and scared I climbed into the ancient fabric covered Auster which Ibrahim fired up, and he took me for a sight-seeing tour above Baghdad and to the confluence of the Tigris and Euphrates, pointing out the Gardens of Babylon. What an introduction to one of the world's seats of civilisation. Ibrahim knew his history – if only I'd had a tape recorder, and had been more relaxed, less nervous and less suspicious.

After my Auster flight induction into Baghdad, Ibrahim drove me to his Dad's office which happily had my luggage in it as well as my passport. I presented him with his grand plaque marking his fifty years as the Phillips Distributor. Tears and hugs ensued on this my very first visit. Phew! When I left Baghdad Haji Abdul presented me with a gift of three watches each named – one for me, one for Mrs John Macnaughtan, and one for the new Raleigh chairman, Tom Barnsley. I was always careful over gifts, pleased to accept a key ring or corporate item like a pen, but would never accept a carpet or such and anyway these watches were named and presented. To refuse them would have been an insult. I received them with pride. However, to move to the end of this story – when I came to pass on to Tom Barnsley his watch he refused it with disdain telling me 'we should never accept gifts' and that I was to thank Haji Abdul and tell him this watch would be passed to the Raleigh Athletic Club as a prize. I duly wrote to Haji Abdul. A month later two watches arrived in my post the one inscribed as a gift to the Victor Ludorum at the Raleigh Athletic Club and another to Mr Tom Barnsley to wear his watch as a special token from Mr Haji Abdul!

I refused the gift of carpets from my customers, but I learnt one interesting thing – how is a valuable carpet identified as such and what it is worth? This is what I was told: when the villagers from outlying districts come in with camels laden with their carpets, from places like Isfahan, the traders in the soukhs buy in bulk and then sort the carpets. When they find one, they believe to be valuable they lay it out on the floor of the market place where it is trodden upon, spat upon, and abused by the masses. When it is nice and dirty it is then carefully hand cleaned. If the colour holds and the carpet returns to its original look, he has an expensive carpet.

Meanwhile from Baghdad I flew via Basrah to Kuwait where another experience awaited me. My well used and labelled suitcase I noticed, when I went to collect it from Customs, had a chalk mark on it, and it was stopped and opened. At the top of the case and on top of my clothes were a number of bottles of whisky. Kuwait was a dry State. I protested my innocence of the possessions therein, which sounded very hollow. I was apprehended. To cut a long story short I eventually was sent up to the Head of Customs where in front of subordinates I was given a lecture on the decadence of the West and was presented with a book on the evils of alcohol. The head honcho then dismissed his staff and in the most civilised English he apologised to me, explaining that his counterpart in Basrah had placed this whisky in my case, marked it so that he could pick it up before it went to Customs, and he apologised for any inconvenience caused and would I accept a gift in recompense? He had just received some tie-pin microphones which could be connected to a small tape recorder put in the top inner jacket pocket – I took it, and left.

Front page of the booklet on the evils of drink

I covered the amazing Gulf States in a week from Kuwait down to Oman and then flew to Beirut. This was a long-established Raleigh business route with flights taking off and landing early morning and late at night so it was possible to complete work without staying the night in some of the States. This itinerary also worked well with Distributors attending meetings promptly and prepared and usually organising meals and pick-ups and drop-offs. So, from Kuwait to Bahrain to Abu Dhabi to Dubai to Oman. In each case an order-taking agenda (with Friday as a day off). Every trip is also a learning experience because who rides a bike in 50 degrees Centigrade? The answer is only fanatic road cyclists, but the Double Top Tube Raleigh Roadster with Balloon tyres ends up on Dhows trading from Pakistan down the African coast or sold to Bangladeshi's taking them back to Dhaka. Traders find sales routes and customers untouched by clever advertisers and exporters.

Lebanon was a paradise in those days and with a strong French influence. A day was needed with each Distributor, Tiger Tamraz, the Raleigh man, Tamer Freres, the Phillips people, Boustani representing Rudge. The hardest thing was to have the stamina for the entertainment at the end of each day. The Casino du Liban was in full swing in those days and the performances therein outmatched in grandeur and expense anything from Broadway or the West End. I had met two Iraqi girls when I was in Baghdad who were holidaying in Beirut for a few days – Kawther and Awatuf. Kawther was the fourth wife of a 65 year-old general in the Iraqi army. She was 24 years old, and her friend Awatuf was unmarried and only 19. One evening Tiger Tamraz asked me to have dinner with him followed by a 'local show'. I asked if I could invite my two friends. He was delighted. In fact, the invitation lasted over 22 hours as he showed off Beirut and his wealth to me and the Baghdadi girls. Boat trips on his yacht were followed by a visit to a very old Lebanese club where palms were read and hookahs smoked, followed by a most seductive dance of the seven veils which Kawther claimed was amateurish and poor. 'Can you do better?' asked Tiger. 'I am the best,' retorted Kawther. Half an hour later we were in Tiger's car going up to his

Awatuf, Kawther and me in Beirut

house in the mountains. He opened his wife's wardrobe and told Kawther to help herself and come down when ready. My job was to light a fire in the corner of Tiger's living room, while he found the Arabic music, the Arak and dates, and, when we were sitting on the sumptuously carpeted floor on luscious cushions, in walked Kawther. Her black Iraqi eyes flashed evilly at us. She was dressed in silks and lace and swathes of material with jewellery from Tiger's bedroom adorning her. The Arab music wailed, and the open fire in the corner lit the room. Kawther's performance was mesmerising. She clearly had been trained to perform. Not one move was wasted as the thin silks were discarded. The intoxication of the liqueur in our blood was accompanied by an intoxication of the brain accentuated by the music it heard and enchanted by the sight our eyes feasted upon. When she had taken off the six veils, she used the seventh to cover alternately the top and the middle of her body to cover her femininity. My whole being was alive, in love, transported into a new-age type drugged trance. Then she threw off her last veil and replaced it with a gown and screeched a laugh of triumph before joining us on our cushions. Tiger and I wanted to devour those two girls. The girls knew their power with Kawther, knowing the consequence of any liaison, and Awatuf needing to have a show of blood on her wedding night to avoid the same consequence – death.

From Lebanon I returned 'home' via Athens, which by this time I knew well, and my friends the Gounaropolous family owed me big favours after I had appointed them as sole Agent for the Sudan. This was taking away the Raleigh agency from the family Khatchikian, a cultivated and rather broken and displaced Armenian. Taki knew that in the longer-term Sudan would follow the other failed states after African independence, and he had to rebuild himself in the interim back in his home country Greece, and also because of his two children – I came to know Dino his son well too. But after my Middle East trips Taki thought I needed feeding up, entertaining and restoring, because he had observed my arrival from Libya in poor condition. This time, fresh from Beirut, I was in great form. It was still the time of the Generals in Greece when the dancing clubs of Athens were characterised by the smashing of plates and dancing on the tables. After a day of unneeded sympathy for my Islamic experiences, and with a 24-hour soft landing, I would leave Athens in further need of R&R.

I could not help but add some of the cartoons from my souvenir from Kuwait, the book on the evils of alcohol

The Middle East
TURKEY
Istanbul
GREECE
Athens
MEDITERRANEAN SEA
SYRIA
Beirut
Damascus
LEBANON
ISRAEL
Amman
JORDAN
IRAQ
Baghdad
Basrah
KUWAIT
ARM.
AZERB.
Baku
CASPIAN SEA
TEHERAN
IRAN
PERSIAN GULF
BAHRAIN
DOHA
QATAR
ABU DHABI
DUBAI
OMAN
UAE
MUSCAT
SAUDI ARABIA
RIYADH
JIDDAH
MECCA
YEMEN
SANAA
RED SEA
EGYPT
Cairo
SUDAN
Khartoum
ERITREA
DJIB.
ETHIOPIA
SOMALIA
ARABIAN SEA
AFGHANISTAN
HERAT
MAZAR E-SHARIF
Kunduz
KABUL
Kandahar
PAKISTAN
ISLAMABAD
Karachi
INDIA
EH 21

A Reflection

I refer in some detail to the more social nature of my Middle East experiences, as the business side was covered in full in market reports with action columns and statistics like any businessman's report. But although these social times were also more modest than given to many businessmen, it was the effect on me that was lasting, partly because my customers were not the usual corporate smoothies with entertainment allowances. I was easily absorbed into their lives and families, and they were talking to me not just openly but also with intimacy.

I had, for example, six customers in Baghdad of whom I have only dwelt upon Haji Abdul, who represented Phillips. However there were also agents from Raleigh, BSA, Hercules, New Hudson and Humber in our portfolio. Each had to be visited and made to feel 'special'. All of these 'Agents' had been dealing with Raleigh Ind Ltd for many years and usually since the end of the Second World War. What is more each had been writing to one man in Nottingham be it Harold Dearn, Jimmy Cumming or John Rowberry. What I didn't appreciate was the strength of the relationships that had grown up over many years with the customers and on my first and subsequent visits I was treated as though I was 'that person' they'd known forever in Nottingham. It was often assumed that I was aware of all that had passed over the years; fortunately my nodding head and silent listening gave an impression of understanding that I believe confirmed or won their confidence. The result was always an intense visit, not just because of lack of time but often a huge need for the customer to offload to 'their friend'. In my case, the naive belief that I could be the solution to whatever issue was thwarting their quality of life and always made for some intimate confidence being imparted. Often it was simply to be their contact in the UK for a son or daughter being despatched there for further education and I was to be '*in loco parentis*'. It was like with Tiger Tamraz in Beirut who had married one of King Farouk's daughters which I thought must be special, until I learnt that he had dozens of daughters. But with such reverence did I address Tiger, believing his status to be high, that he confided to me all sorts of outrageous intimacies inappropriate to my tender years at the time, let alone my limited experience. All the social, political and personal intimacies to which I was subjected were growing experiences for me as an only son, but which fed my reflective nature.

After my first year at University, I found I enjoyed my subject – History – it would be a sad man who didn't. I left University with a good knowledge of 'historical method' for approaching 'facts' and their verification. I knew all about the essential reference to sources and 'doing my documents' to back up my conclusions or value judgements where subjectivity had crept in. However, my intense trips to the Near and Middle East, my childhood allegiance to the Far East and my Scottish background combined to upturn any feeling that I was a man of any worthwhile knowledge of what the world was all about. What a man was Alexander the Great (356 – 323 BC). I'd been to a collection of countries all so far apart bearing his name. I had seen the biblical Babylon, seen many 'Jesus's' proclaiming their faith and crying out their philosophies, I'd known Zoroastrians since birth, and I'd seen the effect of their replacement in Persia by Mohammedans. I had read T.E. Lawrence's *Seven Pillars of Wisdom* and watched Peter O'Toole's portrayal of him. I'd been given hospitality out of all proportion to my position. I saw buildings of great antiquity pre-dating Jewry and Christianity let alone Islam. I was in a world of post-Colonialism with independence granted to ungovernable territories by a now bankrupt coloniser. I visited all of the British Embassies in the territories in which I found myself, and met the most educated of inmates. I had seen Greek inscriptions in Northern Afghanistan, oracles brought from Delphi carved on a monument from two or three hundred years before Christ. So much that didn't conform to my university knowledge of history. I reflect now on the world with these memories reminding me of the transience of politics and the duplicity of nations, with the bankruptcy, both financial and moral of the West, especially in the closing years of the twentieth and the first twenty years of the twenty-first century. I cannot help but think of the old trade routes, and the way of doing business where money lenders serve in place of banks, and traders sit on their worn carpets on top of huge mounds of different secreted currencies ready to pounce on a bargain. Trade and trust are a long-proven pathway to interdependence, and it will return. Look at the lands growing up along the old routes from the Caspian Sea into China: the mineral and oil wealth of a Turkmenistan and the mines of Uzbekistan and Krygystan. History teaches me that that these lands have always been important in our global history. Huge melting pots of ideas and languages that add depth to our very being, and these are the future as well as the past. One has only to open one's eyes and release the education which has closed them – or so my travel suggests. My view of history was again transformed. Anyone invested in our now global world should read Peter Frankopan's *The Silk Roads: A New History of the World* (2015, with later editions). This book was a relief for me to read forty years on reflecting how history was, is and is not what I had learnt, and connecting with my life experiences.

I'd enjoyed evenings with Anglophiles who were admirers of the British Empire, of its spread of just laws, of its introduction of railways and education. I'd seen evidence of atrocities, but anything the British may have done was outweighed by the wickedness of the current incumbent or another invader. I had witnessed the flourishing slave trade, and indeed been served by slaves in customers' houses. I then see the West trying to judge their history from a twenty-first century perspective with demands for recompense for offences and hardships sadly endured by their predecessors. Anyone with the view that we Brits have a monopoly of 'colonial' traits (all too often ignorantly meant negatively) should meet M. N. Dhar from Calcutta who accompanied me on my trip to Afghanistan: 'This mountainous mess of medieval mentalities.' There are many imperious M. N. Dhars in India. In the British club in Addis Ababa one evening I encountered an old boy snapping his fingers at the waiter and calling 'Bronchitis'. The waiter duly jumped to attention. It turned out the word in Amharic for 'listen', which was often used to summon a waiter, was in fact 'Asma'. I giggled at that silly English twist of humour.

What was I to make of my knowledge of this and of European history and my happy university introduction to Islam? I was hugely reflective. As the 1960s passed into the 1970s, and after some seven years of non-stop travel in Africa and the Middle East, I found myself in March 1973 being seconded to Australia on a three-year contract to set up Raleigh there. After a three-month reconnaissance, from 23rd February to June 1973, in and around the State of Victoria, which was to be the base for my contract.

It was not long after I returned home from the recce that, in September 1973, Sue gave birth to our son Alistair – and I was at home and there at the birth. What a moment. Most happy though were my parents to have a grandson. I saw more of them than I had done since my school holidays. I also saw a side of them that as parents I had been denied in their quest to make me the 'perfect' fellow. They came up from Tunbridge Wells to stay with us when Sue and baby arrived home. Gran took over the baby and house and Grandad did what he was told with nervous devotion. It was such a delight. When after some three months the time came for me to leave for Australia I did not want to go. When my dad came to bid me farewell I even saw a tear in his eye. This was not the dad I knew, but I do now. I was so happy to see that tender and loving side of my parents, particularly my dad, which was denied to me. It was no wonder then that a year after we had arrived in Sydney they sailed out to be with us for just over a month when I had the benefit of seeing and having the best of parents.

Australia, 1973

I never wanted to go to Australia. During the months between East Africa and the next assignment it had become clear that there was little opportunity for me in Nottingham. Those who remember February 1973 may realise that the U.K. economy was not a favourable environment for manufacturing industries. However, the U.S. bike market had peaked, and another was needed which could consume the U.S. style 10-speed bikes that the factory was making. The 'job' I was then offered was: 'set up Raleigh in Australia or leave'. This was the message I received from my friend with the 'Iraqi' watch, Tom Barnsley. That was the choice with which I was faced. Today I would have left, back then with new wife and new child, combined with my upbringing of loyalty, I felt obliged to stay.

There followed three years of highs and lows I'd never before experienced, and perhaps would not have survived so happily, had it not been for a consequence of my flight from Heathrow to Melbourne. I had broken my journey in Singapore to meet up with an old friend, Francis Taye, ex Robinsons, and now Area Sales Manager for Raleigh Malaysia. After catching up with all things South-East Asia for 36 hours, I re-boarded my flight, and 12 hours after that arrived in Melbourne, checking into the Octagon Hotel. It was 9 March 1973. I unpacked and went down to the bar to 'arrive'. At the bar sat an 'Ocker Aussie', a bearded *oke*, who I thought was best avoided, but who suddenly greeted me: 'G'Day BA006, welcome to Oz.'

The broadest and harshest 'Aussie' accent gave way to a booming laugh. We had flown out together from the U.K. – had had a drink in Bahrain – now here he was in 'my' hotel. Now that was two days and half a century ago, but recognising this very English face and huge humour was a delight, and so began a friendship that has lasted to this day. We would go about our respective jobs, and each evening return to this bar and share our very varied experiences – his in computing, (pre-PCs) and me in the Cyclops (toys) Warehouse, with days spent visiting dealers.

Meanwhile my Raleigh colleague, David Duffield, had been seconded out to 'Oz' for a full month before me to start up Raleigh in Melbourne. I didn't know David Duffield well, as he was Raleigh 'home market', but in the cycling world he was a giant, holding several world records and heavily involved with the sport. With David we worked frenetically, visiting cycle dealers each day, and in the evening writing up and typing the invoices on the orders taken and placing them on the warehouseman's desk for him to despatch the next morning. David had one more month to go before I was on my own, and my brief was to pick up from him, work together for a month before returning to the U.K., where I was to put forward a business plan, and then return to implement it. David Duffield's world was bicycles and bicycle dealers; he loved both with an intensity with which it was difficult for me to identify. His relaxations were to ride his bike, and women. He threw himself into both with intensity.

My relaxation, after having my daily fill of bikes and bike dealers, was to sit at the bar with Bernard and laugh. After several weeks of this routine, I arrived at the Octagon bar one evening to have Bernard announce that he had found rented accommodation into which he was moving. I was shattered by the news. Bernard was my only saviour from my narrow two wheeled world. 'What's more,' Bernard continued, 'it's a mixed flat'. I'd never heard of such an arrangement – I had emerged from the 1960s sexual revolution unscathed. 'The secret is,' Bernard continued, 'that in a mixed flat you never mess with the flat mates, but they introduce you to 'totty' which you'd otherwise never meet.'

I threw myself into work for several weeks after Bernard left, and established a network of dealers in each state. I went up to Sydney and over to Adelaide, and slowly found that Raleigh had indeed a place in the market in Australia. I missed my newly born son Alistair every day. I had been travelling all my previous life, but not after having my own son. I found myself staring at the photos Sue sent of my child with his very bright and blond hair, and spent hours with tears in my eyes.

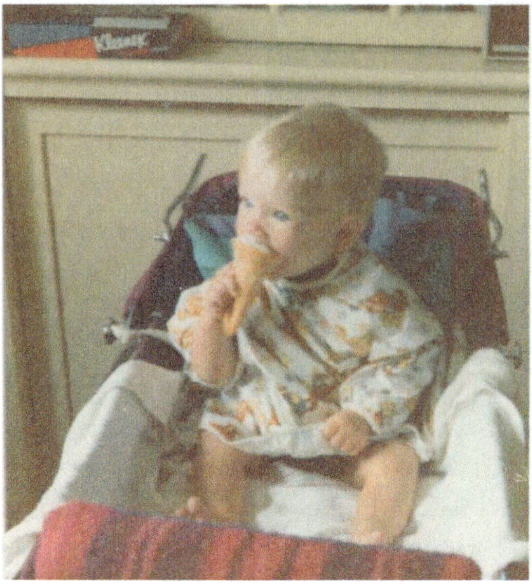

I plodded on though, now without David Duffield and on my own new parish. One day I returned from Sydney, checked into my old hotel – the Octagon – and went into the bar where I spotted Bernard. He was waiting for me. In fact, he was bubbling over to tell me that he'd met a girl, and such a girl. A flat mate! So much for not messing on your home patch I thought. Bernard was totally smitten, and I was happy for him.

A month or so later at the same bar, Bernard was to announce to me that he and Louise were to marry, and would I be his best man? Wow, marriage, now that was different, and I took it upon myself to assume, as it were, parental responsibility for Bernard. I needed to know more about this girl and whether she was worthy of my friend. Bernard had told me a lot before this, but I had only half listened to his glowing reports of Louise. Now marriage loomed and suddenly I felt responsible. So, like a good Hindu parent would do for his son, I started listening and finding out more, and what I found astounded me. Our Louise's mother's brother was the Prime Minister of New South Wales, daddy was a leading Country Party M.P., and in fact the family were one of the most established 'Ozzie' families owning much of the Victoria countryside in the Rochester area. How had Bernard landed such a prize? I needed to meet her and to my surprise found that Bernard had not been exaggerating. She was 'the best' in every way, and I was treated to and introduced to the very best model of 'Ozzie' life. (What a contrast to my world on the high streets with Ozzie bike dealers.) Louise's Dad was a treasure; her mother was a bit more formidable. Life in Rochester was like life in an English Victorian village, with their Lord of the Manor – Michael Clarke – as the benevolent dictator. The highlight of my three years in Australia was the friendship with Bernard of course, and then to become godfather to his second son Marcus.

The Australia I lived in for three years from that March of 1973 was still an Atlantic Island moored between the U.S.A. and the U.K.. Governor Menzies' White Australia policy was evident, but now Gough 'cough-drop' Whitlam was the last of the old guard, calling himself a 'new broom'.

Soon after I landed in Melbourne, T.I. bought the New Zealand and Australian subsidiaries of Triang Pedigree – the toy giants. The upside to this was several visits to New Zealand, and I also took Alistair to places like Rotarua which should have been an education but he sadly remembers nothing, but he has photos to compensate; herewith one, taken at one of the country's hot springs.

The amazing sulphur springs at Roturua, left, and Alistair looking curiously at the bubbling mud, right

Cyclops was the unlikely brand name of the Australian toys, and since its foundation in 1915 had been a household name to all 'Aussies' over a certain age. It meant that after three or four months setting Raleigh up in Melbourne, I had to go to Sydney and work from, and for, the Cyclops factory in Leichardt, New South Wales. This further kept me from flying my 'new' wife and newly born son Alistair over to join me, as I'd no idea where I was going to be permanently living. From working independently in Melbourne, and setting up dealerships interstate, it was a shock to be absorbed into an old established Aussie culture like Cyclops with its own hierarchy.

For any 'Pom' coming to Australia, or indeed the USA, it's difficult to think of either as a foreign country – the Australians drive on the left and it's easy to feel as one with them, but in fact I was to be a victim of the love/hate relationship that Australians harbour(ed) towards their motherland. My time also coincided with Lilly and Thomo smashing through the Poms on the cricket pitch, and when they brought out Colin Cowdrey, the *Age*'s headlines were 'Poms bring out grandad to save them'.

The Aussies are an amazingly competitive breed, as I learnt at one of the Sydney Toy Fairs, where a leading supplier took all his customers out in a Jumbo jet and flew it around Ayers Rock. A journey of some five hours on the most important show day and therefore denying these customers to other exhibitors who had paid for the Stands etc. Cyclops people were upset: I was amazed.

Working at an old office in Leichardt was often a shock. Metaphorical banana skins were put down for me to slip on, to the noisy satisfaction of the natives. It wasn't all one-way traffic though: Raleigh packed spokes and nipples together in one soft wood box, and it was very heavy. The warehouse man offloaded a box from the container by hand and promptly it dropped and fell through the raised warehouse floor. I was called out by the furious warehouse manager to see what I'd done to his floor, along with two others from the office, as the four of us stared at the hole he shouted at me, 'Well, what are you going to do about it?' My retort was not appreciated but I smile to this day when I recall it: 'Shall we say that management is looking into it?'

Funnily enough it was one of the Cyclops Sales managers, Laz Ferencz, who researched a little about my past and to his surprise discovered I was less of a Pom than he'd and others first supposed and he took to calling me 'Jungle Jim'. This name stuck with a certain number of my colleagues in the office and, much later, it confirmed my choice for the title of this book.

Perhaps my funniest example of the swings of fortune is the tale of Jack Walsh at Punchbowl (an ocker Sydney suburb and Jack an ocker Aussie). Jack had a large and successful bicycle shop there, and its decor and pride of service made it a natural outlet through which to sell Raleigh. So, I used to visit Jack nearly every week. I would pop in after my first proper 'sales call', which had got me nowhere. I knew Jack, who was of Italian extraction, was a difficult man, but also like a pineapple – soft in the middle. I had been brought up not to put my hands in my pockets and to walk with a straight back. Jack had picked up on my deportment, and on my third visit to his shop he loudly announced to staff and shoppers, 'Look out gents, here comes bloody Prince Phillip.' The nickname stuck and was my moniker thereafter in the metropolis of Punchbowl.

My Raleigh catalogue had a cover of scenes of the 'outdoors', of surfers and board sailing, which I identified as being a competitor to cycling in Oz. Jack suddenly announced on about my sixth visit that he would stock and sell Raleigh, but in return I had to paint my catalogue cover on one of his walls. I agreed, found an artist and sure enough his wall was truly inspiring. I remember he bought some 25 bikes with at least one of each model in the range. I was ecstatic. I visited him less often thereafter but at least once a month. After about a year I came to see Jack when he'd had a recurring problem with the 'crook clusters' (faulty sprockets) on some of the Raleigh bikes. He got into the habit of opening the carton on arrival, checking if it had a 'T.D. Cross Cluster', and if so, returning the box to the driver without accepting and signing for the order. This meant that a new invoice had to be raised and the product both credited and debited and, no surprise, there were some accounts problems where he claimed to have been invoiced for bikes, he had ordered but not received. Whatever the truth, I arrived at his shop to discuss an equitable solution to find him in a liverish mood –

this was no surprise, but I felt I could handle it with my apparent Prince Phillip charm. This time he was in no mood to listen, and when I suggested a compromise, or indeed queried anything he said, he fumed and then ended up getting a paint brush, dipping it into some whitewash and marched over to the Raleigh mural and splashed paint on the wall saying, 'This is what I think of Raleigh, and you can take all your 'effing' bikes in my store back, and never come into my shop again.' The wall was left for several months in this state of vandalization. I never withdrew the unpaid invoices or took back the stock for which he'd paid. Fortunately, he particularly liked my secretary, a tough, local, pretty lass, and after a suitable interval I sent her round to talk to him. He took her out for dinner. She suggested the compromise I'd tried to offer months earlier, and he said to her now, 'If only that Pommie Prig had offered this there never would have been a problem.' All was sorted in a couple of days, but the question of the restoration of the wall remained. Business to Jack did decline, but it also continued. When I left 'Oz' he was one of the only dealers to present me with a gift which I still have in my house – an original 'Wanted Dead or Alive' poster for Ned Kelly, appropriate, and which I cherish.

Pommie bashing was more of a sport during my visit than it probably is now that Australia is firmly a Pacific island. There were jokes like, 'What's the best sight for an 'Aussie'?' An 'Itie' swimming out of the harbour with a Pom under each arm.' But my retort was not considered so funny: 'Why are the Pommies 'poofters'?' – 'Cos all the 'c….s' are out here!' In a country where all the swear words have become terms of endearment a new hierarchy of words has had to be created to replace the usual 'F's and 'B's, e.g. 'he's a real dill', or 'he's a complete dag' (a dag is the excrement from a sheep clotted on its wool). But nasty occasions did occur and were not done in jest. My Aussie boss more than once asserted his authority over me in vindictive terms. Here again, the word of Grandad Godfrey's wisdom stood me in good stead. After one long week of being 'pommie bashed' by this boss, and accused of doing things wrongly, and being a total dill, and where I knew that any denial or assertion would merely have added fuel to the unnecessary invective to which I was subjected, I retorted in Grandad's words 'Just remember, I can always do worse that you think'. That stopped him short.

Having spoken critically about Oz I should correct the balance as, after the first few months of incidents, not only was life good but I had my wife and son there, and we had happy holidays in Nelsons Bay, and tennis and barbecues most Saturday evenings at home. We lived in Lane Cove, a lovely suburb just north of the Sydney Bridge. Visits to Balmoral beach, where the sea was often calm was ideal for teaching Alistair to swim, and then to Curl Curl, for some real surfing fun. On the Saturday evenings when in New South Wales, at home, I would have an open evening for friends with a barbecue going and play tennis on the flood lit tennis court at the bottom of the garden. Not a bad life.

Both my and Sue's parents came out to stay with us, so we made the most of being so far away. It was also a great place for Alistair's first years, and with both sets of grandparents visiting, it made life very full. I was travelling interstate every month and made many friends. Malcolm Elliot of Elliot Bros, Rundle Street in Adelaide was always a delight to visit and catch up with in the evenings, as we shared an interest in theatre and drama. When the time came to leave, we were all sad. Certainly, one of the best things I got out of 'Oz' was my deep and enduring friendship with Bernard Morris. What's more I loved his wife to bits and don't know how he has pulled off the most difficult of life's tricks in finding such a partner. Suffice it to say that his frequent trips to Europe are 'occasions', and after ten minutes catch-up I feel he's never been away. Cheers, mate!

Bernard and Louise Morris visit Kingston

Nigeria, June - December 1976

Australia wasn't the centre of the world for me. I don't regret leaving Oz, but I'd have had an easier and more comfortable life had I stayed. Life in the U.K. is complicated and stressful, and my compatriots would think I was mad at returning to it. I had travelled a lot in North, East, Central and South Africa, and also around the Middle East prior to my assignment to Australia. I then returned to Nottingham via Nigeria, where I spent six months mainly in the East – Biafra – setting up a components arm to the cycle factory plant and head office in Kano, Northern Nigeria. I'd returned from Australia via Perth – a short stop over to see my Raleigh dealer, Glen Parker. Then on I flew, via Mauritius for a weekend break, to South Africa where Jack Catlin had been replaced by Kevin O'Donovan. From there to Nairobi for more catch up, especially at the Aero Club where little had changed thankfully, and then (3 July 1976) to Uganda. At Entebbe, where on the other side of the runway when we landed were the Israeli commandos who had sprung an anti-terrorist mission. What a success – and now the subject of a film *Entebbe* (2018). A quarter of Uganda's air force was destroyed and 102 of the 106 hostages were rescued – and I was there. So, pleased to be leaving Entebbe, we arrived in Lagos.

'Chaos' is the best term to summarise Lagos. On top of all the traffic and noise there were about a hundred ships waiting to dock, mostly with cargos of cement to feed Nigeria's growth since the end of the recent Biafra war. But I was quickly back 'at home in Happy Africa', and soon to be on the scene of the battlefields. Burnt-out tanks and abandoned trucks were beside the roads on the way from Aba to Enugu. It was good to experience the most populated country in Africa after being in the biggest country – the Sudan – and after learning my trade in the South and East. West Africa has a different flavour from the more picturesque East, but it did confirm my notions of the difficulty of governability of these ex-colonies. Nigeria is country that is not naturally a country, but one created with other objectives. The natural geographical division of the country did also separate the three major tribes from one another – the Yoruba in the South and East, the Ibo in the East and the Hausa in the North. How will these countries' histories be played out over the years ahead? (One of the most gripping of stories of Nigeria's past is Ellen Thorp's *Ladder of Bones*. They were days when the expectancy of life for a Brit in Nigeria was some three months living as they did in the mangrove swamps of Port Harcourt and dying from malaria, and reckoning they were better off at sea rather than on the land.)

Raleigh had its Sales Office in Lagos, where I spent a couple of weeks before departing to Port Harcourt to begin my Parts & Accessory mission. One lives fast on these short but not brief trips. There's always time to go to the bar, beach or to frequent the 'must see' of a place. Also, within minutes one is embroiled in the chaos of business life in such a vibrant community. The one European Sales Manager could only cope with as much as Mike Pedley did by working a ten-hour day every day, six days a week. With me there he simply delegated work to me as though I'd been there forever. At least I felt wanted.

Port Harcourt was completely different, different people, different feel. After the Civil War the whole of the East of Nigeria (Biafra) was run down and depressed, but with that African vibrancy that treated disaster and success the same. Crashed aeroplanes, burnt out tanks, broken army lorries decorated the sides of the roads from Port Harcourt to Aba, to Onitsha and on to Enugu. Life was frenetic, and the very bloody Civil War belonged to yesterday. I stayed at a United Africa Co (UAC) guest house with my own maid and cook and conveniently it was right opposite the Port Harcourt Club.

At weekends we would go to Bonny on the south of the coast near Port Harcourt, and cruise through all the mangrove swamps and then catch fish. While our fresh fish was being cooked on the beach, we took it in turns to water ski. Happy weekends.

Port Harcourt was a dump after the war. But it had life. I used to say that if Port Harcourt was the arsehole of the world, I worked thirty miles up it. This was true as I set up our Raleigh Accessory Head Office in Aba. Aba is the centre of the Ibo tribe. Ibos are wonderful, smart, competitive, cheeky and effective. One really wonders if Eastern Nigeria had ceded from the rest of Nigeria how that country would have done. It has an abundance of oil, lots of natural resources, farming and an amazingly beautiful capital, Enugu. There are tales of business sharp practices everywhere in the world, and the Ibos were masters, gleefully making a few *kobo* on a cleverer way of doing business than their neighbours. In the old days of Raleigh each of the Ibo traders would hold a bank account in Raleigh in Nottingham and draw from it and add to it to allow regular trade to continue despite local restrictions in remitting money out of the country.

I stayed at the only hotel in Aba, as opposed to the usual UAC rest house. I tried to take a shower, but when the usual rusty dribble of water emerged from the tap, it disturbed three rats in the drain of the bath and they quickly tried to escape by clambering up the sides!

An old friend and colleague of mine, Bob O'Donovan, had been the Sales Manager of Raleigh Industries Ltd. Nigeria. He had expected to become the Managing Director but was passed over by Head Office choosing an old 'coaster' – Bryan Dunnill. Bob was an ascetic character but of great ability. I inherited his male secretary who later I put in charge of the components business. He confided in me one day about working for my friend Bob saying, 'We all thought Bob hated Nigerians until we saw how he spoke to Mr Bryan, and then we realised he just hated all people.'

Trade in 1976 was brisk in Nigeria, but one day Jerome Asuquo called his six sales representatives to his headquarters to give them a bollocking. I recall his words and have since used them myself. He shouted at his useless salesmen and ended with the words, 'You've become so used to eating meat you've forgotten how to chew bones.'

I would swim in the local Port Harcourt pool most evenings, one day badly cutting my foot on kicking off from one of the broken tiles at the deep end. I was given my tetanus injections and promptly thrown back in. My local Raleigh Sales Manager, Jerome Asuquo had his offices in the UAC warehouse, and life was just as it had been in East Africa. Our clearing agent was a company called Panalpina. The

Manager of Panalpina was one Raymond Pencherek from Switzerland. What a huge character: we quickly became good friends. He took me out of an evening to have dinner on one of the many ships moored for months off Port Harcourt waiting to offload its cement, with crews coming out and returning without leaving the confines of their ship. Raymond took me to the night clubs near the Port Harcourt airport, where we played the tables at least twice a week. In fact, after spending every night there for a week Raymond called on me excitedly to join him at the tables. He'd been all evening for the past six at the same table of roulette and had discovered how it was rigged. If I would come, we'd share our winnings on a bumper party and night out. Sure enough, the croupier would shout 'last bets', and then place a magnet under the side of the wheel where the smallest bets had been placed. The trick was to bet just after he'd called 'last bets', and provided you covered the three numbers of the weighted side of the table you'd win. You would need to hand back a generous part of your winnings to the croupier, giving him no suspicion that you'd discovered his secret, and by betting on odds or evens or reds and blacks before making another killing on a number giving good odds of 36-1. It was exciting. Raymond enjoyed African life; he loved the largeness of the African ladies in every way. We had a favourite dinner venue – Mama Victoria's at which he particularly enjoyed eating the local fish dish 'egusi soup', cooked and served by Mama Joyce, another large lady with a wicked worldly grin, she was big without being flabby. Her food was spicy, tasty, fishy and hot, and she was all of that too.

Life in the East was sweaty and hard. The roads were downright dangerous, and the sheer stress of getting through the day made the first beer incredibly tasty. But in the East of Nigeria everyone is alive. I completed my task in the allotted six months and ventured north to Kano to report to Bryan Dunnill. What a different world. First, it's totally Muslim, with grand-looking gentlemen smart in their fine flowing white robes. Those that ride a bicycle choose a big roadster bicycle in chrome-plated finish with the Sturmey-Archer gear tied down in 1st gear so that they could pedal slowly and with dignity. The factory was immaculate, the M.D.'s racehorses were grazing on the outside lawn, and life looked good. On being invited back to the M.D.'s huge house complete with garden and outdoor pool, it looked even better. I was given my own room and servant in one wing of the house. At dinner we were served by six servants in their white suits and white gym shoes on their feet so that they could tread quietly. Aba was far away. Bryan, though, was an old 'coaster', he knew West Africa well and deserved all the pageantry with which he was surrounded. This gave Bryan status to the Africans. Here was a white man living as a white man should, and it was a pleasure to serve such a role model. Yet it was not quite like that, for the real local African owner of Raleigh Industries, Nigeria Ltd, Alhaji Aminu Dantata, whose story is very different, was an imperious Hausa Nigerian.

This was illustrated many years later when I was the Managing Director of Raleigh International and Raleigh Industries Nigeria was my Licensee. A meeting was arranged between Mr Mohammed, the Managing Director of Raleigh Kano, and Alhaji Aminu Dantata. It was arranged for us all to meet in Dubai, one morning at 10 o'clock. I flew there from the U.K. only for this meeting. I arrived at Dantata's house in Dubai – a £20 million pad, to be told that he wasn't available that day. The meeting was eventually held two and a half days later! My dismay, surprise and anger, was quickly replaced by a plan which had an amusing outcome. I decided to see a bit of Dubai – a city I hadn't visited since 1968, when it was more sand than brick. I decided to go to the famous 'Burj al Arab' hotel. 'May I look around your hotel?' I enquired of the receptionist. 'Certainly Sir, that'll be $100.' I was shocked and thought the Receptionist was joking, so I playfully replied, 'Oh, but I only wanted to see if my helicopter could land safely on your helipad.' I immediately was given a free and exquisite trip around this extraordinary hotel with its fancy gold tap bathrooms and huge beds covered with silk sheets.

As a contrast, I then visited the 'old museum', and to my delight I soon found walking around the Dubai I knew from 1960s. This was much more agreeable to me than the obscenity of the modern city with its outrageous displays of wealth and waste, and with its influx of Bangladeshi taxi drivers sharing the same bed for seven-hour shifts.

My return to the U.K. from Australia via the six-month Nigerian diversion was a shock. I had missed the three-day week of the early '70s. Britain was running a socialist course under Harold Wilson, Frank Callaghan, and Tony Benn, with a short interlude of Edward Heath, who found that power lay with the Unions and not the Government. Manufacturing was in decline. In cycle terms the brief spell of Japan taking over was now replaced by Taiwan, and soon to be joined by China. While socialism made the EEC look more attractive with its solid democracy, companies were merging and changing. Raleigh decided to split itself into Raleigh Cycles Ltd. – the bicycle company, and Sturmey-Archer Ltd. – the components company.

I should explain here that to include a brand name in a Company title has downsides. For example Raleigh Industries Ltd had over a hundred different brand names of which 'Raleigh' was only one. Likewise 'Sturmey-Archer' refers to internal gear hubs invented in 1902; but Sturmey-Archer Ltd included everything made by Raleigh Industries Ltd, that was not a complete bicycle, i.e. components. Impressively Raleigh Industries Ltd manufactured everything on a bicycle except for the chain, tyres and tubes. So, all single speed, front and rear hubs, rims, spokes and nipples, bottom bracket parts and lugs, chainwheels and handlebars and so on made up the new Sturmey-Archer Ltd's range. Many of these sectors had become uncompetitive to companies concentrating on a particular product, offering a full range and through volume, won economies of scale. Weeding out from Sturmey-Archer Ltd the winners and losers was a key task for the new Company. Undoubtedly the core branded products were Brooks leather saddles and the internally geared hubs and brakes, and a victim became the superb Phillips range.

Sturmey-Archer Ltd. 1973 and 1975-1998

In total I was to spend over twenty-seven of my forty-eight Raleigh years with Sturmey-Archer Ltd. To begin with it was in between my African and Middle East adventures as a subordinate to Ray Bakewell. He led the Sturmey-Archer division of Raleigh before it became a separate company in 1975-6. This was one of the best initiations into appreciating real engineering I could have had. Sturmey-Archer was and is a gem. The gear was a clever design from 1902 involving, among others, Mr Sturmey and Mr Archer – whose origins are a fascinating story in itself, and it is well told in *The Hub of the Universe*, 2020. This product has passed the test of time and the use of epicyclic gearing contained in the size of a cocoa tin on the rear wheel of a bike was revolutionary. Furthermore, to be tutored in the components business rather than complete bicycles was an experience in real engineering which allowed me to meet the major players in the bicycle industry around the world. For example, Sturmey-Archer was fitted exclusively by many Original Equipment Manufacturers (OEMs), most notably by the most well-known American company Schwinn in the USA. To avoid dependence on one manufacturer the other OEM businesses in the USA, Huffy, Murray Ohio, Columbia and AMF, sourced from both Shimano and Sturmey-Archer Ltd. I got to understand both manufacturing, and businesses not just in the USA but around the world.

Being in a way side-lined into Sturmey-Archer also gave me a useful profile, as the more ambitious Raleigh folk were playing the bigger game – I was to be a big fish in the small pond of Sturmey-Archer. SA worked strategically through its subsidiary, Sturmey-Archer Amsterdam, headed up by Alan Clarke with whom I worked very closely for several years, covering all the European OEMs.

On my return to the UK at the end of 1976 I was given my own office along the Golden Mile (that glorious Head Office of the Raleigh world) but was asked to share a secretary with the Home Sales Director,

Frank Donnelly. This was fine by me but not so fine for Miss Vicky. She had been Frank's personal secretary for some years. He took her on UK customer calls dictating to her in the car and she enjoyed his very real flair and professional salesmanship. Miss Vicky was a comely Nottingham lass and a very experienced secretary whose shorthand was certainly at the speed of speech, and her typing close to that as well. What's more she really had little time for foreigners. Here I was bringing her into a world, exciting to me, but one that she did not want to have to face.

I would receive my mail in the morning, put in the typing tray that which needed dictating and when this totalled about 15 to 20 letters, I would call in Miss Vicky. In between the ums and ahs of my dictation she would start to tap her pencil on the desk, when I asked her to stop, she said that 'it was like pulling teeth taking my dictation'. She was right, so I made a point of preparing notes first, before putting letters in my typing tray and then dictating at a speed which I hoped would make her uncomfortable. I failed – she never felt uncomfortable – and it was me that was stretched. However, she would get annoyed at my 'foreign speak', for example when I wrote to, say, a Nigerian with expressions like 'wait small', which in Nigerian English simply means 'please be patient', or say 'Mr X is on seat'. In English we may say that 'Mr X is available', but in Nigeria that is imprecise as Nigerians are always available, but it is difficult to find them 'on seat' i.e., at their desk and therefore immediately contactable. I only gave her good reason to dislike foreigners more, and so when Mr Mohammad from Zaria came to visit me, I thought I would have some fun with dear Miss Vicky.

Mr Mohammad arrived in his beautiful white robes covering his ample frame, and I asked Miss Vicky to bring in two cups of tea and take notes on the visit. Mohammad started sipping his tea from his teaspoon, and Miss Vicky looked disgusted. I then poured my tea into my saucer and started drinking it from the saucer. She glared, and I said that it cooled my tea and that's how I take it. So, the meeting went on, and Mohammad placed a huge order, which I had anticipated, for 50,000 front and rear wide barrelled Phillips hubs, nos. 37 and 39. Even

Miss Vicky was impressed and I then asked Mohammad if he would like to pay for this in cash and give it directly to Miss Vicky as I was not allowed to accept cash directly. To her horror Mohammad stood up, picking up his robes and there tied around his legs were rather old and sweaty, but still worthy, £50 and $100 bank notes which he duly peeled off and counted out into Miss Vicky's hands, making up the £50,000 worth of notes. I loved the whole scene. I would have liked to say he had a $ leg and a £ leg. In fact he had his dollars and pounds in their original bank bundles neatly bandaged around both legs. (I don't know where he would have housed his Euros had it been in existence at the time.) Funnily enough after Miss Vicky saw to what I had exposed her we got on well.

My work with Sturmey-Archer meant attending trade shows around the world. In those days Sturmey-Archer was not just internal geared hubs, it was all the Phillips components business – brakes, roller levers and callipers, single speed front and rear hubs, sprockets, nipples, and rims. Also Brooks saddles, in fact everything except frame sets, tyres and tubes. The largest international bicycle show in the world in those days was the Cologne Show. Raleigh used it as a venue to entertain customers from all over the world. During my first show attendance, briefly in September 1969, my fellow graduate trainee David Cropper, who was a linguist, while also a junior pipsqueak like me in Raleigh, was invited to be the translator of the grand speeches.

On one evening every year at the Cologne Show, Raleigh put on a huge dinner party for all their customers around the world and David very ably translated for this into German and French. To my dismay I found I was not even invited to this prestigious Industry Dinner at which all the top industry grandees from all over the world were present. I was upset at this snub, so decided to invite a couple of my new German acquaintances, who were also competitors of Sturmey-Archer, out to dinner. I went onto the Union Frondenberg stand and asked one Alfred Ludwig what he was doing for dinner and if he'd join me. He was delighted, and I asked him if he could book a table at one of Cologne's finest restaurants. He chose one on the Rhine – *der Bastei*.

Funnily enough, at an adjoining table sat the Shimano team, a small operation then, so I was introduced to Yoshi Shimano, who was to be a useful contact in later years. I suggested to my 'friend', Alfred that he, as a local German, should choose the wine, and between us we enjoyed a superb evening and dinner – until the bill arrived. In those days there were no bank cards, just cash or traveller's cheques. I had a little of the former and a lot of the latter. I therefore had to pay with traveller's cheques and only just had enough. When I saw the price of the wine that Alfred had chosen, I vowed to get my revenge – it was obscene. What is more, when I came to put in my expenses, I couldn't even claim for such an expensive dinner and spent the next few days collecting receipts to cover the cost of the meal for which I couldn't claim, claiming the required amount for other meals not consumed.

When next I saw Alfred, it was at the New York Show the following February. I suggested to him that it was his turn to buy me a dinner one night. He said he would be delighted. I went to the concierge at my modest New York hotel and asked them to recommend one of the poshest restaurants in New York and booked a table for two. At the table, Alfred suggested it was my turn to choose the wine. I did, by looking at the price rather than the grape or vintage. On tasting the wine Alfred, after swishing it around his glass and then almost chewing a mouthful, stood to attention at the table and congratulated me for knowing my wines. That dinner we went from the '*Sie*' to the '*Du*', with both of us standing to attention across the table shaking hands to our new friendship and intimacy. I felt ashamed and promised that at the Milan Show it would be my turn, and another charade was played out with the most wonderful '*grappa*' in Italy. Alfred not only became a friend, my pseudonym of 'Sir' Alfred stood, and as such he was known throughout the industry. He was the only man I knew in the industry whose expenses were questioned by the government tax man rather than his company. 'Sir Alfred' knew how to live expensively on expenses. An amusing episode happened at one New York Show where on our Sturmey-Archer stand was Bob Hill, who during the Second World War was captured at Arnhem, falling into the arms of Captain Fumf without firing a shot. He was then frog-marched to Warsaw, where he saw out the remaining months of the war. Alfred it transpired was also captured but by the American 8th Army and was sent to Marseilles to await a ship to take him to Boston. The war ended before his ship sailed, to his huge regret.

During the process of setting up Sturmey-Archer America in West Chicago in 1976 I had to visit all the OEMs in the USA. Huffy and Murray were the largest and supplied mainly the mass market. The most important were Schwinn in the Midwest, Columbia on the East coast and AMF in the Midwest – mainly in Little Rock. I was in Olney visiting AMF a couple of years later when I met up again with Sir Alfred in our hotel in downtown Olney and he was with his boss, Wolfgang Schluter, who was in the process of establishing a small distribution and supply centre in Olney. To me Sir Alfred was Union Frondenberg, so I was always going to be sceptical about any 'bossman'.

If ever you need to beware of judging a book by its cover it would have been with Wolfgang. I was polite I hope to him, but this tall, blond, very confident, loud, ruggedly handsome and opinionated gentleman summed up all that history had warned me about in Germany. His English was not fluent, nor did he miss anything said, but when he expressed himself it was in loud sound bites, coming straight to the point with a directness that was a command rather than an opening for discussion. In the event that you started to discuss his statements he became louder and repeated them even more crudely. Often starting his counter argument 'shit on you …' And then repeating his opinion with force and conviction against which there (to him) could be no response. It was all too easy to disagree without even hearing the opinion, whatever its relevance. To me Wolfgang was the archetypal U Boat commander who could make his commands clear without the need for a microphone to block out the noise of a submarine's engine. He spoke; you jumped. There was no doubting though that Wolfgang had 'authority'. I met him more socially than for business for several years and in several places all over the world. 'Union' was a respected competitor rather than an enemy, and clearly Sir Alfred deferred to his 'boss'. However, back in Europe I was to see a lot of Herr Schluter and for the extraordinary reason that soon after he resigned from Union, which must have been around 1989, he took up the position of CEO of Kalkhoff Werke in Cloppenberg, one of the largest German OEMs. Wolfgang filled this position in every sense. He soon decided that Kalkhoff couldn't survive in its current form and he set about finding new owners to buy out his employers. He hit upon the new owners of Raleigh – Ed Gottesman and his Derby Corporation – with his usual conviction. I didn't know Mr Gottesman and never got to know him, but this did not stop Wolfgang using me as the unknown 'go between'. I was a party to all of Wolfgang's plans, which as ever came about, and Kalkhoff Werke became Derby Germany, with Wolfgang as the *Oberführer*. It was to be a good purchase, and Wolfgang was not shy about spending any profits or cash in expansion, and soon after the fall of the Berlin Wall set about establishing an Eastern German subsidiary in Rostock on the Baltic (the place where the KGB members used to meet for their summer holidays). I went there for its opening, which was impressive and also rather sad – I had never met so many PhD qualified engineers working on the shop floor, as employment was hard to find. I was amused to see though that Wolfgang spoke to Mr Gottesman in exactly the same manner he used with me: when he queried any comment Wolfgang would subject him to an even louder repetition of his clear and un-ambivalent view, with which only a fool would disagree. Even Mr G was silenced (He was after all Jewish). I flew back from Rostock to Hamburg in a helicopter Mr G had rented after this grand opening where he repeated his arguments, but they still did not impress Wolfgang, who went ahead anyway. DCW, which the company was known as, turned out to be a good investment but the Rostock operation never did succeed. As we flew along in our helicopter between Rostock and Bremen, just to make conversation, I suggested to Mr G that he should invest in a Company Helicopter to save Michael Hancock the dreadful 24 hours weekly journey from Dieren in Holland to Cloppenburg and on to Rostock. Mr G promptly gave me some age-old advice along the lines of 'Mr Macnaughtan if you can drive it, fly it, or fuck it; rent it.' Silence again followed.

Wolfgang has become a good friend, and this I knew when his wife left him, and he came over to stay with me in Nottingham. He never moaned about his wife, a medical doctor, but rather needed space. He was a fun guest and I enjoyed his unaltered expressions of his clear views. Moreover, I had the pleasure of having his second son Martin to stay with me to improve his English while doing a short job with Raleigh. In fact, I enjoyed meeting the older son Christoph and daughter Annette, and indeed, my son Alistair went on holiday with them to the Bodensee. Wolfgang then met and married a most unlikely and very sensible young lady – Helga, a school teacher. I was able to enjoy many nights staying at their home in Cloppenberg in their granny flat.

One dinner was even more memorable – which needs explaining, after an introduction. The Derby owners found Wolfgang's imperious manner hard to handle and they appointed Michael Hancock to have joint managership with Wolfgang. Michael was the very English CEO of Gazelle in Dieren Holland and he used to make the unenviable drive every week from there to Cloppenberg. Michael had a rather depressing top floor flat as his *pied à terre* in Cloppenberg, to which I was invited on several occasions, and shared his home-cooked spaghetti Bolognese. I had known Michael when he was in charge of the Birmingham factories of Raleigh and found him terrific company, which sadly his beautiful wife, Margot, did not. In his flat Michael confided in me that Margot had left him and their three grown up sons, and that he still loved her etc. etc. He then told me, after the divorce, that he used to confide in his Dutch golf partner about his personal problems even to the point of telling him where he had secreted his money so that Margot couldn't get her hands on it – only to find that Margot was leaving him in preference for this very man. Just before Margot and Michael parted ways he and I were invited to the Schluters for 'this dinner' during which Michael explained that he had taken the advice of a doctor friend of his in Dieren that one way of re-attracting Margot was to have a 'tummy tuck' to improve his appearance. The subject would not normally be considered appropriate dinner table talk, but with the characters of Michael Hancock and Wolfgang this would never have been a consideration. He explained over the main course that the good doctor was marking up his body where the incisions would be made and did so with him standing in the nude in front of the doctor, when, after sorting the 'tuck' he declared that the tummy was not the main problem it was Michaels 'family jewels' that would put off any young lady and should be rearranged. In particular, one of his gonads hung far too low and gave a very strange and ugly appearance but that with some attention this could be addressed. Michael then showed us the result of the tuck he'd undergone by dropping his drawers at the table. Happily he did not show us the more offending item, but did explain that the one over-size testicle had been removed, and that it was rather like peeling an onion reduced to match the other. Michael was very happy with the result. It must have been true, as a couple of years later he was to marry the Mayor of Arnhem's daughter, quite a catch. It was a hysterical dinner with even Helga shaming herself for laughing so heartily.

Enough of Wolfgang, who has remained a true friend, and whose company always is shockingly uplifting and who together with his family has stories enough for a good many dinners to which I look forward.

In 1976 on returning from Oz I was asked to head up all of Sturmey-Archer's export business. It took me back to my global trading routes again, but this time spending much time in the USA, as well as catching up with customers all over the world. There were to be few long trips from the years after 1976 but more time was spent on them, and time issues made each more focussed, and with fewer social diversions. The UK manufacturing environment in the 1970s was in a sorry state of decline, as were wealth-creating industries more generally. One immediate result, and probably overdue, was the decision to separate Raleigh's bicycle business from its component business. Raleigh Cycles Ltd was charged with addressing its cost and competitive base, and increasing its domestic sales profitably in the light of falling exports; while Sturmey-Archer had to address its product base and redefine its market base. Sturmey-Archer's turnover in 1976 was still in excess of

£100m of which £38m was exported with the balance being sold largely to Raleigh and some to UK wholesalers. Redundancy and restructuring was inevitable. I found the following years full of opportunity and was allowed a free hand although I didn't realise at the time that I was not always bringing my colleagues along with me, and didn't feel the need so to do when the bosses supported me – or so I thought, especially as I could often bury my failures without even bringing them to light. I hope that the following gives a brief summary of the next many 'business years' that absorbed me for some 20 years. They gave me a quality of life that was great fun but also produced personal side effects where I squeezed in a domestic life in far too business-like a manner.

Sturmey-Archer's MD was the charismatic Mike Smith (MSMS). He was by nature a man to lead from the front, less interested in cut-backs but more in identifying new opportunities or markets, investing in them and driving the business to offset uncompetitive product sales and to overcome all with a harder work ethic. Leading from the front MSMS had just been persuaded that a new forging technique could halve the cost of conventional forging by a process of squeeze casting melted material. This would press out air bubbles and provide the strength of a fully forged product. He called it 'hyper-forging'. He recruited his best engineer, Alan Macgregor, to head up the new venture and located it in Birmingham, an area which was under greater threat of redundancy in the Phillips component range and therefore had a ready workforce for retraining into hyper-forging stems and cranks.

In Australia I had been introduced to the new Taiwanese OEMs to whom Cyclops turned to reduce their cost base and whose attitude to risk was more open than their traditional suppliers, and where cosy relationships had built up between supplier and customer. I saw too that the Taiwan manufacturers relied upon 'Trading Companies' to organise their purchasing, and all the Sturmey-Archer's products were sold through them. I had by chance struck up a good rapport with Grace Tseng the sister of Ike, who owned Merida in Taichung. Ike was a Japanese-trained Taiwanese with huge ambitions, a sense of humour and he liked to gamble. Luck had it that I struck gold on one short trip to Taichung, and Ike was ready, not to buy Hyper-forge products but to manufacture them under licence in Taiwan. The match between Ike and MSMS was uncanny, and some three months after this trip led both of them with Grace and myself to meet up at the Goodwood Park Hotel in Singapore where we did the deal. In fact so taken was Ike with MSMS that he named his son and heir 'Michael', and Mike Tseng is now the owner and boss of Merida – nice story. But one with a sadder end, as about a year after Hyper-forge was introduced the whole technology of forging leap-frogged and newer squeeze forging techniques were offering better products at cheaper prices. A tough world, but Ike held no blame and said it had been 'a good adventure and learning curve' and had given a year ahead of the game for both Sturmey-Archer and Merida.

In parallel with this two year adventure I had immediately identified the American market as the most critical for Sturmey-Archer in the short term. Sturmey-Archer was the 100% supplier to the leading USA brand of Schwinn, who like Raleigh had felt their place to be invincible in the market. I saw that Shimano and to a lesser extent Fichtel and Sachs were quickly gaining ground in the mass market, non-dealer, growth segment in America. I thought of the success that Sturmey-Archer Europe had had in Amsterdam with a local sales arm in the market keeping close to the entire customer base, in the same time zone and with a locally available after-sales service. I saw too that Alan Clarke who had been seconded to SAE in the early 1970s, was crammed at the local convent to learn Dutch, and soon had a lean and reliable asset to Sturmey-Archer's customer base. Also, invoicing in Dutch Guilders kept the price locally stable and incidentally allowed currency gains to pass straight to HO. MSMS backed my proposal to set up Sturmey-Archer of America Inc. and invoice in US dollars.

So it was that a few months after being back in Nottingham that I hot-footed it to the USA determined to set up Sturmey-Archer of America Inc. I knew little of USA Corporate law and simply asked my colleagues at Raleigh International America (RIA) in Boston at the time if I could use their legal partners. I also quickly concluded that the location of Sturmey-Archer USA should be close to its biggest customer

Schwinn in Chicago, who happily and freely supported me in my quest. I got to know all of the management of this great company, and that American inclusive spirit saved me days of work by their spontaneous advice. These two high-handed decisions saved me much time and debate maybe at an overhead penalty price, but in line with my philosophy of putting the market first. Bruce McWhirter, the legal eagle from Raleigh America, flew in from Boston to see me at my Hilton hotel at O'Hare airport in Chicago. His huge experience was a delight and for a full day talked to me of tax and law and people costs. Bruce was immersed in his knowledge and it took me all of 10 minutes to know he was 'my man'. He actually started his 'clock' on his hourly rate after about half an hour of 'free' coffee. Together we completed a mocked-up business plan with him costing for me the set-up legal liabilities and the facility based in a couple of locations, and projected employee costs and current sales, which left me left me to fill in the actual costs and addresses etc. as they unfolded. I never met Bruce again but worked with him closely and with a great sense of fun for the next several years. On day three, I started interviewing my candidates for General Manager, again at my hotel. The most memorable being a young man from Kentucky who was quite the most polite, charming, upstanding gentlemen of all-American values; a god-fearing guy from USA's Bible-belt. I doubted not his integrity, devotion to work, loyalty and intentions but tried to picture him into fitting into my customer base of clever and fast Jewish wholesalers, and a trade that required a strong liver and a dark, quick and sometimes deprecating humour. That interview was an experience for me. The obvious choice for General Manager though was John Temple, an ex RIA man, living locally and closely interested and aware of the cycle trade. It was also the easiest decision which I knew wasn't wrong and anyway only time ever tells if such decisions are right. I decided to chance my arm and pick him; indeed I brought him along in my quest the very next day to find premises, which we did in West Chicago. It came in at under the projected costs in my Business Plan drafted the day before.

I knew MSMS wanted action and I knew too that my immediate boss, Bob Forsyth, only wanted a robust plan by which he could measure me. So after three days I started filling in the Pro Forma Business Plan Bruce and I had developed. I remember then pausing and going to talk it through with my new friends at Schwinn. Their accountant, Bill Long, gave me long-winded but great advice. Their marketing guy Jay Townley showed off his huge market intelligence (he later became an Industry expert and lecturer on the dealer trade in the USA, and we spent some together both in the USA and on a trip to the UK). A fund of knowledge but very bikie dedicated. To cap it all who should I also meet working at Schwinn was a very youthful Bill Austin. They say old soldiers never die but nor did Bill fade away instead this happy meeting was a prelude to a long relationship as he moved on to be the President of Giant USA and then was selected to head up Raleigh in the USA at their new HO in Seattle. So we were on the same side again and despite him being on a higher level than me our relationship proved mutually beneficial and happy for some 30 years!

The evening after my meetings with his staff Eddie Schwinn took me out for dinner that night and tested my liver, and it was a pleasure to hear many Schwinn family stories which are rich indeed. I was made to feel a member, which paid off well in joining them on their generous bi-annual conventions all over the States. I was able to nuance my business plan with all sorts of uncorroborated flesh and blood material. I concluded this amazing week over the weekend at RIA's annual golf day – as I shall relate shortly.

Sturmey-Archer's wonderful accountant, Ernie Mellors, soon translated my Board Presentation into Anglo Saxon, and apart from severe reservations about John Temple, supported the initiative but he thought I was mad at getting involved in the USA at all. A month later I was to return to USA to get started with John Temple in our new West Chicago premises and went around all of the USA OEMs to tell them of our commitment to their market and ask for their support. Here started a twenty year close relationship with the American market. We became members of the Wholesalers (BWDA) and Manufacture (BMA) organisations in the USA and soon were part of the USA Industry scene and considered as 'locals'. I am left now with huge memories of Schwinn Conventions on the Great Lakes; partying at Boca Raton;

meetings at the CamelBack Inn in Phoenix Arizona; visiting Key Biscayne in the Florida Keys, not to mention the New York and West Coast Cycle shows. Oh to be blessed with short sleep and a good liver.

Many side adventures came our way in the USA, for example getting into the growth wheel-chair market with the largest supplier 'Invercare' in California, selling them Sturmey-Archer hub brakes as an option in their wheels. Then in getting to know the USA market proved invaluable to understanding the Far East manufacturing base, where I was able to chase the Taiwanese not to fit the more locally available Shimano product and thereby hold our world markets. Short visits to Taiwan resulted, plus accompanying American customers to new OEMs to keep the UK industry relevant as a supplier was necessary.

Getting to know Shimano itself should have been even more important, as I soon met the three brothers Shozo, Keijo and Yoshi separately and together. We struck up a surprising working relationship even to the point of their considering using Sturmey-Archer as a partner in their European strategy – but this involves bringing others with you in the UK! Not so easy.

Managing time is hard and especially to a personality not accustomed to the word 'no'. To do this in a time of decline and fall of UK manufacture, but with clever UK engineering design, is especially galling – still then world beating in terms of innovation if not in its production methods or costs. I was to watch over the demise of many of my customers, and not just the Cycle Makers both in the USA, Europe and elsewhere, but also to witness the devastating effect on their old local suppliers like the seat maker Person Majestic or the demise of the much loved Italian company of Tagliabue et fils (dear, dear Gianni) to name only two. To see the likes of Charlie Persons endure so doggedly the setbacks that befell him into his final fall, after three generations, into bankruptcy is hard to take. History is written for and by the survivors but life is lived uniquely and precious for all, and I remember all of them who had to reinvent themselves usually with pain and qualified success. But no time to dwell. Another unforeseen adventure was to pass my way: The Itera plastic bike concept in Sweden.

A group of Swedish engineers at Volvo in Gothenberg had been working for over five years on the development of a plastic car, which Volvo then aborted. In return they offered these engineers a year's sabbatical to develop their knowledge of plastics into other applications. So started the 'Itera' bicycle. I was approached to offer a press fitted Sturmey-Archer hub into the hub of a plastic wheel and to be part of their adventure. I went to Gothenberg with Gerry Beardshaw, Sturmey-Archer's clever technical Director, and with his knowledge of sintering components, and stress lines on moving parts, he soon became a hit with the young Swedes of Volvo. It was a privilege to sit in on many technical meetings way above my head but listening to solutions to problems that I never would have thought about. From inception to product this project raced ahead and before I knew it a prototype had been built and tested, and I was invited to a pre-launch of the product with a selected gathering in the botanical gardens at Gothenberg. I am no cyclist and especially because of this I was nervous about my ability to ride a vehicle which had inherent problems of lateral stability. The chosen few, some twenty of us, duly rode our bikes around the beautiful gardens and were all impressed with the quietness of the product, its smooth ride and easy handling. I had spotted a Viking burial ground within the Gardens and asked if I could try the product off-piste on my own. I reached the top of the mound breathless, but with no fault attached to the bike for that, and then found to my dismay the other side was stepped, and before I knew it I was being propelled down them. Sure enough the bike was hard to control both laterally and vertically as it successfully overcame all shaking except my own. In a five minute nightmare I had exposed the downside of a less than rigid frame where I provided the suspension often in conflict with my bicycle. The Itera boys were unfazed by my experience saying they were aware of the problem and had solutions using a stiffer plastic. Suffice it to say that we sold them 35,000 three-speed hubs, but the bike never really was brought to market. A shame, but not without a happy outcome in that the boys had developed with Bosch in Germany the right mix of plastics for use as the vanes of the wind driven windmills about to become established for wind and solar energy. I think our Sturmey-Archer hubs were hardly used and are languishing somewhere in Lapland where the bikes were (cheaply) assembled.

Meanwhile SAE in Holland had consolidated itself, losing some memorable customers like Batavus. A trip up to Friesland didn't succeed in retrieving this business but rather losing it to Fichtel & Sachs. But we gained others less prestigious in the mass market and then extended SAE's reach out of Holland and into Germany in much more depth, with Alan Clarke's appointment of Horst Sudbrack – a German OEM casualty from Far East competition, allowing him to recreate himself with his son, Olaf, now taking over Sturmey-Archer and the Holland Mechanics agency.

We visited every European manufacturer – well over a hundred of them from the Tagliabue's in Italy to Rog in Llubljana to all of the French and Belgian markets (The Belgian market was aptly described by Ray Bakewell as a 'dog's breakfast' but ably run by Jean van Stappen who thrived in a muddle) and all in Norway, Finland, Denmark and Sweden, and soon after we were ready to tackle the Eastern European customers. Nothing beats personal visits especially in a 'close' trade as the bike business is. Bringing together these intense and long-distanced visits at the annual Cologne and Milan Shows made the Sturmey-Archer Booth a busy one and it was well manned now. This left me free for one day in the Autumn of each year to pop over to Düsseldorf to spend a day with the Japanese enclave there responsible to their home market for marketing information. The 'Japan Bicycle Promotions Institutes' statistics must have been the best in the world, and as these guys found some of my market knowledge useful they were quick to share their conclusions with me and show me their research, as I was seen to be independent and not a cycle maker! Their statistics were difficult to understand as they were wrong but were in fact statistically accurate – you had to read the qualifications so that year on year a very clear pattern emerged, which while wrong in detail, was spot-on in analysis and highly reliable as a marketing tool. This connection which I kept to myself made me feel like a double agent at the time but it hurt no-one, and I had a regular source for the best Japanese meals in Europe in downtown Dussledorf. It was to lead to a very tangible opportunity in Japan itself which follows.

Japan

I was excited when it was first suggested I should visit Japan in 1977. The Japanese were our family's Second World War enemies – not the Germans – so the inherited press I had received was negative and peppered with stories of cruelty and barbarity with the only compliment being 'but they were good fighters'. Indeed the only advice my father gave to me was to ensure that I worked with 'efficient Japanese not inefficient ones'. In our house Dad would have no products of Japanese origin. I did note though that Dad loved his 1939-bought Japanese Ikon 35mm camera, and swore it was the best lens on any camera he ever used. Clearly an efficient producer. Dad was one never to talk about his war experiences in Burma, but Mum and Grandad told me of many horrors.

I had two jobs to complete on my short 1977 trip. The Suntour company had ventured into the internal gear market and was aspiring to take on the giant Shimano with a slew of innovative products and 'would I put my nose into this and advise'. Secondly, my mission was to understand the upsurge in sales of Brooks branded leather saddles, and whether it was sustainable and why.

Tom Field and I at a press conference with an interpreter

Suntour's CEO, Junzoh Kawai welcomed my visit and was flattered that Sturmey had recognised his initiatives, and with a great sense of fun revealed to me the most ambitious of engineering opportunities he was exploring. 'If someone doesn't challenge Shimano now they will become a monopoly in the cycle market, and this is not healthy,' declared Kawai-san. It was clearly a drain on his resources and cash to enter the internal hub gear market, and it didn't take a genius to see the opportunity for Sturmey-Archer here, which is the main subject of this chapter.

But the more exciting side of this visit was actually the Brooks saddle sales. Brooks had a Japanese competitor, Kashimax, who complimented Brooks by copying them and promoting leather, but not quite having the brand cachet of a genuine Brooks. By chance Brooks had the most eccentric and engaging of distributors in Hiro-san. This guy was a human gem and his daughter a concert violinist of the highest order. Funnily enough he saw the after-market opportunity for Brooks through non-cycle channels and with devilish delight asked me if I would stay for a week and man a tiny stand, consisting of one desk, in one of the new and fancy and sophisticated Shopping Mall high end stores, which he proposed to rent for a week. We arranged a special packaging for each saddle and increased the price by some 30% in order not to alienate the existing trade and see if there was a demand

Making a point to Junzoh Kawai

for a premium product. In that week the two of us sold nearly as many saddles as Brooks had sold in a full year into the traditional cycle shops in Japan. I learnt so much from this experience and have oft repeated the moral of this story. But as an aside I got to see the sheer energy, hard work and cleverness of the Japanese, and to see someone whose charm was combined with a great love of the Arts and classical music, and who found his day-time job such a joy by contrast. This was not the caricature of the Japanese I had in my prejudiced head, and set me up well to get much joy myself from this extraordinary island race.

But the reality of another order soon arrived on my return visit in 1979, and this brought me into the real difficulty of trading in Japan. Like many countries and quite understandably, the Japanese are highly protectionist. This is a bigger issue in Japan than just their Government enacting legislation. It is the industries themselves that will place 'conditional selling' on their customers i.e., Shimano (Sturmey-Archer's biggest competitor) threatened any customer buying a Suntour 3-speed hub with their ceasing to supply to that customer, thereby making our whole deal unviable.

We were able to take this up with the Government authorities at a press conference. At this meeting, impressively, was the French ambassador to Japan. We got nowhere. The Japanese patiently listened and very politely made a virtue of not understanding the problem. The meeting ended amicably and without issue.

The ambassador later explained why to me. In fact, he invited me to his Club in Osaka, as he was surprised to learn that in my many visits to Japan, I had not been expensively entertained, since the Japanese companies usually have a Club membership expressly for this purpose with expenses deductible from tax. The ambassador was not just very bright, but also fluent in Japanese and clearly enjoyed Japan, but he was also realistic about the chances for trade from Europe to succeed, and was intrigued to know more about my initiative. We had, for me, a memorable night, and when he dropped me off at my hotel after 3 a.m. I was so mentally stimulated that, with the help of a report he gave me, I wrote up what I had learned. In re-reading this I find it worthy of repetition, and include it as an appendix to this little book (see Appendix 2). It is dated but still illuminating. The episode demonstrates the importance of market visits and 'following your nose'. Business will go awry if the context in which it is carried out is not seen in context. In our case, and even with the bravery of Junzoh Kawai, (Suntour's CEO), we were always on to a loser, and even though we did sell some Suntour hubs to him the project floundered because of the culture and context of the Japanese market.

On a later trip to Japan my Managing Director, Mike Smith, asked to accompany me. What he didn't tell me was that he had spent some of his 'war years' in Sumatra. He went on to confirm, what I already knew about the cruelty of many of the Japanese soldiers. However, he then said that by the end of the war 'we were as bad as some of the Japs. Do you know how we cleared the sewers in Sumatra? We shoved the Japanese POW's down them with bamboo rods until they emerge at the other end'! If only the story could have ended there, but no, that wasn't Mike Smith.

Mike Smith and I in Tokyo

He was treated so well during our visit and with the grace that only the Japanese possess. He was asked 'would you like a very Japanese dinner Mr Smith or would you prefer Italian?' Mr Smith replied with aplomb 'Japanese of course'. Our hosts were delighted and on the way into the restaurant we passed an aquarium full of fish and the host asked him if he'd like a sample of what was to follow. 'Of course' he replied. Whereupon our host scooped out a fish, cut out a small portion of the fish's body and passed it to Mr Smith who took the tiniest of bites and declared 'absolutely fantastic you try this John' and passed me the large portion to swallow! We soon found ourselves sitting cross-legged on the floor while a table of raw meats and fish was laid out, with a live lobster cut in half as the centre piece and with its tentacles swaying for much of the meal. I thought I was stiff limbed and with short hamstrings, but sure enough so was Mike Smith. We both sat inelegantly around this picturesque table and very soon Mike Smith dominated the conversation, becoming more voluble by the glassful of sake. Until sure enough so happy was he in such gracious company that he proceeded to relate his war stories including the one just mentioned. 'Of course,' he said, 'by the end of the war we were no better than you lot' thinking this made us all equal and the mates which his sake dictated that we now clearly were. The Japanese just nodded quietly with their inscrutable smile and Mr Smith was totally at home with his new friends.

I kept my father's own experience strictly to myself. I hate to think what the Japanese hosts were thinking. I was no 'war denier'.

The Bike World, 1976-1989

The old guard of the '60s whom I had known – the Wilf Dawes, the Schwinn family of the Mid-West, Murray Ohio, the Smith family from Huffy's, Columbia, Middlemores, Haden Bros, even Raleigh, had all changed beyond recognition by the 1980s and a new generation of players was up and coming. There should be many books on each one of them and what eccentricities and scars they bore… The great thing that still exists from this rich heritage is The Centenary Club, established in 1939 and still very much alive. Please look up their website: https://www.thecentenaryclub.co.uk/ and follow the links to the 'Gallery' and to their Instagram account where there are some splendid photos covering the last 70+ years. They show the captains of the cycle industry actually going out for a bike ride together. For most a bicycle was for making and selling and not for riding. Indeed, if you ask any of us 'oldies' why we have stuck within this industry I guess nearly all would tell you 'because of the people in it' and that is really true.

The late '70s were the last gasp of the old bike industry. The famous Maillard derailleur gear ceased production and the Huret family sold out to Fichtel and Sachs in Germany. The cycle market changed again with the arrivals of the likes of Decathlon. Some of our OEMs ended up merging, like Peugeot and Gitane, while others ceased production as cheap Far East goods made local manufacture unviable. At St. Etienne, the bicycle and components centre in France, I saw that not everything had changed for when I was with M. Balouzet of Stronglight (makers of chainwheels and cranks) for lunch the '*garcon*' yelled out '*un bifteck Jeanne d'Arc pour l'Anglais*' across the restaurant, relaying my 'ugly' request to have a steak well-done and causing huge amusement to the superior French clientèle.

The trade shows always gave rise to stories. I have only related a few. These shows are proof that trade breaks down barriers and encourages interdependence, and makes war less likely. The Cologne Show, with its 40-50 local cycle manufacturers, was the industry's shop window to the world.

I was pleased to come across this photo below in the course of writing this memoir. Taken at one of the Cologne Shows in the 1990s it shows many of the 'oldies' of the industry. At the front, in the red jumper, sits the late George Flegg, who was rarely outside of the Brooks Smethwick factory where he worked for over 50 years and was known as 'Mr Brooks'. He only retired when Brooks was sold to Selle Royal. Next to him, and now also passed on, is Trevor Wilkinson, now probably in heaven with his binoculars bird-watching as he was that day he stole during a Long Beach Show to bird-watch from the Ritz Carlton hotel onto Laguna Beach. Alongside Trevor is Charlie Persons and with him his long-term business partner Dick Sanderson. Next to him, at the back, Brian Montgomery, a well-known face in the bike trade who lived in Paris, but is no longer with us. On the right-hand side of the photo is Horst Sudbrack – a one-time bike-family OEM in Germany and now representing Sturmey-Archer and Holland Mechanics in Germany, which his son, Olaf, has taken over. Next is Joop Balster who for all his life worked in Sturmey-Archer Amsterdam only to die some weeks after retiring. Alan Clarke has named the Sturmey-Archer museum after Joop. Then we have Jari Kommulainen with two of his Finnish customers.

There were colourful personalities throughout the industry. I think also of the likes of the old guards Gerry Burgess and John Cross, not to mention their German counterparts Herr Schwerdhofer and Herr Kronauer from Fichtel and Sachs or the old Schwinn family from the Mid-West, accentuating their eccentricities and strutting around the globe asserting their superiority. America's new guard meanwhile were hot footing it to Taichung and Taipei to re-source not just components but the whole bike. How offended I was to see the likes of Bill Kerns and Karl Barton of Raleigh Industries of America (RIA), amongst many others, teaching Giant and Merida how to make bikes suitable for the U.S. market – giving away the very hard-won production tricks of Raleigh and Schwinn etc. I was caught between knowledge, and even love of, the eccentric oldies, but with a grudging respect for the energy and direction of the new guard.

In those days I was away from the U.K. for some 140-150 days in the year, and I remember that the only way I kept up was by working Saturdays to follow-up my trips. My domestic life suffered – and Susie and I divorced in 1984. Happily, Sue's new house was around the corner from me, so I spent weekends with Alistair, and soon afterwards he came back to stay with me. I employed a housekeeper to help out. I had businessmen as bosses. M.S.M. Smith exuded a leadership that won the war where loyalty and even harder working was not an option. The rewards on return from my safaris were satisfying; it was easy to become absorbed in work. My boss from 1977 – 1983 at the time was Bob Forsyth, a formidable Yorkshireman with all the pluses and minuses of that breed. Although, he died in 1983, from too much good living, he was and is still the subject of many a colourful story.

On one occasion, when I was in the final throes of setting up Sturmey-Archer America in West Chicago for Sturmey-Archer and had been away for over two weeks, I was asked by Raleigh Industries of America (RIA) if I would like to join them for their annual golf competition to be held at the Pheasant Run in Chicago. I was due home on the Friday and had social appointments on the Sunday, but I rang Bob Forsyth to discuss this offer. 'Of course, you must play John – don't worry about the family. I'll look after them. You get to know the Raleigh America boys out of the office.' Come the Saturday I not only played in their championship, but I actually won and had a huge American trophy. I was so proud. In fact I elected to carry the trophy back rather than risk damaging it in my luggage.

At Heathrow Bob Forsyth had driven down on the Monday morning to meet me off my flight. As I emerged from Customs, I spotted him in the crowd and raised my arm with the trophy held high shouting, 'I won Bob!' He went apoplectic. 'John have you no sense? I told you to play, not to win. This is RIA's Annual Championship and you go and show off without realising what this means to them. You bloody idiot, you can find your own way home.' Whereupon he stalked off, got back into his car and drove to Nottingham alone. I was left to get a tube into Central London, a train up to Nottingham, and a taxi home from the station all the while clutching my trophy which had become a symbol of my ineptitude and thoughtlessness for winning.

Being awarded the (forbidden) Raleigh America Golf Cup at the Pheasant Run Resort in Chicago, by John Baggott, the President of Raleigh Industries of America on my right and Eric Thomas from Raleigh Industries UK on my left.

I have to say that Bob and I soon made up after this incident, and in fact when I returned to the USA the following February for the New York Show he proceeded to show me how to behave in America. One incident suffices. Bob had lived in the New York of the 1950s when he was with Hoover. He declared one evening that he would take Bob Hill (a Sturmey-Archer technician) and me to his 'Club' for dinner. He duly reserved three seats at the 'Pipe Club'. On arrival, Bob was asked for his membership card and number. He couldn't find it. He then remembered he'd looked it out prior to leaving and left it on the hall stand back in Nottingham. 'I've left it at home,' he told the concierge who replied that 'he should ring his wife, and if she could advise his membership number that would suffice.' (There were no mobile phones in those days, and transatlantic calls were not cheap). He dialled his home number and screamed at Mavis, 'what's my bloody number?' To which she replied, 'I told you you'd forgotten your card, and you didn't listen to me.' 'Alright, alright, just give me the number,' and after more loud invective she shouted out the number and he plonked down the phone and we gained entry. Bob loved his drink, and in fairness he could hold it too. 'Perfect Rob Roy' was his tipple in the U.S. He'd had at least three by the time the maître d' came to our table full of apologies. They'd had trouble locating Bob's clay pipe but after Bob's three cocktails they had eventually found it, very brown and abused it looked too. The maître d' said it had been put up in the attic along with several hundred others from members who had not visited for some years. But now, along with a saucer of best tobacco shag, the maître d' thanked him for his patience and said his drinks were 'on the house' for the whole evening – his not ours. I cannot remember how many more 'Perfect Rob Roys' Bob consumed, but he was well oiled, for when coffee arrived, he announced to us that he was going to make a speech. The club was now full (men only). 'Not a good idea,' we told him, and when he went to stand up, Bob Hill and I held him down. Not to be outdone he rapped his spoon on his glass vigorously until silence descended in the room. We had to let him go and he stood up (which was a miracle in itself) and made a speech on the value of 'tradition' and how in the U.K. we had it but didn't value it, whereas in America they valued it but didn't have it. This club he asserted was one of tradition in America, of the highest order, and of which to be proud, and he added that 'after not coming here for 25 years they even found my pipe.' He held it up in all its brown and faded glory and promptly burst into tears. The Americans love tears, we were hosted to drinks, and made to join one table after another. Bob continued to consume all he was offered. I don't know how we got back to Bob's hotel at the Plaza, but I do know that the three of us blokes passed out on his bed fully clothed. A few hours later it was Bob that got us all up with coffee delivered, and we went to man our stand at the New York Show in the clothes we'd worn for the past twenty-four hours.

The Bike Industry was changing fast in the 1980s. My job was to 'feed the elephant' of production in Nottingham, while reconstruction, redundancies and new strategies were put in place to meet the changing world. The centre of the world's bike industry was no longer Nottingham – it had moved to Japan, and then quickly from Japan to Taiwan. Raleigh had won an expensive court case in 1978 not to have to supply Argos with Raleigh branded bicycles. Two years later, desperate for sales, Raleigh was supplying Argos. Meanwhile Sturmey-Archer was separated more fully from Raleigh, and it wasn't long before all of the Birmingham Phillips operations were closed down with another 2,000 redundancies. In the early '80s the energy expended to make the industry survive was huge. Britain's manufacturing ability declined, and the stories of personal difficulties increased. This was reflected in the politicians' optimism that we were alone and needed to sort ourselves out, rather than leave it to our trade unions or to government. Charlatans appeared, made money, and some were exposed. It was the world of the Freddie Lakers and DeLorean whose thriving proved ephemeral.

Eastern Europe, 1991 - 1994

When in 1989 the Berlin wall was torn down my sales territory was expanded to cover all of Eastern Europe. Did these markets offer new opportunities for Sturmey-Archer, I wondered. I had met on several occasions, either at the Cologne cycle Shows or during their visits to Nottingham, the CEOs of the State Trading Companies of Poland and Czechoslokia and they were both impressive ladies. I had also come to know some of the members of the Nottingham Polish Club, and they were always good company. We, Britain, went to war on September 3rd, 1939, when Germany invaded Poland, yet at Yalta we, the USA and UK, handed over Poland to the Russians. I was surprised that those Poles I knew, bore no anger for the West. Instead, they looked forward to Western investment helping the country reap the benefits and opportunities of capitalism.

It was in June 1991 that I had ‘all my ducks in a row’ to enable me to embark on a grand tour of Eastern Europe, visiting potential business partners and customers throughout Poland, Czechoslovakia, Hungary, Romania and Bulgaria. I was not to be disappointed; I was to be educated. The timing was not good, however, for the West was heading into a recession. Indeed, it wasn’t long before many in Eastern Europe hungered for the return of the ‘old days’, after all, everyone was educated to a high standard, and all enjoyed annual State holidays. The harsh climate of capitalism has its downsides too.

I started in Warsaw with a visit to a company called ‘Universal’, where I already knew the chief executive, Hilaria Glowacka and her sidekick Bobby Cwiklak, as both had visited me each year at the Cologne show and in Nottingham. Both were clever ladies and in the art of political dialectic they were to be avoided. They knew the arguments of political dialectics and were not shy. On arrival at the huge Universal office, I made plain that I wanted to understand the infrastructure of the bicycle industry in Poland. They took me around each of the nationalised ‘Romet’ manufacturing operations in Bydgosc, Kowalewo, Posnan, and then on to ‘Kolesczewski’ in Bytow, on to ‘Bike Sport’ in Wroclaw, and ‘Planet’ in Krakow and ‘Olpron’ which was in Olomouc, over the border in Czechoslovakia. So, I travelled the length and breadth of Poland and got what I asked for, including long boring rides in a car on B roads. At each venue I was feted, not with grandeur, but with attention and openness. Each of these operations was looking to keep going by being privatised. They saw me as a potential ‘white knight’, whereas I was hoping to sell them our UK products!

I was shown huge engineering prowess especially in Posnan. I was particularly interested in their production of a product which had been discontinued in the Sturmey-Archer range because we couldn’t compete with the Far East. Here in Posnan was a robust ‘coaster hub’ at a lower price than available from Shimano in Japan. The meeting took on a different agenda when they saw my interest. Some ten weeks later, I brought out to Poland the Sturmey-Archer MD, Peter Wittering, and he in turn brought out the technical guy, David Rayner. I thought there was going to be collaboration with at least this 'Romet' organisation headed up by Mr Nowikowski and his technical team Mr Kariewski and production engineer Mr Duda, but after many visits to Romet Posnan nothing materialised.

These trips always had amusing moments which the lively Poles enjoyed. Happily too we found a small market for our Sturmey-Archer 3 and 5 speed hubs and avoided getting involved with Romet whose companies all sadly closed. Typically English, our guys made nicknames to get their tongues around the Polish names, Bobby Cwiklak became 'Quick Lick' and the formidable Glowacka became of course 'Glow Whacker', Duda needed no change. Quick Lick knew men. She had a tolerant husband who put up with her lover, Bogdan, and when Peter W. made provocative remarks during our long journeys from Warsaw to Posnan she stopped the car in the middle of nowhere and gave the driver some instructions. He came back from nowhere after a few minutes with a tray of excellent Russian champagne and four glasses which she filled and proposed a toast saying, 'I am now going to answer all your questions Peter, including those you have not yet asked, and the answer is Yes.' We solemnly raised our glasses to 'Yes'. Sure enough Peter W continued to ask increasingly more provocative questions to which Bobby simply replied 'you already have your answer'. When we arrived at our rather faded but one-time grand 1930's hotel in Posnan with its huge marble foyer Peter W said to Bobby 'shall we dance?' Bobby promptly and in front of the hotel staff, grabbed Peter and waltzed him around the foyer. Strange, embarrassing but there we are.

Among the team at Universal was Juliusz Kabath. He was both a sportsman - Sturmey-Archer became sponsors to the basketball team he played for in Poland - and a diligent colleague who, years later, I ended up appointing as a Raleigh Licensee (see his picture on page 211). He was also to become a good friend and I was delighted when, in August 2017, I was invited to his daughter Paulina's wedding which took place in Warsaw.

On another visit to Poland, I met up with a huge character, Mr Andrzej Wawrzyniak, curator of The Asia and Pacific Museum in Warsaw. He possessed one of the best collections of Burmese art and artifacts, much of which he had bought through my old friend in Yangon, Kyi San. Small world. He was in his 80's when I met him, but it was a pleasure to listen to his world view. I was told that his fellow Poles found his thoughts boring, but to me they were not just enlightening but useful.

I have often witnessed the strength, wit and generosity of the Polish people, and it is testament to the character of a nation which has seen a great deal of adversity. On one trip, I arranged to visit Auschwitz. I went with a hundred questions to ask as, like others, I felt I knew the story. I asked none of them. I was numb with horror and sadness. I remember thinking that our species did not deserve to exist if the Earth was to flourish.

I was excited to go on to both Prague in Czechoslovkia and Budapest in Hungary. The former I expected to be sophisticated and modern and the latter with more echoes of the Austro-Hungarian Empire. I was right, but my superficial views were overcome by the reality. The Czech Republic, as it later became, had already moved on with a brand called 'Author', started up by one of the smart guys at their State Trading Company. 'Csepel', the state trading company in Budapest intrigued me but I was beaten to it by 'Schwinn' from America who went forward with a joint venture – 'Schwinn Csepel' – this famous American company identifying the clever technology therein. 'Csepel' had developed a system of developing magnesium frames. Their engineer and GM Laszlo Nogradi demonstrated the welding of a magnesium frame in a vacuum: the problem was not in making one but in producing these in any volume. I too felt this could be the future, and maybe he was right, but the future has still not happened. I arranged for our own very clever design engineer, Steve Rickles, (who later joined Andrew Richie at Brompton) to come over. We came with wives and had a lovely trip with visits to The Gellert, the original Roman baths which have featured in so many films. It was a pleasure to soak up the culture and atmosphere of Bratislava as well, to sit in the large open baths and play chess with someone who spoke no English, and then to sail along the Danube visiting both Buda and Pest.

On my first visit to Budapest, I had a happy experience when one evening returning to my hotel, the Sheraton. I asked for a table for dinner, the maître d' said the restaurant was closed and 'you must go down there'. I was sure most guests simply thought 'no I mustn't' and went out. I was too exhausted to go anywhere else and sure enough found that I was the only guest, and there was a classic band of four artists waiting. No sooner was I installed, next to the band, when I was asked what I wanted to have them play for me. I knew Eastern European musicians were masters of the violin and the only tune I could think of was the 'Devil comes to Georgia'. The band struck up with the most amazing rendition, and sure enough more guests soon arrived, but I was the hero. I was asked what I wanted to eat, I didn't know and suggested they feed me, and they did. The first course was caviar served in a circular glass bowl sitting on another bowl of ice and served with Russian champagne. I asked the waiter what the band would like to drink to which he replied that the best would be a genuine Scotch, which in Bratislava was very expensive. It happened that I had an unopened bottle of 'medicinal' Scotch in my room. I went up to my room and handed it over to the band. It was one of the best investments I ever made, and the evening was one memorable beyond suitable description. From there to Bucharest and on to Sofia which was also enchanting.

In Bulgaria the 'Cross' company intrigued me because not only were they an OEM manufacturer of Cross branded bikes, but they needed an international brand to give them domestic credibility in the trade. A perfect fit for Raleigh which I embraced. Leaving business to one side, my trips to Bulgaria were interesting. Sofia is fascinating architecturally and historically, but of course I was bound for the grubby manufacturing areas of Bulgaria, and to Montana in particular. Spending hours with the clever Cross managers though was an experience, as their views of Europe and life are worth recording. Here's an example. I went up to Montana in the North-West corner of Bulgaria. I was told that this was the poorest area in the country and the poorest in all Europe. 'Why and how,' I asked, 'did Bulgaria qualify for entry into the EU?' To which I obtained the prompt reply that 'the reason was political, as Bulgaria was a buffer state between Russia and Europe, and an ally against any silliness from Russia or the Balkans.'

'Surely though, the EU rules would be a cost issue for Bulgaria?' 'No, it's been our salvation, you see out of our population of 12.5 million people, eight million are Bulgarian and four million are Gypsies. We positively discriminate in favour of Gypsies giving them free education, free transport to schools etc., but they are not interested. The birth rate of Bulgarians is about 1.7 per family, whereas the Gypsies' are at nearly eight per family and therefore in thirty years there will be more Gypsies than Bulgarians. Happily, though, now that we are part of the EU, we are exporting so many Gypsies to Spain and Italy that the pressure has been taken off us, and let the EU see if they can sort them out better.' I haven't researched the veracity of these assertions, but this 'beer talk' in the middle of the poorest corner of Europe made me view life differently, especially because not many politicians or tourists come to this region, preferring the beaches of the Black Sea, or the culture of Sofia.

Back To My Bike World

The benefit of my early trips to all of the Eastern European countries was in getting to know each market at a time of great change. The huge State companies were underfunded, over-staffed, and suited to a 'Command Economy'. Their demise was inevitable. I was able to put my market knowledge to good use in the 2000's when, as Director of Raleigh International Ltd, I was quickly able to set up effective Licensees for the Raleigh brand and sometimes, especially in the case of Bulgaria, a good supply source for some of my other Licensees as a welcome alternative to their Far East sources. This underscores my life's experience that there is no substitute for good personal knowledge of both your supply chain, your markets and especially knowing your customer's customer. This can only be accomplished by in-depth personal visits, and not from a head-office desk or behind a computer. You can then direct your operation and add to it rather than let your customer choose his own way unchecked. He may usually be right but not always. If your advice is backed up by first-hand knowledge it will be appreciated, and you respected.

As the eastern Europeans were soon to find out, naked capitalism doesn't have a pretty face. For when economic growth came it covered up all sorts of unpleasant realities. The recession of the early 90s hit Sturmey-Archer Ltd hard, as did the UK's withdrawal from the European Exchange Rate Mechanism. I was now in a position of some responsibility so had to act accordingly. One day we were making redundancies, another we were pressing for investment, productivity and innovation.

A very human story played out over the in-house manufacture of BMX foam frame guards. These were all made in Birmingham by 21 ladies stitching using Singer sewing machines. The sole customer was Raleigh, who announced that these could be brought cheaper from Taiwan, and a final three months' order requirement would be placed and then this business re-sourced. The Managing Director of Sturmey-Archer, Peter Wittering, saw this as a sales problem, and therefore it was my job to either persuade Raleigh to change its mind or make the 21 ladies redundant. I spoke to the Raleigh Purchase people and discovered the Taiwanese offer was just over 20% cheaper. This was greater than the profit Sturmey-Archer was making, so there was no alternative but to make the ladies redundant. Since this was deemed to be my job, I drove to Smethwick, and spoke to the ladies. They were a happy, closely knit team, and after I'd explained the situation, they asked if they could discuss and see me in half an hour. They did so and announced that they would take a 15% cut in their wages. I was amazed, as their salaries were already at below what we would call the minimum wage today. I promised to revert back to them; I re-did my sums and to keep the business I offered Raleigh the next day a 20% price reduction. We kept the business – six weeks later I was informed that the Taiwanese had dropped their prices by a further 10%. I kept the business for six months longer, but the ladies were then made redundant. It hurt.

In 2002 Raleigh closed its production totally, with all their bikes resourced largely from the East. I watched as all the big European brands went the same way. The American brands – Huffy, Murray and Schwinn – had already ceased to be made in the USA during the 1980s. There had been investment put into Raleigh in the early '80s, but little into Sturmey-Archer Ltd. In 1987 the CEO of Tube Investments, Chris Lewington, sold Raleigh to his American International lawyer, Ed Gottesman. I entered an alien world. In 1976 I had been the youngest Divisional Executive in the Raleigh Industries Company. Twelve years later, when Ed Gottesman took over, this layer of management was disbanded, and each group company was to have one Director who had also to buy a share in 'Derby'. Sturmey-Archer apparently needed an engineer for that role and so I was excluded. This allowed me to think about the new Group almost from the outside and during the 2000s I came to realise that there were actually only two pearls in the Raleigh oyster: Sturmey-Archer and Raleigh International's business, in which I would include their trading company in Taiwan. The attention, however, was all on Raleigh UK and Raleigh USA (with the Raleigh Company in Germany being sold off to Pon, and Gazelle in Holland to Accell). When Ed Gottesman bought back Raleigh USA from Huffy (to whom Tube Investments had sold the company) they must have thought it was their birthday. But Ed was an American and wanted to own the American Raleigh. The good side of this was that I was left largely alone, but it was galling to see the rewards that went to the hard work of the Raleigh UK and USA employees. I noticed that my business practices were different from those of the oncoming so-called global age. Raleigh had some hundred short-term inter-company loans, and at the end of the financial year these were used to minimise the tax bills. Short-term borrowing at high interest rates could save the company from paying tax while enriching the lender. I was brought up with the attitude that success was to pay lots of tax and have a low golf handicap. The one was socially responsible and the other personally beneficial. My upbringing had taught me that life was a relay race where success was to take over the baton as smoothly as possible and to pass it on in a better state than when it was received. The 1990s made the race metaphor redundant. New global possibilities broadened the game. You had to be smart and quick, but not in the energetic sense of yesteryear, you had to be clever and cunning and then incisive. You needed good lawyers, and to play survival games on a number of levels. Loans and borrowings are just good vehicles, and as far as gauging the worth of a company it's no longer a question of the Price-to-Earnings ratio and Profit & Loss. It's 'debt' and 'perceived value' that seem to count. It wasn't my world, and it was probably for this reason that in time, I ended up getting involved in other business enterprises, some of which, such as river boating in Burma, were completely removed from the cycle industry.

Family Issues

1994 was the year that my dear Dad died. It also seemed to mark a turning point for me as a new orphan. I had gotten into the habit of spending any free weekend driving from Nottingham to my home in Tunbridge Wells. With my very close Grandad Godfrey dying in 1986, then Mum from cancer in 1987, and Dad having a major stroke in the midst of all this, our life was 'family based' at a great distance for nine years. My Grandad (captain) Godfrey's passing affected me deeply. He had however lived life to the full and died at a good age. The same was less true of his daughter, my Mum, who died a year later after enduring huge pain, with her typical humour and grace, throughout five years of dreadful cancer. She was a real 'mum' to both me and also to Alistair and her ready and easy laugh and wit were infectious. This period was one of great reflection and much personal pain and anguish, and not one I wish to re-live even in its repetition here. During this time, I was so grateful to Ninoo (who lived near to our home in Tunbridge Wells) for all the love she showered upon Mum and Dad, especially as she was not going through the easiest of times in her working life as a school teacher. We chatted regularly. I was also travelling in my job a lot – for some 140 days in a year (I had to keep records for my tax). Son Alistair had just left university, and was embarking on a gap year to go to India. My friend Algy, from my early days at Tube Investments, gave him a job in his tea business, involving some three months in Madras followed by three months on the tea plantations in Kerala. This was a happy thought for me, as he not only reconnected with my birth country, incidentally making a point of visiting my birthplace, but he also visited our Indian family in Bangalore when he could get away from Madras. Ninoo's mum met up with him, and her sister and brother-in-law, Nergez and Roy, put him up.

As for me I was 'free' and alone and had met a wonderful girl, Ane Marie, who seemed to put up with my overseas absences and who indeed was often overseas herself. After my Dad's passing, and with Alistair in India, my weekends were mine for the first time in many years. The new owners introduced a different culture to Raleigh – with consequences – which allowed me to indulge my other interests. I'll talk about this now with bias, but certainly with love.

Mum and her younger brother Ralph in typical gay form

Burma from 1995

My connections with Burma run deep. Both sides of my family lived there and loved the people and country, and spoke Burmese of course. I had a Karen nanny, and my father collected books on Burma, which collection I prize today. He has fascinating original material on the country and its people, with many newspaper articles of the Irrawaddy Flotilla Company during the Second World War. It was my intention to collate some of this material and this is still an ambition. Burma has cut itself off from the world for long periods and for better or worse much is still preserved in that country that would have been swept away by 'progress'.

I only wish to introduce this land of the Nats (Spirits) and its Theyavada Buddhism to you here as a prelude to another projected work to follow.

The Shwe Dagon in Yangon

This 'Golden Land' and this 'Country like no other' are epithets oft applied to Burma. Such terms scream out for definition and a visit reveals their meaning in abundance. With every village sporting beautiful pagodas and temples; with artistry and lacquerware that delight; with pretty faces neatly covered in *thanaka* to protect delicate skin from the sun. Thanaka is acquired from the bark of a local small tree; it is an anti-oxidant that replenishes essential nutrients for the skin and reduces wrinkles and been in use for over 2,000 years! The charm of a solitary fisherman in his boat, guiding it along with his leg entwined around the rudder-come-oar and casting his nets – these are the simple skills of an old people, honed and perfected over time.

Fishermen on Inya Lake

There are villages where the old ladies indulge in a meditative smoke over a huge cheroot and put the world to rights. Where the old are respected and revered for their wisdom and experience. In other areas we have the long-necked Padaung women still plying their trade of weaving. Visit this land and you'll never be the same. It touches you.

Burma is also a land of poverty and neglect, poverty in economic terms though, rather than in any spiritual sense, but neglect, yes. I have delivered many talks on Burma since my return there after forty-eight years of absence. I have travelled along its rivers approaching its western border with India; to the east nearing its border with China; luxuriated and swum in its western seaboard on the Bay of Bengal; climbed Mount Poppa in the middle of the country; got lost in its markets and bazaars; and been led astray in its tea houses and homes with lively gossip.

This 'Golden Land' though has been mismanaged since its Independence. The richness of its many tribes and hill tribes has been neglected rather than embraced. The talents of the hard-working Karen, up in the Shan States, and the skills of the Chins and Kachins have been deprecated. Now these old 'principalities' are homes to petty warlords who grow the odious opium, rather than the rice or tea whose price is too low to sustain them, and they buy arms to protect themselves from the Burmese army. This rice bowl of the world has been lost with consequences felt throughout the world. We, the British, should be ashamed. Instead we are merely ignorant, which is perhaps worse.

The West has ignored this land since the end of the Second World War, suffering perhaps from an unnecessary and uncalled-for conscience from a misunderstood past. So the country has been isolated

Long-necked Padaung Women at work

Ngapoli Beach

and happily, and lucratively, mismanaged by its ruling 100 families. Now Burma is there for the taking by its Eastern neighbour, who has populated and supported it for the past fifty-five years, and their patience could pay off. China has long wanted its 'California of the West', and the Arakan and the beaches of Ngapoli would provide it. Those of us who should have been born in Burma and educated in some of the world's best schooling, returning each holiday, understand that the vast and lovely resources of its peoples and land could have been integral in its rebuilding after the devastation it suffered at the hands of the Japanese during the war.

Buddhism becomes too easily the opiate of the people, believing misfortune or misrule or worse are to be seen as 'Karma'. It can support a lazy arrogance of virtue amongst its army or in its civil service. The Burman is a literate person and clever, and Buddhism has trained the mind and body to be content and happy. The outside world is taught to be acquisitive and how to make money as an end in itself, only recently learning the value of 'mindfulness'. Burma is blessed too with a rich soil replenished twice yearly by the melting of the Himalayas, with huge rivers depositing fresh and nutritious topsoil. A warm climate allows clothing to be simple and even uniform (men and women will wear a *longhi*) differentiated by exquisite colour and inventiveness and tied and knotted differently. With a full tummy, a trained Buddhist mind, and natural heat, what better than a palm tree and quiet meditative sleep? How easy it is to ignore that human greed for power that sweeps through politicians and leaders whose country has inadequate checks and balances in its Law and in its Civil Service. If the Army is in charge then how easy is it to close one of the threats of disquiet – the universities – and prevent an alliance between the intellectuals and that other powerhouse of Burma – the monks in their monasteries?

So this hasty Independence from a bankrupt imperial power with its ignorant and unworldly paymaster – the US – has lost more than a land and its people; it has lost the opportunity of the integration of a rich philosophy. Many of its former businesses and businessmen would have returned to Burma after the War and Independence to rebuild their businesses and the country. Experience has been lost from a breed of professional men and women who spoke the local languages, and is now replaced with temporary NGOs with no stake in the country. It took several hundred years to build the Indian Civil Service, but at least India has an infrastructure of trained Indians in sufficient numbers to check the excesses of a Ne Win or worse!

Apart from its gorgeous abundance of forests populated by flora and fauna that are either unique or made extinct elsewhere in the world, this land has inherited wealth from its soil, from its oil, its precious stones of ruby and jade which abound in Moguk, and from a diversity of clever indigenous people occupied now by survival rather than developing their talents.

The famous Irrawaddy Flotilla Company (IFC) is a case in point. The Irrawaddy is to Burma as the Nile is to Egypt – a 'free highway'. Roads are not the priority, but there is one the Chinese are building, and destroying trees and wildlife in the process. The villages of Burma lie along the Chindwin, the Irrawaddy and even the Salween. The teak forests and paddy fields in the upper regions provide real assets that are wanted by the world and the teak and rice transported cheaply along the Irrawaddy direct to the ports in the South. However, for the greedy, teak grows too slowly and the price of rice too low.

We are where we are – in a pickle, which is hard to unpickle. There were many in the 1930s who could have avoided this situation and given of their labour and love to realise it. I know because my family were amongst them, and my grandad would have loved to continue to manage Rangoon Harbour and Dad and his fellow IFC Scots would have returned to the largest inland water company the world has ever known and rebuilt a flotilla of paddle steamers with trade restored. Instead, we have petty warlords in the hill States trying to resist the Burmese Army's attempts to dictate to them. This takes money which is easier to earn by growing crops like opium, rather than grow rice and teak, which is now felled prematurely and is improperly cured. No sooner had I finished writing this chapter than I heard of the military coup. This should not come as any surprise and follows the pattern of 1962, 1968 and now in 2021. The only thing that was a surprise was Aung San Suu Kyi's going to The Hague to defend the army against genocide charges. Anyone wanting to buy me a beer can hear my views which say more about the West than about Burma. The best comment is still the humour of one of the witty students explaining that 'General elections are those which the Generals win'. So it is and will remain, and given where we are the best the West can do is set a good example

Teak floating down the Irrawaddy

which all too often it doesn't. However, there are still individuals of the old school who do set an example: one such is my dear friend Mark Tippetts who lives in Yangon. He not only supports two orphanages in which his family teach on their weekends or days off. He employs these students when they leave in his enterprise based on the Pun Hlaing Estate near Yangon. That Company and Mark in particular gave much aid and assistance freely at the time of the terrible Tsunami in the Delta region. He sets an example too by living tastefully and surrounded by local beauty and treating all with respect yet demanding high standards. This has huge unseen effects on everyone he meets, although the European generation of today seem either unaware or think it clever to reject either good manners or speaking intelligibly (if the UK is to rethink its place in the world, we shall do well to relearn these British values, which are respected abroad). Mark first came to Burma in 1964 by Land Rover and then went on to Hong Kong where he worked for many years before joining up in 1995 with one of today's movers and shakers in the Burmese business world. Serge Pun has invested heavily in Burma over the past 25 years, his buildings ranging from hospitals to Golf courses. Mark is his perfect Ambassador in the Pun Hlaing enterprise and entertains the Great and the Good from all over the world. My family was honoured to be Mark's and Yeon's guests recently in 2018.

Our paddle boat is just visible here, making its way to Mark and Yeon's place in time for dinner

Among the many books within Mark is his epic 33,000-mile journey out to Rangoon from Warwickshire. He said in a letter to me, ‘I was 19 when I made that journey ... we also drove up into the Himalayas to Kathmandu and back down to India, but we never got round to painting Nepal onto the driver’s door for the 18th country which we crossed. Half a dozen of the countries we traversed, in both directions, are now war zones … How lucky we were.’

Sundowners in Mark's house is always an intoxicating experience

Burma - Family Reminiscences

There is little that can match cruising along the mighty Irrawaddy on a colonial ship designed just for that river. The river can rise and fall by 80 feet and many a boat has been grounded, or worse, caught in a whirlpool. The flat-bottomed paddle steamers introduced by the Irrawaddy Flotilla Company were the solution. Their captains could read the river, helped by a sailor on each side of the boat who chanted out the depths with bamboo poles. These boats are still on the river to this day, operated by the modern incarnation of the Irrawaddy Flotilla Company, and it has been my privilege on a number of occasions, to step on board for a relaxing drifting cruise past scenery of a timeless biblical quality, made all the more luxurious by the Burmese cheroot and the gin & tonics they serve so well.

While on these cruises, fellow passengers can be persuaded to give a talk in the evening and on one particularly memorable occasion we had an opera singer who transformed the whole ship into a pageant of sound that awoke the slumbering sailors below deck. I was not quite as noisy when my turn came one night in 1999. Instead, I told the assembled passengers about a memorable time in my family's history that made this trip going along the Irrawaddy's main tributary, the Chindwin, all the more special.

This river and its hinterland has its own atmosphere and the villagers delighted to have your company. Combined with this sense of welcome was the realisation that it was across this very river that the British Army of the Second World War had to cross in order to survive to win the most important battles of Imphal and Kohima against the Japanese. In the higher reaches of the Chindwin, starting from Kindat, you become aware of the absence of any European faces and you become a curiosity to the villagers who are also quick to offer you their precious stones of ruby and jade, or for young ladies the chance to beautify you and protect you with Thanaka from the sun. In this magic atmosphere I gave my little talk, but let's start with this map to show not just the significant towns and villages mentioned but showing how the country of Burma or Myanmar, if you prefer, was born and built up.

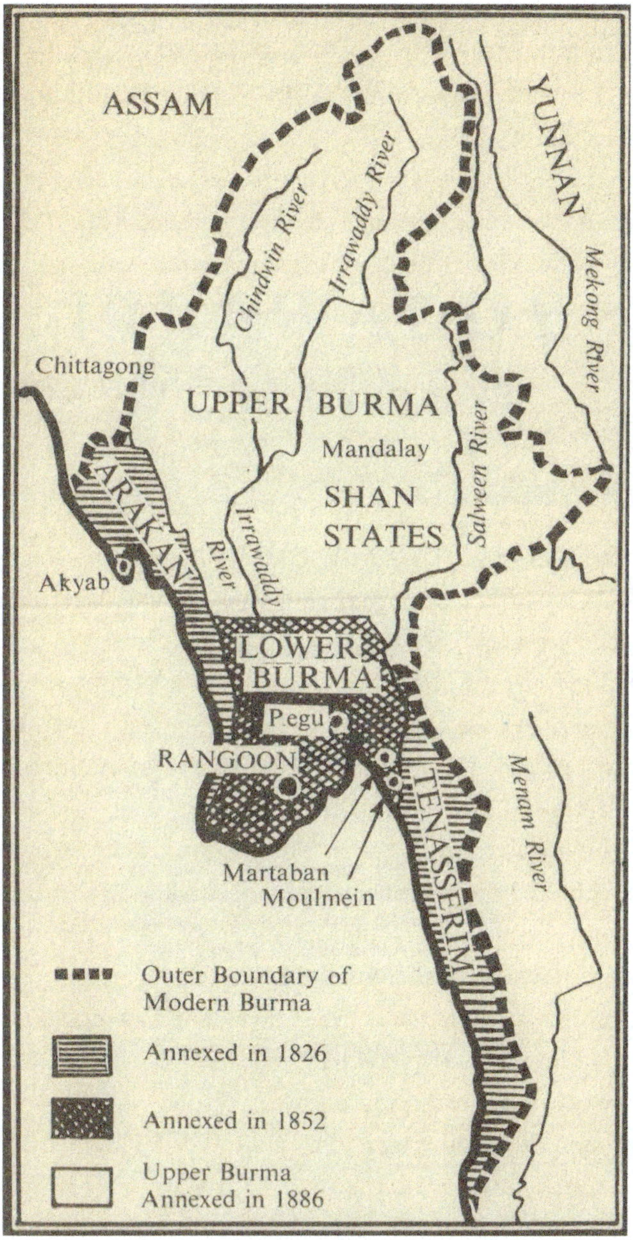

From Irrawaddy Flotilla *by Alister McCrae and Alan Prentice, 1978*

Irrawaddy Flotilla Company Talk,

delivered 23rd September, 1999, at Mawlaik on the Chindwin

My return to Burma (after 47 years) was coincident with the first voyage of the newly founded Irrawaddy Flotilla Company (IFC) of which I now proudly own a 20% stake. On the 27th September 1995 I arrived in Rangoon and went immediately to the Shwe Dagon Pagoda to try to calm my excitement – unsuccessfully. I then contacted U Taw, a former employee of the IFC, who had kept in touch with my family each Christmas since 1950, and who sent me the most wonderful letter on hearing of my Dad's death in 1994.

U Taw arrived the next morning at the Inya Lake Hotel with his wife and granddaughter, Aye Mar, clutching a photo of the Irrawaddy Flotilla managers in which both he and Dad appeared. The photo was taken at Belmont, the house we lived in prior to my Dad's enforced departure from Burma. U Taw was in his 80s and frail, but his memory was sharp. As we drove around town he told me the British name of each renamed road or street. He listened to the BBC every morning he said, and extolled the virtues of all things British. His Karen wife corrected the balance a bit, saying that after the War the Brits changed. Pre-war they didn't really mix and talk to the Burmese in Rangoon, but after the War they were greeted like long lost friends.

After tea at their house at Perami Yerktha, U Taw retired and Aye Mar, with car, was put at my disposal. I asked her to take me to the zoo. The zoo was a clear childhood memory. We went in, but I was disorientated. It wasn't until we got to the tigers' abode, 'cage' is not a grand enough word, donated by the Prince of Wales in 1900, that I found my bearings – immediately walking to the 'real' entrance – now closed. It was here that the distorting mirrors were placed where I would stand, as a child, one minute being long and thin another fat and silly. From here I quickly found my way, across the road, to 'my house'. The Flotilla houses are now occupied by British Embassy staff, and in fact it was on the now British Ambassador's tennis court at Belmont that I celebrated my third

The Chummery in which Dad lived from 1932

birthday (my first real memory). We had donkey rides and a big cake in the shape of a shoe – Old Mother Hubbard's. I looked up at the cluster of lovely IFC houses and tennis court from what is now the British Club, and memories flooded back. My Karen nanny, Tun Tin our lovely Burmese house boy, Grandad's pet monkey and his chow dog. Are things ever erased from the mind, and what else lies there that cannot be recalled but which helped form me?

From our old house, which I later saw inside thanks to the Ambassador, Robert Gordon, Aye Mar drove me again downtown. I remembered names: Monkey Point where my parents had their first house when they married. The Mayo Marine Club, where my Gran and Grandad lived, and where I learnt to swim. Those Sunday curry lunches followed by Gulamalaka. I drifted back.

Both sides of my family were in Rangoon. Grandad Godfrey (Mum's Dad), an old Merchant Navy Captain, ran the Ports Commission, bringing out his wife, daughter (my Mum) and youngest son (my uncle Ralph) in 1929. Captain Godfrey was one of life's colourful characters who deserves a biography of his own.

Dad went from Glasgow Academy to join Henderson Lines, a large shipping company majoring on trade with New Zealand, and particularly to that other Scottish enclave, Dunedin, on South Island. The ships came home empty, and so took to stopping over in Rangoon in the early nineteenth century to take on board the teak, rice and semi-precious stones from Burma – the Indian trade being too well served by English companies. So it was that Hendersons developed into inland water transport, buying up a few Government boats in 1864, and forming the lrrawaddy Flotilla Company a year later.

Dad joined Hendersons in Glasgow in 1930, and within two years was sailing out to Rangoon. In those days a tour away from home lasted four years before home leave. You could not be married, and behaviour was controlled and strict. These IFC Scots were all very Presbyterian, disciplined with a high moral code and probably not much fun.

It made it easier perhaps to obey the rules and to endure the hardships that were to come. On arrival they were housed in a 'chummery'. In the case of the IFC boys theirs was owned by the great trading company Steel Bros. Now that 'chummery' is a hotel, and stands opposite the IFC managers' houses that we were later to occupy.

A paddle steamer

Work started early in the morning and finished at 4.00 pm. Tennis and sport were then played, followed by sundowners (though my Mum told me, not approvingly, that not a drop of alcohol had ever passed my father's lips until he was past 30!). A priority for these IFC assistants though, was to learn both Burmese and Hindustani, written and oral, with salary increases dependent upon exams passed.

The IFC was a huge organisation, moving nine million passengers a year and over 1¼ million tonnes of cargo. The Company pamphlet, which I have, and the frontispiece of which is in the newly formed JFC newsletter, describes the cargo carried:

> *Great bales of cotton, bags of rice, blocks of jade, lacquerware, silk, tamarind, elephants, woven mats, maize, jaggery, bullocks, marble Buddhas, oilcake, tobacco, timber. Upward bound cargo consisted of various imports from Europe: motor cars, corrugated iron, condensed milk, matches, aluminium ware, sewing machines, soap, cigarettes, cement and whisky.*

The IFC was a river network. IFC houses were in each of the main towns upcountry. Many still exist. It operated 57 different services, with a sophisticated timetable showing the arrivals and departures from nearly every village from Myitkana to Mandalay, Bhamo to Prome, along with Chindwin and into the Delta. The captains were usually Chittagonians who seemed to 'read' the unchartable lrrawaddy river. Groundings were rare with the paddles themselves providing an effective dredging action in the dry season when the water was low. The lrrawaddy rises and falls some 80 feet, and has whirlpools and shallows that demand no loss of concentration on the bridge. Still today two members of the crew stand in the front of the steamers, calling out the soundings as their bamboo poles are thrust into the river to gauge the depth, which is chanted out in a rhythmical and continuous fashion. What is more, these paddle steamers were big (sternwheelers i.e., the smaller ones, were some 200 feet long and 36 feet wide), and often very full with cargo and passengers and sometimes with a 'flat' tied alongside also loaded down with goods.

Upcountry secondments, and months on the river on inspection launches, not only improved the linguistic fluency of the IF assistants but taught them the many wily ways of human nature. Ensuring tickets were bought and paid for was the subject of many a discussion and tale. These lengthy secondments were always character forming experiences and the 'assistants' returned older, and with a training unobtainable from any book, or even the highest Head Office experience.

In the heady colonial days on board a Flotilla Steamer, the day for a European passenger started with Chota Hazri, a large, late breakfast, then later an afternoon tea and late dinner. First class menus, served by Madrasi butlers, were extensive and voluminous. A passenger once commented, 'following a meal of gargantuan proportions, sufficient to tax the capacity and digestion of a python, the menu concluded with the words God save the passengers'.

Otherwise, whilst a steamer was underway, most passengers indulged in talking, eating, sleeping or in two of the national habits: smoking a whacking white cheroot or chewing betelnut. My uncle wrote:

> *This white cheroot is a fearsome contraption, sometimes measuring one foot in length with a diameter of over an inch. The outside covering is comprised of maize leaves, giving the white appearance. This is stuffed with what looks like chopped hay, but is, in fact, cheap tobacco leaf mixed with herbs previously boiled in palm sugar. Part of the smoking ritual required a pot; partly to provide a resting place for the cheroot while it was handed round for others to share, but more importantly as a safety measure, for they were prone to burst into flame showering sparks over nearby passengers. The shared smoke was communal and included babies at the breast who were often seen being given their chance to have a puff.*

He wrote less politely about betelnut because of the stain left on the steamers deck when the scarlet expectorant was spat out.

The Irrawaddy Flotilla Company became the agents for Imperial Airways in 1936, the forerunners of BOAC. I remember my first air flight on an Imperial Airways seaplane to Bangkok.

The IFC was therefore the main communication provider and supplier to all business in Burma. Employees of Bombay Burmah, Steel Bros, Rowe and Co, the upcountry teak traders and Forestry Commissions, Government officials etc. all talked of their dependence on the IFC paddle steamers. What went unmentioned was their reliability – simply because they were so reliable and kept to strict time-tables. As ever good news is no news, and the tough and unrelenting work to keep and maintain these steamers and their schedules, upon which imperial Burma depended, went unsung. Reviving, even in our tiny way, this service makes one appreciate the dedication and effort of the IFC team in those days.

The grand head office in Phayre Street in Rangoon is a testament to the importance and status of the IFC, still in exactly the same building today, with little improvement or alteration after sixty years, and used by Inland Water Transport who took over the IFC affairs upon Independence, when the company was nationalised.

Life was busy for all the Europeans in Colonial Burma and regimented in the sense that not only were jobs clearly defined but their reliance upon one another meant that you never would let colleagues down. When upcountry, the IFC Assistants were usually alone and trusted. The IFC had a network of houses in many of the villages along the Irrawaddy where the steamers would stop and off and on-load – many of these houses are still there and used today. My uncle Alan (Prentice) often told me of his life in Bhamo, which he loved and where he was stationed for a four-year stint. Fortunately today some of these men have recorded their experiences, and there is a rich library of their daily life. The common thread was their love for the local people, and this seemed a two-way affair. In his spare time Uncle Alan formed a football team and called it the 'Bhamo Rangers' (guess who he supported back home!) and paid for them out of his own pocket to sail down to Rangoon to take on the IFC team there. I was never told who won.

In Rangoon my parents' photos show a round of fancy dress parties, formal dinners, weddings and regattas at the various clubs. I proudly own Grandad Godfrey's pewter pint pot embossed with the words 'Monsoon Regatta 1931 for Rowing'.

There was the quaint but effective practice of delivering your visiting cards upon arrival, without which you did not exist. Then there was, of course, golf.

The Rangoon Open was one of the biggest and most prestigious annual events in the Burmese Colonial calendar. That of 1925 was memorable. Well known dignitary, Mr X, had gone round with a nett score of 80 shots while his big rival Mr Y had hit 81. However, on scrutiny of the card returns, it transpired that on Mr X's third shot on the 5th the ball had lodged itself in a tree whereupon Mr X declared it unplayable and dropped his ball not nearer the hole and added one penalty shot to his score. Mr Y disputed this ruling saying that he should have returned to where the ball was hit and counted two penalty strikes – for stroke and distance – in which case the scores would have been identical or at worse Mr X would have flouted the rules and his card disqualified. The Cup could not be presented at the dinner gathering that evening and all had opinions on the sacred Rules of Golf. The Committee announced to all that it had been decided to ask the Honourable Gentlemen at Royal St. Andrews for a ruling, and that the presentation of the Cup would be postponed accordingly.

The case was duly written up, signed by both parties and sent off by steamer to the U.K. the following day – the journey taking a month and of course with another month's return. By the time that the Honourable Gentlemen of St. Andrews had met another month passed, but sure enough after three months and three days the post duly arrived whereupon it was decided to open the ruling in front of the whole Rangoon Club:

The reply simply said, 'There are no trees on a golf course...'

The impression is of a good life, perhaps too consciously good, living for the day, tinged with a homesickness suppressed by activity. Home news was late and scarce and thirsted after. News from India being more common, e.g., 'Ghandi on hunger strike again'. I cannot think before or after of any doubting the good effects of colonisation. After all, it was evident that the Burmese were unfit to govern, and the British had not only protected the minority tribes but even the Burmese themselves against the excess of cruelty of their own Kings, and brought Christianity and enlightenment to empty established religions and superstitions. So it was with a kind of well-meant arrogance that a group of English Ladies wrote a code of conduct for their Burmese counterparts which included exhorting them to bathe at least once a week, to the horror of the Burmese who bathed twice a day at least.

This idyll, this 'safest of places', was then shattered by war.

Mum's family experienced the bombing of Rangoon in December 1941 from their home the Mayo Marine Club. This property is now a naval base, with entry prohibited, as I know after spending many hours sitting around while permission was sought and not granted for me to visit. (It is nearly opposite the Strand Hotel and therefore right on the Rangoon River.) Uncle Ralph, my mother's youngest brother, wrote of this episode:

> *The first air raid on Rangoon was traumatic. After the sirens had sounded people were still sitting in the streets and the Jap Zeros came in wave after wave. [Your] Dad, Mum and I were still up in our apartments. We went out onto the veranda only to see a Zero nearly level with us and we could see the pilot clearly. He bombed Watling Street Wharf. After the 'all clear' came, the main street outside the Mayo Marine Club was littered with the dead and dying and both sides of the harbour were alight.*
>
> *In between the following air raids, troops and ammunition ships came to unload. The Indian workers were terrified during any raid and difficult to control. Offloaded Ghurkhas with their mules were quickly moved out into the jungle. One huge ship was unloading ammunition at the wharf right behind us in the Mayo Marine Club. Horrified, Dad quickly and personally operated one of the tugs, got the ship's Skipper and crew to cast off, and helped manoeuvre the ship to a buoy in the centre of the harbour. If this ship had been blown up alongside the wharf, half of Rangoon would have gone with it, let alone all the stores and provisions already unloaded. Such acts of spontaneous heroism went unsung.*

We stayed at the Mayo Marine Club throughout the heavy bombing, living in the cellars for most of the time. After one particularly heavy raid, Dad took me up to the top of the Mayo Marine Club from where the whole harbour could be seen. It and the riverbanks were one mass of fire as far as the eye could see. It must have been appalling for him, as harbour master, to see.

Mum and I came out of Rangoon on the last ship to leave and went to India, and up to the hills of Darjeeling. Your mum flew out on a Short Sunderland Flying Boat – the last of the IFC planes to leave. She stayed in India to await your Dad who walked out.

Amazingly we all met up in Calcutta.

As you know my Dad (Captain Godfrey) refused to walk out through the jungle. Being an old sea-dog, said he would rather die at sea than in the jungle. He took an old river vessel, boarded up her sides and with 100 Indian crew took on board the last women and children and moved out of Rangoon into the Bay of Bengal as the Japs entered Rangoon City. They arrived safely at Akyab some 10 days later. As the only qualified Seaman, Dad never left the bridge all the time to negotiate those hazardous seas. In Akyab the British army requisitioned the boat to which Dad only agreed in return for safe passage to Calcutta for all the passengers and crew. (As a postscript Dad applied, on eventual return to the UK, to captain a ship for the D-Day landings. To his dismay he was told that he was 'too old'. It even happened in his day!! He started making parts of aeroplanes in a workshop from a garage at the back of Grandad Sayers house in the Uxbridge Road, Ealing. What a fighter.)

Back in Rangoon the experiences for my father and the IFC boys were very different. Under the leadership of their peace time boss – John Morton (the IFC General Manager) who now reported to the British Military, they had an immediate testing mission: to help evacuate the British army from Burma into India, while not letting any of the river fleet get into enemy hands. (Alister McCrae and my Dad were both decorated for their efforts in getting the British troops across the Chindwin at Kalewa. Stuart Macdonald wrote an official report on his/the IFC employees' escape from Burma, which I read in Australia in 1973, where he retired to be with his son Alasdair, an architect. I must see if Alasdair has kept this record.)

In selected groups they sailed and walked their way out of Burma, scuttling their beloved fleet on the way. Uncle Alan Prentice, the IF Manager at Bhamo, walked out into China. McDonald, McCrae and Macnaughtan did as instructed by John Morton, proceeding up the Irrawaddy and Chindwin into India. John Morton wrote in his diary on 28th April 1942:

> *Mandalay was evacuated yesterday, the I.F. being the last to go. The army is retreating up the Chindwin. Our men won't be many days at Monywa, and I expect them to retire up river and so through Manipur. Macnaughtan has been at Semeikon (below Mandalay) ferrying the Army across the Irrawaddy. I have a guarantee from General Slim that he and the crews of the steamers there will be taken safely to Monywa. We are being chased out even quicker than was expected and I have orders for more sinkings here at Kyaukmyang. There are over two hundred of our fleet sunk at Mandalay. Imagine how I feel drilling holes in their bottoms with a Bren gun.*

My Dad never spoke of his war days to me, although Alister McCrae told me of their having carried out the Army's crossing of the Jrrawaddy at Semeikon, where they established at the Shwegyn/Kalewa the crossing of the Chindwin; yet another battle honour for the IFC. The Army was safely crossed at Kalewa and the Flotilla party, with every steamer capable of running, along with the 481 Brigade, made for Sittaung.

It was here they scuttled the Sternwheels – i.e., the Pandaw predecessors. Taking part in this scuttling was Major Eric Yarrow, a Sapper officer and member of the family who built the sternwheelers – now Sir Eric Yarrow, and proudly aboard Pandaw at this time last year!

Dad arrived in India a walking skeleton like all the others, suffering from beriberi and dysentery. Alive at least, and delayed in their journey by injecting morphine into those crucified alive on trees by the Japanese. Some joined the army and others became part of Wingate's famous Chindits force, Dad joined the Burma Navy, saying that he had had enough of walking, operating along the Arakan Coast – the BRNVR had at least four boats! He was on board a little Corsair and went back into Burma, trying to keep open some of the sea routes into Burma, and thereby hold down some of the Japanese troops in these coastal townships.

Instead of being born in Rangoon, I therefore emerged with other escapees in Calcutta. An unhealthy place even then. Mum and I were quickly despatched by train to South India Coonoor in the Nilgiri Hills. There was no compensation for our family's losses, and the Burma Navy pay didn't allow for the cost of rent at a European establishment, so I was brought up with an Indian family – the Bhagwagers (a whole story on its own). Pershotan Hall was on the edge of a tea plantation and near Snooty Ootie. Altogether a lovely place, but not 'our' place.

Mum and I returned home to Rangoon in 1946, staying until just after Independence in 1948. I was at a Convent School in Rangoon. It was never the same, and with a kind of sad inevitability the post war days drifted into a mixture of trying to recreate the past, trying to rebuild the present and overhung with an insecurity which developed into reality.

Burma achieved Independence prematurely. The country had been devastated. The few educated Burmese were impatient, and before the country could be rebuilt, before the infrastructure was sufficiently Burmanised, independence was granted, and what was restored quickly crumbled, as did the IFC. I remember Dad saying of Aung San, 'a good intelligent man but misguided'. Those who were here feel for the minority tribes and most especially the lovely, tough and cheerful Karens. They felt they'd been let down, and Atlee and Mountbatten were not their heroes!

Back in the UK, Gran, Grandad, Mum, Ralph and I lived in a small terraced house in Ealing with little money. Mum and I then went up to Dad's family in Helensburgh until he returned from Rangoon, which he did in 1950. He was the last of the European managers of the old IFC to leave.

Alister McCrae stayed with Hendersons in Glasgow. Macdonald, Prentice and Macnaughtan worked for Stonegate farmers in Kent and established a successful company. Board Meetings were held in Burmese.

They came back to the UK – but never left Burma.

After my talk I took several interesting questions from fellow passengers. Night had fallen some time before I finished. On reading it through I felt it was still apposite and worthy of inclusion here in setting the scene especially if you read it with a G&T in hand and pretend you're on board too.

Back to the Day Time Job

The next three to four years from 1997 were heady ones for me. My company Sturmey-Archer, part of the Raleigh Industries Ltd Group, was sold to American investors and then sold on by them to a bunch of near-crooks. They know who they are. Soon after, it went into liquidation and was sold to Sun Race in Taiwan for a pittance. Incensed by all of this, I took the gamble, with Adrian Williams, of buying the Brooks leather saddle business in Birmingham – a Sturmey-Archer subsidiary. Sun Race in Taiwan bought out the Sturmey-Archer hub gear side of the business. Another bid had been put into the liquidators for Brooks which we had to fight (my business partner in Pashley Cycles and me). We won the deal in a Contract Race and bought Brooks in 2001 – this iconic brand and product would otherwise have disappeared from the cycle world as so many of the others have done. (This is neatly summarised by Tony Hadland and Alan Clarke in *The Hub of the Universe*). Happily, when buying Brooks, I also had an exit plan. I had flown over to Selle Royal to ask Ricardo Bigolin, the owner and founder, if he would take a share in Brooks. He refused, but told me to go ahead with the purchase and if and when we wanted to sell, he would pay more for it than we bought it for.

Indeed, two years after taking on Brooks we did decide to sell, only because we realised that was best for the business. It required more time and money than we were able to provide if it was to reach its potential, which it certainly has since done. What is more Selle Royal duly paid us more for it than it cost us. Also, as part of the sale I reached agreement with Barbara Bigolin and Massimo (owners of Selle Royal) that my staff would be kept in situ for the first twelve months at least. To understand this you would have had to know Gordon Nixon, whom we had made General Manager. He was congenitally blinded at age 13. He was a 'toughie', who didn't suffer fools gladly. He was a favourite in the Centenary Club, riding as stoker on his tandem with Roger Airey in front. Stories abound about Gordon in the Trade – all endearing – but I knew that the Italians would find working with him difficult. I was right, and so during his year he re-qualified as a 'counsellor', and when the Italians put in their own man Gordon followed his new profession with some distinction. Likewise, Nick Sanders, my Sturmey-Archer colleague from Nottingham, whom we appointed as Commercial Manager, needed shielding from any quick Italian replacement. At this point a brief sporting aside involving Nick when I was captaining the Exports Department cricket team. We used to meet at the Raleigh sports ground after work, in our case at 5.30 p.m.. Nick was captaining the Hardening Department side, which stopped work at 4.30 p.m.. When we came to play, not all of my team had turned up, and before we stepped onto the pitch to toss a coin to see who would bat first, I suggested to Nick that as we only had four people at that moment it would be sensible if we batted. 'No, we'll spin,' he said, and we stepped onto the pitch; he won the toss and elected to bat. We started to field with about six players with the other five turning up slowly. I was furious, and when Nick came into bat at No. 3 I called on my mate, Bill Alexander, to bowl. Bill played cricket at a high level and was a fearsome fast bowler with a mop of red hair. I instructed Bill to bounce his balls aiming at Nicks head rather than go for the wicket to soften him up. Many years later Nick joined my Commercial team in Sturmey-Archer, and neither of us forgot that incident. Yet both of us got on really well.

Brooks marketing under Selle Royal (SR) was interesting. For at least two to three consecutive years, in the late noughties, they exhibited at nearly every 'Fashion Show' around the world. They were exploiting, to a non-bikie audience, the 'hand-made leather' quality story, thereby attracting a new market, showing that a leather saddle, like a leather shoe, moulded over time to fit 'your shape' giving real personalised comfort. Indeed many bought a Brooks saddle who didn't own or ride a bike! I was often asked to address the Brooks customers at the Brooks/SR annual dinners. It was rewarding to meet many 'old' faces and typical of the bike world, a group of people who were also interested in my other 'made in England' ventures. Bikies can't always afford the best but if they are convinced of the quality, and buy the story, they then cannot afford not to have one. It is a fun and slightly incestuous business.

Brooks never sold these saddles below, with portraits of the Ayatollah and Saddam Hussein, for fear of a fatwa. They belong to a trio made by Persons Majestic, Brook's distributor in the USA. The third, which I leant out and did not get back, bore the portrait of Colonel Gaddafi. They were dreamed up by my dear friend Charlie Persons and his sense of humour that overcame commercial considerations. Apart from this trio of 'kiss my arse' saddles Charlie decided at one of the Californian Trade Shows that customers came to see him rather than see his products and so he turned his stand into a Beer Garden with three armchairs and a barrel of beer with tankards. Popular though this was, the show organisers were not impressed.

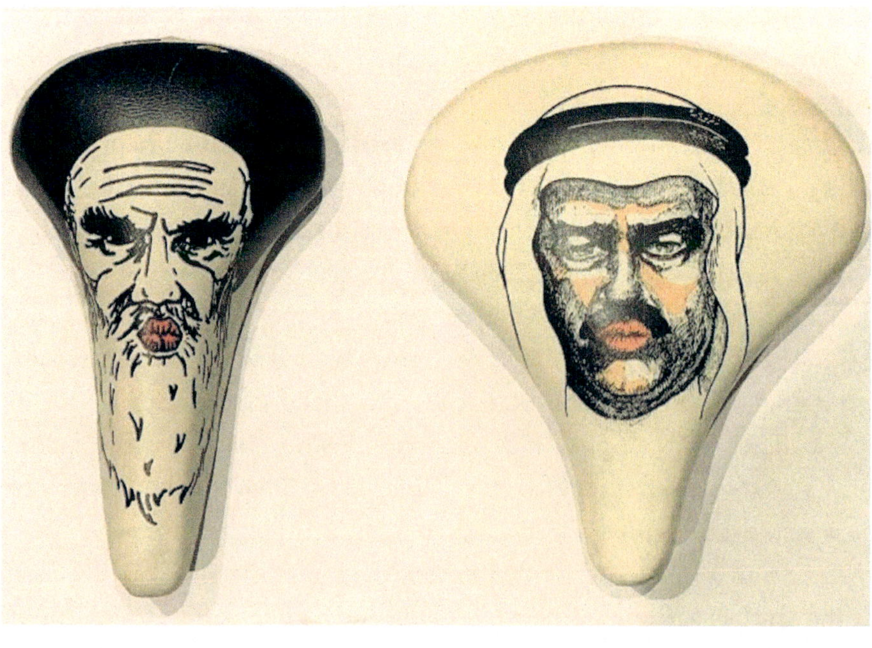

Mixing Family and Business

With Sturmey-Archer gone (for me, in 1998), my business portfolio included Brooks and Pashley. I was also the Managing Director of Raleigh International and a Director of the IFC along with some Insurance broking through Hampden Agencies and I felt my business life had to come together. Alistair was working in London after his sabbatical year overseas. He then surprised us all in 2002 by deciding that he needed a business qualification and enrolled with the American University in Prague on an MBA course. I was very proud of and for him – he excelled himself not just in obtaining his MBA with Distinction, but at the same time finding a smart and clever wife. Lorena and Alistair arranged the most perfect wedding in Prague, including a lunch-time tram tour complete with champagne and a guide in each tram followed by a grand dinner. They repeated this extravaganza in Transylvania (in Azuga) by hiring a horse-driven sledge to take us through the snow from the church to the dinner party in a Forest Lodge.

Meanwhile Ane Marie and I had moved into a new house, Kingston Hall, in 1998 and I was ready for everything – except for what did happen. Ane Marie became pregnant – and with twins! Amazing. I'd never known anyone so happy (just look at the photo opposite) with being sick and having a big tummy. She made the most of her ever-changing condition with huge enjoyment. One of the best experiences in my life was Ane Marie's pregnancy and the birth of twins Timothy and Amalie.

I had no idea how we were going to cope, and it was tough. Ane Marie turned out to be the tiger-mum she was born to be, which was just as well as the twins consumed the day. We only had one set of relatives and they lived in Denmark, but Inge Herluf, Ane Marie's mother, was very involved when she was able. She was a remarkable lady, selfless

Ane Marie, the expectant mother

and generous to a fault, she made the world a better places each day by her presence and by her actions. She was one of life's unsung heroines. I was delighted, therefore, in the course of writing this book, to rediscover this old photo, on the right, of her coming down our stairs with Ninoo just behind her. She was a leading Civil Servant and for over 20 years she was the Head of Social Services in Zealand's second city, Roskilde. Her many heavy responsibilities included the care of those less fortunate or less able or vulnerable. Long hours and dedication in her social and family duties was her daily fare, and she gave her all, without thought for herself. She always took a warm and active interest in Timothy and Amalie, and she was a vital source of support to us throughout those early years of their lives.

Inge Herluf

We were also lucky to be living in a village with very competent helpful girls to give us a break both over weekends and even helping us in our home in Denmark. We got through a day at a time. I went to work for a rest.

However, I couldn't let this get in the way of my job, could I? – plus, my job was overseas. It was then I came to a decision. I was 60, I had worked all my life, was never busier, but rarely had put my family first. If I were to have children I didn't want to repeat my experience of missing Alistair when I was in Australia, and so this time the kids would have to come into my world, not me theirs.

Ane Marie was a 100% Mum. An event drove me to consummate my decision: when the babies were just three years old my new Raleigh Licensees in Shanghai needed me to come to their Raleigh Launch in 2004. 'What's the date?' I asked. 'December 25th,' they replied. 'Small problem,' I retorted. 'If I come, I'll need to bring the family.' 'Ah no problem,' … 'And also hire an *ayee'* (Chinese for Auntie). Again 'no problem', they said. What a Christmas 2004 proved to be.

'Forever', the largest distributor of bicycles in China, selling over four million a year, had booked not just the largest hotel in Shanghai for the launch, but four entire hotels to accommodate their thousands of national dealers. We were the only non-Chinese at Forever's Annual Event. When the prize giving ceremony took place on Christmas Day I was sitting with the Forever Board on the top table on a stage, staring over these thousands of dealers stuffed into a room where the partitions between adjoining rooms had been taken down. From 8.30 a.m. till after 5.30 p.m. that day I had to clap whenever a dealer was awarded his 'prize', clap again when he came onto the stage to receive it, and then clap when he returned. The whole day passed with this monotony of clapping and only Chinese spoken. Fortunately Ane Marie and the twins were spared this ordeal, and had a day of sightseeing with the a*yee*.

Boxing Day was similar, but more corporate. No wonder then, as the day concluded, that we adjourned and met up for early dinner,

Christmas Dinner with Forever. I am in the middle

that everyone was ready to get drunk. Once again I was on the top table though, not with Ane Marie or the twins who were at the dinner and kept occupied by our accomplished a*yee*. When I went over to see them there they were being fed by 'long' chopsticks being offered sheep eyes and chicken feet and being encouraged to spit out what they didn't like – I was more worried about the things they did like. They loved the mess and noise of their happy table, with Timothy showing off about eating anything that the table challenged him with. I shut my eyes, and the three days of a well-named Forever Christmas passed. Then I was free, and with a nanny and on expenses, and so off to West Lake in Hangzhou I took my brood. They say in West Lake that if you live to be 100 and eat three meals a day you need never repeat a meal. To help with the social life there I had gathered our Phillips Licensee – Mr Chen to join us with his team. It turned out that we had given our children Chinese names – Amalie became Mai Lee (Beautiful), Timothy was Tim Fei (Flying Warrior). Having twins, and one of each gender, was to a Chinese a double blessing, earning them the accolade of being Dragon and Phoenix. To be seen with Dragon and Phoenix, and especially ones with very blond hair, was a gift to all who could behold it. So, whenever we went out they had some followers with a*yee* totally in control and any fingers touching the twins' golden hair being scolded by the fearsome a*yee*. Timothy relished the attention, whilst shy Amalie played her part as the reluctant female, and the crowds grew and grew.

I didn't tell my guests that in fact I had first visited Shanghai in 1947 (pre-Mao) by ship, moored off the Bund area. When the ship anchored it was immediately invaded by hundreds of swimmers laden with goodies they hoped to sell to the passengers by climbing up the ship's sides. Most were repulsed by long bamboo poles and dropped back into the water, but surprisingly many succeeded in boarding, and even in selling their wares.

After Shanghai, Suzhou, West Lake, etc., we reluctantly said goodbye to our, oh so competent, *ayee*. She was no spring chicken, only spoke Shanghainese, she was serious and competent. I wanted to take her home, and on our departure, I asked about her background and learned that her previous job was as a 'Madam' – a brothel keeper; I could have done well with her in the U.K. then!

Thinking we needed a rest – not to mention a Christmas – I then arranged our return to the U.K. via Malaysia, a country in which Ane Marie had worked as a teacher to the family of a rubber plantation director, and to me a second home. We spent time with the Ng family and Ken Ng took this lovely picture of the twins on a Pangkor Island beach.

The twins on Pangkor Island

We then went on into Kedah State in the North of Malaysia where my new Licensee, Quah of Montana Ltd, resided. I had never been before, but knew it would be different. It was nice to have the family with me as we were shown around the museums and sensed the cultural background of the sultanate. I learnt too of what was termed a 'Macmichaelism'. Mr Macmichael was the last British Governor of Malaya, and had gotten on well with the Sultan of Kedah State. But he was an impatient and high-handed Englishman and gave the Sultan a no-choice offer when it came to Independence. 'Join the new Malaysia, or be part of Thailand (an old enemy).' Both were anathema to the Sultan, but he trusted Mr Macmichael. So Kedah State was part of Malaysia, although not reconciled to it.

This was not the only trip for which the whole family joined me. What I found was that having Ane Marie and the twins was for my Agents/Licensees/Customers an opportunity to include their families, and what's more, leaving the husbands and me to work, but to look forward to dinner each night to catch up with the full day's activities of our despatched families. So after 'Forever' we travelled as a family a lot from Sun City to Kuala Lumpur to Bangkok, to Yangon and Chennai, not to mention Cloppenberg, Amsterdam and Aarhus. We became better bonded with a group of businessmen and their families than Raleigh could ever have foreseen – let alone me.

Still today if you are in Bangkok and mention the name 'Vitya Lee Issaranikol' you might raise a knowing smile, soon followed by an outpouring of reminiscing of outrageous memories. His father made his first million pounds from selling Raleigh bicycles in the 1930s, and Vitya not only never forgot but honoured this start by his continued non-judgemental support. If the order book at Raleigh was low, Vitya was always good for 1,000 bikes – the stock held by Vitya's family company, Seng Guan Hong, was huge and old on Vitya's death in 2010.

When I last met him in the 1990s, he told me that he was standing for Parliament – I was shocked – 'Why?' I asked. He promptly replied, 'I've taken so much from this country and it's time to give something back.' He spent a lot of money on this venture but failed to become elected.

It was Vitya who introduced me to Ane Marie in 1983. Vitya had bought tickets to attend a very traditional, very old and prestigious Thai evening. But he declared that he couldn't make it, but I should attend. Just as I was saying that I really didn't want to go on my own, this apparition appeared at the check-in desk at the Oriental Hotel. Vitya went up to the apparition and promptly asked her if she had any arrangements for that evening, and three hours later Vitya's chauffeur picked up Ane Marie and me to take us to the show. It set a standard that I still have to live up to.

The next day Vitya, grateful to Ane Marie for accepting his ticket, included her in more lavish entertainment in one after another of his hotels, including dinner at the latest Japanese restaurant. He embarrassed us by sitting low on the floor so that the waitresses had to serve us by wriggling along on their tummies with food held aloft thereby keeping lower than their guests, Ane Marie was not impressed; which added to Vitya's pleasure.

I'll allow myself one Vitya story: he loved, he said, to know how rich and famous men relaxed or spent their down-time. He owned Chrysler Thailand, and had decided to visit his daughter at her university in Buffalo near New York, and combine this with an appointment to see the President of Chrysler – Lee Iacocca, no less. 'To my horror,' said Vitya, 'I was given an appointment for Wednesday at his office between 8.25 and 8.30. My first reaction was of offence and decided to decline this meeting. Then I became intrigued and very formally confirmed the five-minute meeting. I turned up at 08.15. Lee had eight secretaries so I simply sat down after introducing myself 'Vitya Lee – Lee Iacocca 08.25'.' At 08.20 word came down that Lee Iacocca would see me now. 'I looked at my watch and declined but a minute later,' Vitya went on, 'Iacocca came out of his office to my seat and ushered me, with his arm around me, into his office. With a 'How are you Vitya? A good journey? Where are you staying? How long are you here? and so on.' After all this largesse, which consumed many minutes Iacocca finally said 'so Vitya, how's business?' I looked at my watch to see it was exactly 08.30 and so replied 'I'd love to tell you, but it's 08.30 and we're out of time.' Iacocca replied, 'You're right, my goodness, what are you doing on Saturday?' 'Seeing my daughter at Buffalo.' 'Tell you what, I'll get my helicopter to pick up your daughter from university to join us for a little cruise on my yacht which has its own helipad, and during luncheon you can see her on your own'.' And so it happened.

Meanwhile the twins had been everywhere, eaten everything but memory-wise could remember none of it. The next step for growing kids was 'education'. In Denmark school starts at six or seven years old, before that it's all about 'playing' and learning in other ways. In England you start to learn to read at three. So it was that we hit upon the Danish model of 'Forest School'. This has now become known throughout Europe, but in Denmark it was not only well established, but could not be repeated elsewhere, if only for insurance reasons. Based in our flat in Charlottenlund in North Copenhagen, that we had with Ane Marie's Dad, Erik Herluf, the twins went to 'Forest School'. I was often able to use Copenhagen as my 'hub' from where to visit the world of my Licensees and thereby spend weekends in Denmark. Once again, I led a double life. I should add that Ane Marie only spoke Danish to the twins from birth, and then their linguistic competence was ensured by our decision to send them to Danish summer school (for overseas Danes) straight from their schools in England for one further month each year. The idea of Forest School is simply that 4 – 6 year-olds learn through their environment and all their senses rather than by rote. Reading and writing are not encouraged, nature teaches you. They get to use their gross motor skills by climbing trees rather than fine motor skills by writing letters. Research indicates that this use and emphasis on the gross motor skills is beneficial for a child's development and may help their ability to concentrate later on at school.

Each day between 8.30 a.m. to 3.30 p.m. you are dressed appropriately (for rain, snow or shine), and sent into the forest. Here the teacher will pick up insects, snakes or spiders and flora and fauna, pass them around with explanations about their place in the cycle of life. There is a rule that each parent also has to spend one day in the forest, and in Ane Marie's case, hers was a fishing day and the kids had gathered their 'catch'; the teacher selected the biggest fish caught and explained to all the children that this fish was to be special and to be their teacher. It was duly stunned, with the other little fish thrown back, and the 'teacher fish' duly dismembered with each part of its body explained to the children – 'This is its liver and as in our body it cleans the blood, this is the bladder,' and so on. Only Timothy could be trusted to say at the end of this display – 'Teacher, can you now put it together again and throw it back?' Their lives were filled with many walks in nearby forests and beaches with singing and drawing and also with visits to the theatre, cinema and museums on really wet days

The diploma displayed on the page below was awarded to the twins showing the levels they attained at the Danish Forest School, and is very descriptive of the activities in which they were engaged.

Interestingly it was not straightforward to convert to the English education system, where reading and writing was encouraged from an earlier age. We certainly learned of the cultural differences between the British and Danish education systems.

In Denmark education is, more than learning, a process of socializing and integrating the child into the Danish society with its belief system. The education is dogmatic and teaches established Danish social values and views for the child to adopt rather than challenge; e.g. rights, democracy, vocal expression, egalitarianism, anti-elitism. Being told how – and what – to think is undoubtedly good for the homogeneous society – if you all buy into it.

The unwritten 'Jante Law' (no-one is better than anyone else) then ensures that your child and the adult it turns into, is careful about appearing to do better or be more privileged than 'the average person'. In Danish schools there is, within the boundaries of conformism to the taught way of thinking, an emphasis on self-realization, self-expression, on articulating your own needs. We wanted our children to put the needs of others before their own, to be good listeners and give others the talking space, as they need it more!

SKOVBØRNEHAVEN

DIPLOM

Det bekræftes at

TIMOTHY EMIL

har præsteret følgende:

Gået ca. 1200 km. I løbet af Troldens tid i Skovbørnehaven-
Derefter opholdt sig samlet ca. 1100 timer i skoven.
Trolden har klatret i ca. 350 træer.
Og spist 240 madpakker.

Ud over alt dette har skovtrolden vist sig som en god kammerat ved altid at have øje for kammeraternes ve og vel.
Trolden har også vist at med lidt fantasi kan man snildt lege hele dagen uden andet legetøj end det man selv opfinder.

Held og lykke fremover og tak for den tid vi havde sammen.

Ulla Thisen   Magnus Berg   Sanne Adser   Celal Sayir   Anom Puspa

***Translation**: It is hereby Certified that Timothy Emil (and Feodora Amalie) has completed the following: walked over 1,200km during the Trolls time in Forest School; stayed over 1,100 hours in the Forest; climbed approx 350 trees and consumed 240 packed lunches.*
Over and above this the Troll has proven to be a good friend by always keeping an eye out for the well-being of his/her mates. The Troll has proven that with some imagination you can play all day long without any other toys than those you create for yourself.
Good Luck in the future and Well Done.

In Danish schools the atmosphere is casual and informal; pupils address their teachers by first name and get away with being disrespectful. In English schools the atmosphere is kind, respectful and formal; teachers are addressed by last name and 'Sir' or 'Miss'. Politeness and manners is by many Danes considered old fashioned and not particularly important. In Britain traditional values such as politeness and good manners are part of a child's schooling. Politeness does not cost anything, and if you cannot do anything else in life, you can at least be polite.

We wanted our children to learn and to be encouraged to do their best in every subject; in Britain learning and excelling are legitimate prime objectives with less emphasis on the societal role of what you are taught. In Denmark encouraging excellence smacks of elitism; British schools encourage excellence and for a child to be taken as far as it can in each subject.

Danes are generally not good at tolerating other views than their own, and other ways of thinking; we wanted our children to grow up with intellectual freedom and able to listen and engage with other peoples' viewpoints.

Danes pride themselves on being amongst the most creative thinkers in the world. Whilst there are many creative Danes in various fields, intellectual creativity seems more accepted as long as it conforms to the Danish boundaries of thinking.

Danish parents think independence from a young age is very important and they tend not to fuss over their children. We wanted a close, tender relationship with our children with no rush for independence.

Ane Marie was taught and found that Danes are still spoon-fed into believing that Denmark is a superior country to others (elitist nationalism!), that they have the best society, the best system of education; that they do things the best way. Ane Marie did not believe that these views have any real basis. (I would have loved to have this debate with the twins when they are about 30 years old.)

Our 1912 hut in Denmark

That said we have been lucky to have Denmark as a second home. We treasure our time there in a safe society and one with many attributes including wonderful films, food, art and architecture, all of which has become part of our twins' DNA.

After some interesting experiences up to the age of seven, Timothy proceeded to Maidwell Hall School in Northamptonshire as a full boarder for six years. A traditional English all-boys preparatory school and being exposed to a schooling very different from anything equivalent in Denmark. We could not speak highly enough about this experience, which was very close to the education I had received and thought no longer existed. From there he won a drama scholarship into Radley College. Amalie went to a combination of a lovely little prep school combined with home education before also boarding at St Mary's Calne, an all-girls school, where she excelled and gained entrance into the prestigious Fonact College in Fontainebleau for drama.

Meanwhile eldest son Alistair had returned from Prague and Bucharest to live in Nottingham, and Lorena had produced the most handsome of grandsons, Tod in 2008 and then in May 2011 a beautiful granddaughter, Mia. No sooner had she accomplished this than she set

L-R, Mia, Lorena, Alistair and Tod

about doing her PhD in Digital Health, which subject still confounds me. She is not shy at describing me as the dinosaur which I proudly am. A mighty animal.

By the time the twins came back to the U.K. in 2006, my business life had simplified. My involvement in the Burmese river boat initiative had sadly ended in 2004 after a lost court case when my partner and I parted ways. This is a story that needs telling, but elsewhere hopefully. Also, we, Adrian Williams and I, had sold Brooks to Selle Royale that same year. Meanwhile my job at Raleigh International though had grown, and from 2001 to when I left in 2012 attained double digit growth year on year, and it was all based 'at home'. Can you remember where that was?

Raleigh International

Raleigh International Ltd was a separate company. It had grown out of its overseas factories, where Raleigh, to save its markets, had invested in local manufacture. The result was Raleigh Malaysia, Raleigh Nigeria, Raleigh East Africa, Raleigh America, Raleigh Canada, Raleigh Germany, and so on. These companies reported to Head Office in Nottingham, but were really very autonomous. Chris Handley had been handling these areas very effectively after T.I. had sold Raleigh to 'Derby' (Ed Gottesman and his hired-hand, Alan Finden-Crofts). Chris's retirement coincided with my departure from Sturmey-Archer, and it was a job I felt I could develop in a direction that could benefit from the experience gained in my earlier travels.

I would love to relate the many tales of trips to Iran, South Africa, South America and especially the Middle and Far East. My pay may have been modest, but I had a rich life, and it was made richer by a full and happy home life with amazing twins whom I was often able to include in my job – when a longer trip allowed me to bring them along, and always to the joy of my Licensees.

In return for a modest percentage Licence Fee, the Licensees became responsible for developing their sales and enhancing the brand – the 'rub' was that each year's model range needed my approval. We were operating in about 10-12 markets in 2002, and by 2012 were in some 35 others. I would visit each Licensee annually to agree their marketing plan and approve their product range. (It was a plum job for me). Over the fives years from 2003 to 2007, the key markets were covered in Cycle Press, a monthly Japanese magazine read by members of Cycle Industry around the world. Many of the these stories came from press releases which I had written.

At Raleigh International I was able to develop a theory summed by my mantra of 'Think Global but Act Local'. Raleigh was a truly global brand and hugely unique and possibly, as far as its overseas spread is concerned, undervalued in the UK. But while the Brand Raleigh is known world-wide it actually means something different in each country, and it is this difference which profits from understanding and exploiting. I set out this philosophy in an article for *Cycle Press* in November 2004, and it lived on in a fresh publication, titled *Raleigh International in the 21st Century*, which brought together numerous articles covering the work of Raleigh's licensees around the world. Reading it again now, I find it worthy of publishing for a third time, on the pages below, for it provides a great context for this chapter.

The cover of Raleigh International in the 21st Century

Raleigh International Limited

'When it comes to world brand names Raleigh is to cycling, as Coca Cola to drink. You don't ride a bike, you ride a 'Raleigh'.

'The Raleigh bicycle started production in Raleigh Street in Nottingham in 1886, and quickly, under Sir Frank Bowden its owner, grew to be the largest producer of bicycles in the world and its place as such in the Guinness Book of Records went unchallenged for decades. Raleigh as a leader of cycle production and innovation set its own standards. These are still used as the basic standards for cycle design and excellence in the world today.

'For over one hundred years, Raleigh placed Nottingham in the centre of the cycling world. When the centre of the cycling world moved to the Far East, Raleigh, like many other traditional European companies, struggled to redefine itself. Now by concentrating on it core in Europe and North America and then by strategic alliances in other key areas where its name is a by-word for bicycles, Raleigh has regained its dominance.

Over 30 Licensees Worldwide

'Raleigh International Ltd, (RIL), a Raleigh Cycle Ltd (RCL) subsidiary, grew out of the exports from Raleigh UK in the days when Raleigh in Nottingham exported well over 70% of its production of some 4 million bicycles. Raleigh bicycles were sold in over 144 countries and the UK factory had over 60,000 unique models in its range. These exports reduced due to world economics. The resulting rationalization meant that many parts of the world were denied what the local population thought constituted a Raleigh bicycle. RIL, therefore, was born to exploit this need

'Overseas factories and distribution companies are licensed to sell under the Raleigh name or other Raleigh owned names like Phillips, BSA, Triumph, Robin Hood, Carlton, Humber, Hercules, Rudge, and more recently Diamondback.

'RCL Registers its Brand names throughout the world with well over 1000 registrations. Mervyn Jones, the Company Secretary and Commercial Director of the Group, who manages the company registrations and their use, says, 'we jealously guard all our brand names and we have an ongoing battle with infringements. It is said that to be copied is to be flattered; but it is an expensive business. However, that's all part of the responsibility of owning internationally renowned brand names. They need protecting and caring for.'

'Today there are over 30 licensees around the world and these, together with the RCL subsidiary companies in Canada, USA, Germany, the UK, Switzerland, China and Taiwan, make up the Raleigh family.

'The challenge that Raleigh faces is that the brand is positioned differently in various parts of the world. In countries as far afield as South Africa and Israel Raleigh is the Brand leader. In the UK the name has a 98% awareness amongst the population. Not many brands can boast such distinction.

'In Africa, advertising posters depicted that on a Raleigh you are saved from the lion. In England a policeman on his Raleigh could be relied upon to catch his man. Whether you are the proverbial onion seller in France or the conveyor of palm oil in Nigeria the only way to conduct your job with security, safety and ease is on a Raleigh. The thread of consistency in what the brand represents is, however, strong. Today the Danish range of excellent Raleigh bicycles, marketed by V N Cykler are exceptional bicycles at the top end of the specification spectrum with such things as sealed bearings as standard. The Bike Total Group exploits the same theme with a Dutch range of Raleigh bicycles where the detail reveals the care and the value of an 'A line' product. In contrast in Indonesia, a Raleigh has to be strong and reliable but also meet a price point to make it saleable but it still has to be an 'A Line' product. In Australia and New Zealand, Sheppard Industries, the Raleigh Licensee, has rebuilt the brand name and over the past few years has enjoyed double figure growth year on year, a tribute to the product management team that has carefully selected a range or Raleigh bikes to suit the market needs that means Raleigh to the consumer. In Japan where Raleigh is seen as the bike for the English 'Gentleman' and has the look/image of a Rolls Royce, Araya has created a range that shows 'class' and 'pride' and an understated elitism. In the November Japanese edition of Cycle Press a whole article is devoted to Raleigh in Japan.

'This pragmatic approach is very much the style of the Raleigh management today. Alan Finden Crofts often says about this industry 'you must think global and act local'. So it is left to the Raleigh Company/ Licensee in its part of the world to create the range of Raleigh branded bicycles that reflects what the name stands for. If distribution is through the dealer only, as is the case in the USA, then the Raleigh bicycles must provide features and returns that allow the dealer to sell successfully against the department store down the street. If mail order is the distribution medium as in Finland, then other factors come into play regarding the specification and pricing. Raleigh is an international name without a global image and that is its strength (i.e., it means what the consumer wants it to mean in each area where it is traded; unlike its sister in the RCL stable, Diamondback, a real global brand). Recognising and bringing out the essence in each of the strong Raleigh Cycle Companies stable of brands is core to the success of its business.

'The Director of Raleigh International, John Macnaughtan, is well known in the Cycle Industry and has visited all of the Raleigh outposts in the world. He looks with pride at the renewed Raleigh image which he has done much to foster. He concludes, 'What is demanded by RIL throughout the world is that any bicycle bearing the name Raleigh should represent value for money, be backed up by service and warranty to maintain the respect which Raleigh has built up over the 117 years of its existence'.'

I would meet with many Licensees at the annual world-leading bike shows in Taiwan, Eurobike in Friedrichshafen, Germany and in Long Beach, USA. This lifestyle was almost the perfect culmination to my life of exporting.

Licensing out the 'Raleigh' and other Raleigh International brands, could have been anathema to me, but by 2002 Raleigh had closed its manufacturing plant in Lenton, Nottingham, and moved into offices and warehouses in Eastwood, also in Nottinghamshire. What is more, the U.K. range of Raleigh bicycles were all being bought in from the Far East and, to my mind, the value of the brand was compromised as a consequence. I resolved this was not going to be repeated overseas. I determined that whatever the brand Raleigh stood for in each market that had to be respected, and that the product had to reflect this heritage. As I was largely left alone to appoint Licensees and agree their product range, my philosophy went unchallenged. Anyway, I knew that Raleigh was a much bigger brand overseas than it was in the U.K.. It was the leading brand in Denmark and Holland, known in Germany as the best value for money, in the 'comfort' segment. In Japan the brand was a 'Burberry', a U.K. legend, and in most of the Commonwealth the Raleigh name was synonymous with 'bicycles'. In South Africa Raleigh was simply the best-known brand which had fed the market through the apartheid years and boycotts, and we needed to have a full range in every segment to exploit this. In India I inherited a 24 year-old court case with the original Raleigh India Company from Assansol, north of Calcutta, claiming ownership of the brand name. I recognised this (court case) as an old Indian scam when the market was closed and protected, so that when the market opened up you found that you didn't own your own name. To close the case I took an expensive but one-off payment, after which I was free to choose my own man and, after a false start, was happy to appoint Rajesh Kalra and his company, Sun Cross. I was told by friends at Hero, Avon and others that my decision was wrong. I stuck by my instincts and now congratulate Rajesh on the hard work and success he has since enjoyed, and I am also happy that we and our families have become good friends.

Establishing the licensing business of Raleigh International suited me well, and I could repeat the Tabarrok or Rajesh story with Robert Pasnau in South America, Mark Ackerman in South Africa, Sanjay Shah in East Africa, Tuncay Cetinelli in Finland, Bike Totaal in Holland, Polbike in Poland and the most important Uwe Reinkemeier Lay in DCW, Germany, to name a few.

One of my most precious relationships is with the Ponpipom family in Bangkok, and while I haven't seen Somchai for eight years, he and his daughter Mananya, are not just close to me, but I know I can ask anything from them. My visits to Somchai haven't been recorded here, and the reason is simple, because they went smoothly and with no drama. Our annual meetings over a long period were spent in his lovely house and over excellent meals. A good strategy was always agreed between us, Mananya was brought in and the plan delegated to her for implementation. Then we would go for an excellent meal, or to his night club, which was managed by a Thai family who always spoilt Somchai's guests and where I was considered a regular, and then the day was rounded off with 2-3 hours of hot baths and massage. Somchai knows me too well and I him.

Then I have not mentioned the most amazing times and very English adventures with Tom Field of Reynolds Tubing in Tyseley, Birmingham. Ours was an unlikely friendship: we sparked off each other's differing personalities. Our adventures in Japan, Taiwan and in particular America were memorable. We were coming out of a BWDA party (Bicycle Wholesaler Dealers of America) in our hotel in San Diego at 2.00 a.m. We had staggered to reception and thence to our rooms when a huge limo drove up and out stepped Dean Martin from one side of the front seat and his bodyguard from the other. No attention was paid to Tom and myself as they drove up by us and rudely stopped us in our tracks; so as 'Dino' plus bodyguard got out of the car Tom and I got in with Dino's girlfriend sitting in the middle of the front seat between us and we drove off. She had seen the whole charade and thought it very funny and was quite relaxed. We drove a quarter of a mile to the gate-house of the hotel where a, probably armed, guard waved us down. We got out of the car saying to him 'It's all yours!' kissed the girlfriend and walked off. A silly episode, the girlfriend loved the prank and said Dino would too, and deserved to be 'put out'. So many incidents with Tom and his Black Country wit make me chuckle even now. Likewise, with Rob Pasnau from L.A. who looked after Latin and South America for me. He introduced me to the natural hot spring baths in the mountains skirting Taipei, which were used by the

Japanese kamikazi fighters before taking off on their last flight. Rob would always research his trips beforehand and take charge of me to make life special for a moment and energise us before the rigours of manning a stand at a trade show and meeting a hundred customers. He even took a cruise along with his Mexican customer, Alberto and Itzel Moreno, on the Brahmaputra with me and Ane Marie in 2018, prior to attending the Taiwan Show.

Finland was another story in the company, first with Jari Komulainen on the one hand or Tuncay Cetinelli on the other. The former's adventures were always larger than life, like his rent/purchase of four Juliette class Russian submarines, one of which he succeeded in sinking in the Skagerrak just outside Danish territorial waters. Had it sunk within Danish waters, the Danes would have made him pay for the salvage – in the event the Russians had to write off the vessel. This occurred as he took one of submarines to Naples and another to be a tourist attraction in Florida. Jari's personal life is even more worth recounting, but I shall resist.

Tuncay Cetinelli is a Turk living in Helsinki with a wife and daughter living in Turku, Finland. He lent me his apartment when I visited along with the twins and Ane Marie. I had appointed Tuncay as

In discussion with my Polish customer, Juliusz Kabath, in Helskinki, prior to the Russian Juliett class submarine heading off to Florida

the Raleigh Licensee for Finland, and many a Finn thought I was crazy; indeed, I saw the racism to which Tuncay was subjected. However, I knew my man and proceeded, and we devised a strategy to bring Raleigh's brand recognition up to No.3 from its current, in 2005, position of No.15 (it was deemed impossible to replace Tunturi – the Raleigh of Finland) and to do so in one year. From selling a handful of bikes to specialist stores, we put ourselves into the prestige national stores making Raleigh the discerning Finn's choice of a bike 'as good value for money'. This required much effort but in Tuncay I had a dedicated workaholic and sourcing his bikes from Turkey was a surprisingly happy choice, financially and logistically. I judged him to be a smart entrepreneur, who certainly educated me in this marketing process, which, of course, I endorsed, and it worked.

The biggest success in the Raleigh International portfolio though was in Germany, and here again this was a happy union of Raleigh's history and loyal dealer network of over 1,000 stores, plus the management of Uwe Renkeimeier-Lay. He understood the positioning of the brand in the 'comfort market' and didn't try to enter the 'junior' or 'race market'. Indeed, as e-bikes took off from 2010 Raleigh Germany was perfectly placed to exploit this rapidly growing sector. I stayed near Uwe's house and worked happily with his amazing German work ethic. What a star.

When the Dutch company Accell bought Raleigh in 2012, I was pleased to move on, especially as the Dutch didn't want to listen to me – they knew bicycles and brands better than me and wouldn't be told. At the Eurobike Show each year on the Thursday evening of the Show I hired a ship on the Bodensee to entertain and thank my Licensees over a delightful dinner cruise. This became a 'known event' but was not one that the Dutch continued. I decided in 2012, coinciding with announcing my retirement, to have a more formal dinner. (My speech is in Appendix 4.)

I saw a documentary programme on British TV, 'Pedalling Dreams' in 2019 which was later repeated in the History Today magazine. I don't doubt the veracity of the story, it showed Raleigh in the UK in an endearing human manner, but it is poor history, and gave a false impression of the incredible world, nay empire, of Raleigh

Industries Ltd. Like the Gold Medal Campaign, such films are good for brand awareness but not for the balance sheet or the full truth. When I look at my pension today after over 48 years with this group, I could be forgiven maybe for being a little bitter, but I am not in the least, as Raleigh has been the vehicle for giving me the very richest of lives. I have been blessed to be surrounded by love and support whether today it's in the Moulton offices, or Woolley Grange Hotel, where I lived, or in the back streets of Kabul into which I ventured. I am reminded of it annually when I receive the pistachios from Khosro in Iran every Christmas, or the oranges from Eyal Brahms in Israel, or the generosity of Somchai in Bangkok, or that of Rajesh Kalra laying on chauffeurs from anywhere in India. I know too this could not have happened without my having the parents I had, a grandad of immense charisma as an example, and the Parsee Indian family's support in our family's hard times, and then to Raleigh which have all combined to have given me a rich experience.

As I reflect on my life, I see that I only really 'came alive' when I was overseas. 'What do they know of England who only England know', was Kipling's lament on the scant knowledge of his neighbours about English achievements around the world. The England I knew was not that in which I had been schooled, nor was it the one in which I had been trained – also within Tube Investments Ltd. I was trained in a tough world but one that was rooted in solid principles where money was not a goal, money came from hard work, but in that old world sense as a 'measure of work', rather than an end in itself and bringing with it huge responsibilities. Right up until the millennium I had had secretaries and was even dictating emails. I had enjoyed long and alcoholic lunches on many days in a week and maybe was less fit for work in the afternoon. My trips were of a duration that demanded all of me both socially and mentally. I forfeited the chance to play regular sport, so important to me in my school days, but when called upon to play a game of cricket in Australia or go on a horse 'drag' hunting in South Africa, I never declined the offer and never disgraced myself either. However, I am now more displaced than ever in this e-world which dominates our lives. I have tried to embrace it and be a part of it, as I recognise that it is our hope as well as our reality. I reflect though on all that has also been lost in this fast world of fast foods, fast decisions and where little time is given to context. The time to build relationships, the space in which to nurture interests is often lost in the apparently necessary greed that drives us to find ways to avoid the paying of taxes. The latter seems misguided as well as time consuming. Wealth creation is supported, but by politicians devoid of any experience of that world, yet called upon to administer it. As the Irish playwright Sean O'Casey said 'The world's in a state of chassis'. There is so much to be done, and if we humans are unable to do it our species is doomed – and we now know it. It was summed up to me in Taiwan back in the '70's when I wanted to go diving off their East Coast, and the Taiwanese dive master told me that 'there were now no fish to see because in the struggle to better their quality of life it had been over-fished and then polluted by the waste from a successful economy'. He said the next step was to address this. What a step. What a challenge and what hope? Old men plant trees they say, now we need our young to do this work, but in an environment in which the costs of 'human rights' outweighs the necessities of 'survival', making the task doubly difficult. Too many nations want to have a better life in order to get around to bettering 'life'. Think on't. I have been fortunate to have been given the space to breathe in many rich, and also in other polluted airs. Is there anything I can teach from my experiences? If time allows, I shall try e'en now to work on it.

The Present

I don't know if my Burmese/Far East background is the explanation for my eclectic life. Perhaps it is, instead, my upbringing to do what I was told and see life as a responsibility, perhaps it is my inherited sense of duty, which was always in the forefront, or perhaps it is my simply not knowing the word 'No'! It was this, after all, that took me to Australia and before that into sorting out the Libyan debacle. I realise now that when in 2008, aged 65, retirement became an option, it was this that caused me to stay on at Raleigh as it was a bad time for Alan Finden-Crofts to sell the company. I eventually left in 2012, when Raleigh was bought by the Netherlands group Accell. At this point my shareholding in Pashley encouraged my fellow shareholder to ask me to take a 'temporary' posting in Bradford on Avon with the Moulton Bicycle Company (MBC). I thought this would be a 12 - 18 month secondment.

MBC has proved to be a fascinating endeavour. I had known Dr. Alex Moulton since the 1960s and was involved simply by being there when Alex persuaded Jack Catlin to manufacture the Moulton bicycle rather than the Raleigh RSW16 down in South Africa. On my return visits to the U.K. I often bumped into Alex Moulton, and I believe that he always associated me with a happy episode in his life, and he subjected me to frequent intense discussions. With no natural successor it was not surprising that Alex Moulton selected Pashley to buy his company, as he had previously sub-contracted the manufacture of some Moultons to them in 1992, when the first APB was launched. It might surprise some to discover that we didn't fully understand what we were buying. We thought that we knew Alex Moulton and that we knew his company. Only when we saw the books, and more importantly the way it was run, did we find that we had bought a company that wasn't making a profit and was run rather extravagantly by Alex, almost as a gentleman's hobby. He treated his small staff of some fourteen craftsmen (and now women) as an extension of his life. Even after giving up control of the company to Pashley he couldn't stop engaging with the MBC employees, to whom he would always be the 'boss'. When he wanted his Bentley washed, or when he had to visit the dentist or barber, he would get one of his, now our, staff to drive him into Bath, wait until he had finished, and drive him back.

This behaviour eventually led my fellow shareholder, Adrian Williams, to write formally to Alex Moulton to request that he not go into the MBC premises without prior permission. What an affront to someone who bestrode his empire like the engineering Colossus that he was. Moreover, when Pashley engineer, Dan Farrell, was seconded to MBC to work on new Moulton designs, he found that the Cambridge educated Alex Moulton was a design engineer rather than a production engineer. Dan found himself having to produce new component drawings to ensure that products could be manufactured without having to be 'interpreted' by Moulton's clever workforce into a finished product. Commercially his great nephew, Shaun Moulton, was in charge of MBC sales. Shaun was certainly a Moulton, had been in the Army for twelve years prior to being given his 'opportunity' by Alex Moulton. Alex Moulton was never a father figure, he was used to being obeyed unquestioningly by his staff, and when he was wrong the staff were expected to put things right and do what Alex Moulton had meant all along. Shaun was undoubtedly grateful to his 'Edwardian' great uncle for providing him with a house and a job, and to come into the 'family firm'. His army training suited him to a world of obedience as a Sergeant Major. But then again, this Sergeant Major was a Moulton, sensitive and wanting to please, but with a determination to assert himself. Shaun was a fine standard bearer for the brand and a great favourite with our overseas markets; He lasted with his uncle for some sixteen years, but then perhaps inevitably moved on to make his own way at the time of Alex's passing in 2012.

Combined with this was the whole question of the security of tenure for Moulton bicycles at the impressive ancestral Hall and in the converted stables (where the bicycles are still made). Would the Trustees of the charitable trust set up by Alex Moulton be forced to sell, and would the National Trust take over and save the Trustees from such work or would there be some other outcome? MBC was on a short lease, and a figurehead was needed ‘to be there’ during this interregnum. I never guessed this ‘interregnum’ would last for over eight years. The ride has been absorbing, intriguing and even fun, and it happily consumed me. It also allowed me to get to know bright, dedicated, fascinating and experienced team of people there and them me.

Moulton bicycles are a niche product and partly as a result of this they benefit from a global appeal. MBC exports 95% of its production to every continent of the world bar Antarctica. I was accustomed to the business of exporting, and I knew bicycles and the markets. MBC seemed to defy attempts to rationalise and grow the operation from a hobby into a business. My first year at MBC was not easy for me. These Moultons were selling for anywhere between £2,000 and £15,000; what was drawing customers to these costly machines, and

Moultoneers camping on the lawn of The Hall, Bradford on Avon, for the annual ride each September, attracting over a hundred members

The 'Boys' who make the bikes at the MBC factory, 2019.
L-R: Ben, Mike, Roy, John, Eddie, Fred and Rob

how could some volume be built into their business model? To a European or an American a small-wheeled bicycle was not a high-performance bicycle, rather a stunt bike or a folding bike. In these areas it was not easy to explain to newcomers that the bicycle was selling for four or even five figure sums. In effect my contacts and experience of world bicycle markets was not of great use to MBC. It took me a full year of 'being there' before I fully understood and allowed the product, the dedicated workforce, the Moultoneer enthusiasts, and the overseas distributors to teach me this business. After the best part of a year in MBC, and with the departure of Shaun Moulton, I agreed to stay on provided, after my year in Bed and Breakfasts, I had a flat to live in. I thought in 2013 this decision to rent a flat was to be for a few months only and not over a year. Hence my surprise when after four years I was still there, but with an expectation to move on after some six months in 2018 when new staff were recruited. However, the old team functioned better than the new, so again I continued on, but had given notice on the Bath flat so stayed in a hotel – the best – thank goodness for Woolley Grange. It became a second home and the staff spoilt me. I was there right up until the summer of 2020. The trouble was that from a job in which I found I was either walking through cobwebs, or fighting off-site colleagues, I have become one of the spiders myself. That said, Moulton's sales have quadrupled from 2017 levels and it's been both challenging and fun, and I leave a good team in place. These last nine years with MBC have allowed me to travel, influence, direct and reminisce, and I'm grateful for that.

I have said too little about my involvement with my 'partner', Adrian Williams who had invited me in 1997 to take a 25% share in Pashley Holdings. At the time I might have left the bike industry and pursued plans in the travel business on the rivers in Burma and South-East Asia. But I didn't and anyway I liked the way that Adrian had gotten hold of a 1927 very English Company and kept its core and reputation solidly in the English tradition, offering quintessentially English products at great value for money, putting brand above profit in to survive. He has had more than his share of difficult situations, dealing with unexpected surprises and rising to many challenges, be they in dealing with the Post Office, the buying of Brooks or the takeover of Moulton Bicycles or simply remaining in the manufacturing business in the UK. He has remained a loyal friend and I thank him for letting me manage the Moulton Bicycles part of the business for the past nine years. We have had fun and some long days as always; I remain today on the Board of this organisation and hope to continue to be of service.

The Spring Ride of the Indonesian Moultoneers through Jakarta, organised by our local distributor, Tjandra Kisnata

Afterword

My planned life though has been put on hold, or so I thought. My 77th birthday heralded in the news that I had terminal cancer, and this 'other' adventure is now absorbing me – mind and body. This little memoir is my Chemo project.

On the eve of my birthday (18th August 2020) Ane Marie and I were asked to come to the Urologist's office in Holbæk hospital in Denmark to hear the results of my CT Scan after a week of being tested/ investigated. In blunt Viking English he announced that I 'had incurable cancer which had spread to the liver, kidney, lymph glands and the prostate.' If I did nothing, I would be dead by Christmas. If I immediately sought treatment, maybe I could last longer. 'The latter would involve having an immediate biopsy and also castration, and the origin of the cancer would be established, and the type of chemotherapy agreed'. I didn't even know that I had cancer, let alone that it was terminal.

After digesting this, talking to my UK GP, I decided to fight my condition as recommended. I needed a project I thought, for the months allowed to me, outside of the chemo torture to which I would be subjected, to keep my mind otherwise occupied.

I hit upon the idea of asking my one-time secretary from Sturmey-Archer days, Anita Dennis, to type up some of my scribbles, as she was the only one with a chance of reading and interpreting them, and then to see where it led me. Anita seemed delighted to take on the challenge, and she tells me that after a couple of pages my idiosyncratic hieroglyphics came back to her after the 30-year break. Thank you so much Anita. I proceed between bouts of nausea and a variety of pains.

In these last few years, I seem to have been going from one funeral to the next. In every case the deceased has been a part of my life, and yet at their funerals I was introduced to a slightly different and greater person than I had known. If you cannot command a eulogy at your funeral, when can you? I am not talking of regrets or personal sadness, or relief at being amongst others at sharing a loss. Nor am I struck by the harshness of any life lost, but rather of the revealed humanity.

When her two elder sisters expressed their love so beautifully in the Haycombe Church in Bath directly to their youngest sister, Cindy Williams, Adrian's wife, it was the depth of Cindy, and her civilised, human and happy core that was revealed. I felt a joy to have known her, and that she had lived and enriched this life. When Adrian Yorath died, all I knew about him was his understated, brilliant mind and quiet humour. But I met a huge person at his funeral, a religious man, a family man who had brought worthwhile children into the world. People like him or Cindy could have risen to the top of any profession if the need or call had presented itself, but in its absence their example made life precious and rare. It is not my purpose to rehearse each death or life, but rather to note the significance to be found in funerals.

The death of my ex-wife, Sue, on the 12th June 2016 was a surprise; but then death is always a surprise. She had happily remarried a lovely guy, Tony Adams, who had earlier passed away from silicosis, dust on the lung. For some 7 years she had indulged in her passion for travel. On her 70th birthday she threw a dinner party for over 40 friends including Ane Marie and me. Sue looked radiant as I told her when she came to our table but said 'you know John I never catch a cold but actually I think I'm getting one now'. A month later she was diagnosed with stage 4 lung cancer. If anyone was destined to live to be over a 100 it was Susanna. She was never ill, and at her medicals the doctors always said she was younger than her years. Within nine months of her birthday she passed away after being nursed by our son Alistair, as she eschewed hospitals and doctors, preferring to die quietly in his front room, which she did, and to Alistair's enormous credit.

My dear Malaysian colleague and friend David Ng Kon Loong passed away recently. When he had throat cancer I happily visited and stayed with him in his modest house in Selak South where he was living with his wife, who was dying from breast cancer, and also his bright son

Ken whose ambition was to be 'invisible'. David related to me in whispers (much of his throat and speech organs had been cut away) the story of his early life. He never went properly to school and his father, the main bread winner, had been unable to work for many months after a bad accident at work, meaning that the three children and wife needed supporting. He found himself at ten years old the bread winner for the family. However, at the age of eleven, he realised that if he didn't think of himself, all their lives was destined to be one a continued struggle, with disease and early death. He only spoke his native Chinese dialect, Hakka, whereas the language in the news and on the streets was English. He could barely read or write. So, he applied to an English school. Without understanding a word, he copied the prologue from an English book, and submitted it directly to the Headmaster requesting a place in his English school. Imagine doing the reverse, i.e., not speaking Mandarin and then copying accurately three pages of Chinese script. When I knew him, he was fluent in all the main Chinese dialects used in Malaysia, Hokkien, Teochew, Henghua, and Cantonese as well as Malay, and of course English. This was a huge asset to Raleigh, as he could talk to all the dealers in their mother tongue and so not become involved in the rivalry between the different Chinese sects. (In the bike trade Hakka is the mother tongue of most of the dealers). He passed all his school exams, and became the Finance Director of Raleigh Malaysia. He lived through the Japanese occupation of Malaysia, learnt how to keep his head down, help feed himself and his family with the gourds he tried to sell, and then used the evenings to work himself out of a life certain to be full of struggle, poverty and hardships. He was a huge man that you would have quickly passed by on the street.

So if we all have 'a story', and if the numbers of really different stories are all written down over and over again, why add to the pile? I once asked my boss, Jimmy Cumming, the most erudite of raconteurs, why he didn't write down his incredible life. He was born in Zanzibar, fought in the North Italy campaign – won a 'purple heart' from the Americans. Spoke beautiful Arabic, Swahili and even Kikuyu, and then many of the European tongues. A man who hardened bicycle dealers would ask for advice on the suitability of a husband for their daughters. He replied that his life and experiences had all been written better by

Baudelaire, and there was no need to add to the overburdened world another 'must read' narrative.

Well, I hope I can bring back to life a few souls whose path crossed mine, as well as give a slightly different outlook to the world in which we live as a result of my experiences.

We are thrown together with our friends and business colleagues in an arbitrary way, and when we pick and choose those whom we start to talk to and make friends with, we put aside so many others. We soon label those that are boring or weird or not deserving of our attention. Then we start work and find we have to talk to all sorts because we want something from them – either their co-operation or their company or perhaps their money. Once again most are quickly discounted as bores or pains. But, as I told my family, don't cast aside these bores and pains, because there's a book in everyone, and many have within them several books. But if a boring beggar has only one book, and you are forced to be with him, seek out his book and you will have a rewarding experience. Do not write people off.

If Greek tragedies question the free will of the human condition; if the Bible/Koran/Jewish Torah provides us with a moral compass, then good literature teaches us about the human condition. If we start as idealists, become realists and die cynics then we have possibly led a full life. Some do the reverse, usually through finding a faith. In my case the winds and waves have sent me buffeted from place to place, and my experiences and reflections attended by my moods have driven me, and now I have set down in writing a little of the story of my being.

I should close with an obvious admission, that I have forgotten more than I remembered, and I hope have not offended too many by their omission nor denied the reader a lot more tales; likewise with those that I have remembered and featured herein, I trust that my memory is not too wide of the truth. Who knows, I may even have the time to recall more and recount even more if I am granted a remission. One step at a time; my chemo course ends in a few days – April 2021: my deadline for this memoir. Nothing concentrates the mind better than a deadline, in this case a word to be read literally.

Please remember this little book is not an autobiography. It would not stand scrutiny as such and would compromise my educational discipline of historical rigour. This is a 'memoir', an indulgence, a friend to accompany me on an unchosen and uncertain journey. I hope that the many of you who have urged me to write a more breezy account of some of my life's diversions, and the resulting stories, have found the journey as much fun to read as it has been for me to write – it has been a friend to me and helped me smile through many a nauseous moment.

Please note too that for better or worse I have used real names wherever possible. I have been encouraged to 'write down' some of my adventures by several of you. I should also say at this point that I hope that I have avoided telling the *'when I was in...'* stories on return from any trip. I know how unwanted and boring this is. In doing so now, I can say to those of you where the cap fits 'it's your fault for bullying me into writing this now'. It has taken something dramatic to bring it all about. It has proved to be an absorbing companion in the last several months of some chemo agony.

I do have to thank a number of people who have helped me see this project through to completion. Particularly Jonathan Barr for patiently sorting out all my scribbles into something publishable from draft to print. Also to Anita Dennis for her selfless typing skills converting awful scribbles into something legible. Then to dear Dr Roger Kojecky, my old school chum, for keeping me grounded and 'at it' when I was feeling lousy and who proof-read this work, making many suggestions for better expression. Steve Harvey, my colleague at Moulton Bicycles has been a constant source of solutions, like how I might present the maps, and also suggesting alternate expressions, which I probably should have heeded. Susannah Burton kindly turned my vision for the cover into reality and for this I am most grateful. My thanks also to my neighbours at Kingston Hall whose technical dexterity has saved me much frustration in fighting with my 'steam' computer and doing so during this period of 'lockdown'.

My thanks also to my many friends, those I have mentioned and the many more I have not. Their love and loyalty, their letters and their support have helped make this project an enjoyable diversion, kept me positive and made this a rewarding part of my life. Above all I thank my family, my wife and children, my grandchildren, Ninoo, and of course my dear Mum and Dad – I hope they're not too ashamed of their little 'Jungle-Wallah'.

Post Script: *As this memoir goes to print I have just received news that 'the chemo has done its job' and I am in remission. Long may this last but it has been the catalyst I needed to record some of my memories. So 'thank you' to all the team of lymphoma specialists led by Dr Nicolas Martinez-Calle.*

Appendix 1: Macnaughtan Family Geneology

A SHORT

GENEALOGICAL ACCOUNT

OF THE

Family of MACNAUGHTAN, of that Ilk,

(*That is to say, Chief of the Clan MACNAUGHTAN.*)

THIS Family is of very great Antiquity; but, through the loss of Records by the Calamity of the Times, their Origin cannot be so well ascertained. The First of the Family (who appears on Record) is GILLECHRIST MACNAUGHTAN, who obtained a Grant from ALEXANDER the Third, King of Scotland, in the Year of our LORD 1267, of being Captain and Constable of the Castle of Freuch-Island, in Loch-ow, in Argyle-Shire. The Family flourished for many hundred Years: severals of them were Knights-Bachelors; they married with the first Families in the Highlands of Scotland; their old Title was MacNaughtan of Dundarave, an old Castle on Loch-Fine side, in Argyle-Shire. From this Family all the MacNaughts in Ireland, and all the MacNaughts, MacNitts, MacNees, MacNivens, MacNuiers, MacNights, and MacBrains in Scotland are descended. The MacNaughts and MacNitts, in Dumbarton, are the nearest in Blood to the Family. The MacNaughtans in Glenlion, and in Breadalbane in Perthshire, are sprung from a Bastard of the Family of MacNaughtans of Killquhrahty in Galloway, who has an Estate of L. 500 Sterling yearly. In the counties of Antrim and Down, in Ireland, the MacNaughts have Estates of L. 500, L. 600, and L. 1000 Sterling yearly. If the Luss MacNaughtans can prove their Descent, they certainly represent the Family.

Their Arms are two Roe-Bucks for Supporters, a Castle with three Towers for a Crest; they carry quarterly, First and Fourth, two Castles, embattled, (that is to say) with Bartizans; Second and Third, a Rampant Lion, a Galley or Ship, Sable or Black, her Sails furled up, her Oars in Action, a Hand grasping a Heart paleways, (that is) upright, for carrying the Heart of King Robert the Bruce to Jerusalem in a Silver Shrine, on account of his murdering Sir John Cuming in the Church of Dumfries, when at Prayers, in order to make Atonement for the Murder, agreeable to the Orders of the Church of Rome. Their Motto is, I hope in God This Family had large possessions in the Shires of Argyle, Perth, Dumbarton, Ross, Inverness, and Murrayshire; but owing to their attachment to the unhappy Family of Stuart, they forfeited, almost, all.

The Reason of the Roe-Bucks is, the Family were hereditable Forresters, in Ben-buy, to the Kings of Scotland; the reason of the Castle is, they were Captains and Constables of the Castle of Dundarave; the reason of the Ship is, to shew their Descent from Germany; the Reason of the Lion Rampant is, to shew their Bravery; and the Reason of the Motto is, to shew their Zeal for the Religion of the then Times. Their Livery is Red and White; the Red Colour shows Bravery, and the White signifies purity of Heart.

Appendix 2: Notes on Socio Economic Observations following visit to Japan, 21st – 30th April 1979

The policies designed to change Japan from a poor, rural society with a low life expectancy and poorly educated community into an industrial society, highly educated and wealthy with a high life expectancy, have brought about their own problems threatening social cohesion and an ability to compete economically.

The world recession since 1974 has not been a serious threat to Japan, if it were, Japan's exports could not have held up in nearly every field of her endeavour as they have done. While Japan's bill for petrol has increased sharply over the last five years, her bill for all other industrial raw materials, including petrol and petrol-based product, has actually decreased as a percentage of the gross national product. This is the major contributing cause to Japan's balance of payments surplus. Since Japan imports nearly all her raw materials, with petrol being only 10% of the whole, Japan has actually benefited from a high petroleum price and from the resulting depression in the prices of all other raw materials.

The seeds of disquiet, however, spring not from any external problem or imposition but rather from the inherent social structure.

After World War Two three fifths of the Japanese lived on the land and farmed, and still they had to import rice. Japan therefore, gave first priority to higher rice output. Now only one tenth of the population lives on the land and the output of rice has more than doubled to the point where, in the last six years, there is an unsaleable surplus. Indeed, the less suitable a farmer's land is for growing rice the higher the subsidy the farmer gets – all stemming from a legitimate fear of want some twenty-five years ago. But yet, food prices must be the highest in the world in Japan.

The fall in infant mortality from the 1920s and a pre- and immediate post-war high birth rate has led Japan to base their economic strengths on the availability of large numbers of manual workers. Around 1955 the 'baby boom' turned into a 'baby bust', and now the birth rate is at, or below, par.

In 1970 Japan was the youngest of all developed countries - people over 65 represented less than 7% of the total population – i.e. one out of 15 people were over 65. (In France the proportion was 12%.) By 1990 it is estimated that Japan will be close to 15% of the population over 65, i.e. one out of three over 65. It will therefore turn into being one of the oldest populations of the developed countries. The majority reaching retirement age now are manual workers, and the majority entering the work force today are university graduates with managerial or professional expectations. The reservoir of farm or factory labourers has now dried up.

Wages are based on seniority – length of service. A new entrant, however highly educated, receives a third of what the same employee doing an identical job receives after 25 years service. Careers are linked to education. Japan is as complete a meritocracy as exists anywhere, thus labourers, manual workers etc. are those who finish schooling at 15. At the other extreme, managers and professionals are only drawn from university graduates. There is practically no cross-over from one group to another. Pre-war some 4% went to university, and a half went to work after finishing school at 15. Now, more than half go to university and practically every Japanese of either sex goes on to the equivalent of sixth form education – and Japan's social policies push heavily towards the expansion of college education still.

Under the seniority wage system productivity automatically increases as more young people are employed, and the labour costs of companies depend on the age distribution of their workforce. For every year by which the average age in a plant goes up the plant's labour costs rise by some 6%.

This explains why Japanese put their emphasis on sales volume at the expense of profitability. Japan therefore needs a growth rate of 6% to maintain her competitive position in the world, but this rate cannot be achieved in the traditional industries on the basis of available manpower and existing retirement policies. Retirement age was set at 55 at a time when life expectancy was only some 50 years. The life expectancy is now in the middle seventies but the retirement age remains 55.

With an increasing retired population, savings in capital formation decrease. Now a larger and larger share of personal savings are transferred to maintain elders. Older people do not save, they consume. The Japanese economy however, has been based on the assumption of a very large savings rate.

It is interesting to note the current change in industrial competitiveness. It is obvious that Japan should now start to concentrate on high technology items and farm out to low labour-cost countries the labour-intensive industries, and this tendency is well under way, but it has gone further than that. Some years ago the Ministry of Internal Trade and Industry encouraged the export of entire manufacturing plants rather than of the products of such plants. Japan is also prepared to accept payment for these plants with products from the plant.

This will increasingly mean that the surplus of Japanese managers and professionals will find an outlet in designing, building and managing consumer goods plants in developing countries, whose products are going to be paid for by their own output and sold to the Japanese consumer in Japan. As examples one can cite the petro-chemical plant in Algeria, the several industries that Japanese money is investing into Taiwan, and now perhaps the Sino-Japanese treaty will open up new possibilities of production in China.

The alternative to this development is for Japan to dump high cost, labour-intensive products at a loss in foreign markets, exports therefore taking on the traditional cloak of being surplus, and high profits being applied to sales on a very large home market in order to maintain any company's viability. It is partly because of this latter concern therefore, that Japan has maintained a highly protective home industry.

Nonetheless, given Japan's awareness of her social problem, what to the foreigner looks like economic protection appears to the Japanese as self defence of Japanese society. However much tariff barriers and political words of encouragement for free trade combine into making an apparent open society in Japan for imports, it is difficult to see that this will have any real effect in altering the balance of payments situation. There is really no need for Japan to import anything other than raw products because all its requirements are met from the home market. The integration of businesses and especially the bicycle business mean that any foreign importer cannot provide the total service that the current supplier of any material does to, say, a manufacturer; such things as testing and research which are very often combined hand in hand in a central institution. Indeed, leading manufacturers not only work hand in glove with leading parts specialists for new development and technologies, but when they quote delivery times the hour of requirement is specified and not just the date.

If all the foregoing is correct, then this reduces the requirement for foreign goods to an elitist market, a market that wants something different just for the sake of being different or in order to say that it is from another country. This, by definition is a very small sector of the market and because it is small and the imports tend to be small the importer and trading company tend to put a very large mark up on the items to cover the costs for handling such a small turnover.

In conclusion, the social and economic background of Japan does not provide an encouraging climate for the overseas exporter. On the other hand, exporters can be blamed for too readily accepting the situation and not promoting their products sufficiently by advertising and the usual paraphernalia of creating a demand, for Japan is such a large market that a small percentage share is worthwhile.

If this can go on behind a political climate of pressure from developed countries on Japan, and a more responsible attitude of Japan's industry towards the resentment that it is presently building up, especially in Europe, then perhaps a more balanced trading position will result. It is hard not to conclude, however, that this will require something of a social revolution.

Japan has proved its ability to do a complete about turn, so one cannot ever rule out the possibility of this happening again.

Appendix 3: London Chamber of Commerce Breakfast Meeting, 31st March 2010

For 47 years I have been exporting, or importing when living overseas, goods of British manufacture. The mantra in the early 1960s was 'the balance of payments'. This mantra spurred me to move against the tide, moving from the South-East of England up to the Midlands. I have been swimming against the tide ever since because I am in the UK engineering and manufacturing sector.

It is somewhat galling to be here today in front of a senior politician and in our capital to sell UK limited manufacturing when it is these very people who have extolled the virtues of the City against having a balanced economy.

Our backs are now against the wall. As we look around British engineering and manufacturing we find the infrastructure has gone; there is a huge shortage of engineering skill, and now a salary expectation from university graduates set by the financial and service sector that is unrealistic in world manufacturing terms.

Where is the steel and aluminium industry that I joined as a graduate trainee in Tube Investments – a company that was one of the barometers of UK Limited's health? It doesn't exist today.

I am involved with three companies, all major exporters. In Raleigh International 100% of what I do is overseas. When I joined Raleigh it was the largest producer of bicycles in the world; it employed some 12,000 people and made and sold some 4.2 million bikes p.a. exporting over 70% of them to over 144 countries. Even in the last recession it exported £100 million worth of goods all made in England. In 2003 it ceased manufacture in the UK, and today imports some £35 million in continuing devalued pounds. Raleigh will be importing its way through the current long recession.

The other two companies where I am a non-exec director are Pashley Cycles in Stratford on Avon and Brooks in Smethwick, Birmingham. These two companies export 95% of their production and both have an order book of well over 12 months. Their largest markets are Japan and Germany. Exporting for them is not the problem; making is. They cannot get the skills. My personal attempts to entice two solid riveters back to Brooks, one a 53 year-old taking early retirement in the early 1990s and another now a taxi driver, were unsuccessful. Moulton Bicycles has a lead time of 18 months at the moment – it is unable to get braziers. Just think Raleigh used to take on 100 apprentices a year in the 1960s.

Contrast the UK bike business with that in Germany. I visit DCW three to four times a year in northern Germany, and I talk to them most weeks. They manufacture over 400,000 bicycles a year; customers are welcomed to go round their factory where the pride in workmanship and attention to quality is exceptional. The value of 'Made in Germany' is real, and overseas demand at a premium. Over the same period 'Made in England' has a doubtful reputation. Banks in Continental Europe support companies on their order take – a huge help to exporters where the cash return between buying raw material to receiving payment for finished product is long.

George Cowcher, CEO of East Midlands Chamber came back recently from Afghanistan where he saw huge construction work etc. being done by American, German and Italian companies, but not a British company. I know the Afghan market, and have crawled all over the place, it is impossible to sell into that country easily because of the difficulty in getting paid, and the ECGD of yesteryear does not exist. The current business there is being done by governments, and it would seem that American integration between politics and business is closer than our own.

When I started exporting, our embassies overseas were hugely disappointing. The irony is that today just when our exporting has declined, so our embassies' ability to assist has improved. But if you noticed in the *Sunday Times* a couple of weeks ago, Lord Berkley raised in Parliament the question why it was that BMW were supplying the bikes to the British Olympics with zero UK content. Lord Davis replied that the bikes were likely to have EU content. I would reply to Lord Davis that in fact this is most unlikely. Can you see Raleigh getting the bike contract if the Olympics were held in Berlin?

Another thought: Dyson speaks of UK Limited's need to go high tech, this after he has outsourced his vacuum cleaners to Malaysia; and I would even dispute this. The success of those British companies in the manufacturing sector is where they have found their niche. Look at Burberry, look at Brooks; my advice would be to old brand names, if you have lost your manufacturing base then keep control of your customer base and intellectual property, and try and serve the latter by resourcing, and then await the day to re-own your company with local manufacture when the time arises. In fact, I would argue the time is now right for Raleigh to start on a modest scale manufacturing in the UK, making bicycles that reflect quality and value, and the spirit of Britain. We have a huge heritage and a history which the world admires. So to old companies and brand names I would exhort them to repossess their past and try to re-invent their company as we have with Brooks.

We do have clever designers and entrepreneurs, but today they are encouraged, when they start up, to see how they can avoid tax, they register their companies in the British Virgin Islands, they even become a Non-Dom and often pay little/zero tax. UK Limited loses out all ways.

May I summarise. Let's get our country better integrated between government, city, manufacturing and banks. Let's re-establish an infrastructure to get back basic skills which in turn will bring back pride in workmanship; let's sort out the tax issues. Above all we must get the economy strong. A weak pound does nothing for export – this is a myth. It is stability which leads to confidence, an ability to plan and invest and grow. Finally, the world still needs a quality of leadership which those well and humbly educated in Britain's unique and best schools still possess. The world, outside of Europe is still there with a place for us in it. We have lost our way and need to find it again. 'Europe' has been a distraction and limiting; Britain was once worldly with worldly, educated, people. Politicians and parastatal organisations are our masters and not our servants to our mutual loss. Let's define our direction as a nation and individually and then define the tools we need and let's get behind enterprise and let us boys who know how to do the job overseas do it.

Appendix 4: Speech at Eurobike 2012

Welcome and thanks for coming to our annual event. I managed to avoid making a speech last year and therefore avoided upsetting anyone, so I am making up for it tonight as I have an important message and thank you for attending in such large numbers.

What a world we live in. If the global crisis continues by the end of this year only two banks will be left operational – the blood bank and the sperm bank – and before you know it these two will merge, and the whole place will be full of bloody wankers!

I believed I was going to be announcing at Eurobike my retirement. Clearly, I trained my successor, Gerry Appleton, too well as he was offered a job with Rolls Royce he couldn't refuse.

So first may I introduce you formally to the new International team: Greg Vanner has taken over from Gerry. Greg comes with a strong background and direct experience in the bicycle industry with both the independent bike dealers (IBD) and retail accounts.

At the beginning of this year Raleigh International Limited (RIL) took over responsibility for all of Diamondback Europe (DBE) and many of you here today will attest to the energy and speed in which Duncan McCann has taken on this tough role as becomes a tough product. A year ago, RIL took on the services of Lisa Barclay as we were becoming more involved with exporting and in particular DBE.

So, from just one full time employee five years ago, we now have four. I have agreed to stay on as long as they will put up with me and can be of service.

The reason for this expansion of personnel is you.

When Raleigh ceased production of bicycles in Nottingham in 2002 we put the flame up on licensing the brand. I learnt after too many years at Sturmey-Archer the folly of trying to sell anything, and decided instead never to lose an order. So, each year, or on the appointment of a licensee, I simply ask 'what does Raleigh mean to its potential customer in your market?' Provided this can be properly answered, we then went about expressing this in the product and to the extent we succeeded – we sold. Where Raleigh had little meaning we had to create brand recognition; where we have done neither we have failed.

The best examples of the first point, i.e., giving the market what it expects and wants from Raleigh are sitting here today – Germany, Denmark and Japan. The best example of where Raleigh had little brand recognition, but where it has been created, is also here in the form of Tuncay Cettinelli and his colleague Petri Koski from Finland.

What a huge job too has been done in Oz and NZ by Sheppards in positioning Raleigh in its very difficult place in the middle of the marketing triangle, and year on year coming up with a continuity of sales in what has been a declining market. Or PacBrands in Oz and NZ with Diamondback, who had to address a significant market change and then repositioned the Diamondback brand resulting in an enormous increase in both volume and profitability.

Perhaps in 2012 the toughest job of anyone has been in South Africa. Our partners – Probike – were Raleigh for some 30 years. SA was the single biggest unit seller of Raleigh outside of the UK and North America, and overnight we lost them to a competitor with whose business practice we could not identify. Tonight I am able to thank the two guys who have worked their butt off to maintain Raleigh's dominant hold of the SA market – Marc Ackerman and Stewart Miller.

Raleigh was a huge force in the Indian market, a market of 14 million bikes p. a., and had its own factory in Assansol, near Calcutta. The Raleigh name was subject to a silly and very Indian court case, which lasted 20 years, whereby ownership was claimed by no less than the local government of Bengal. We finally won this case, and after a false start we appointed Rajesh Kalra of Naren International from the middle of this year. He received his first sample order of 2,000 bicycles at the beginning of this month. He has spent all of August travelling the length and breadth of the huge sub-continent ensuring that the repeat orders, which he has now placed, were exactly in line with what the market needs from a Raleigh. Initially he is not going for the highly competitive top end of the market; he is getting back to Raleigh's heritage of being the 'discerning peoples bicycle' and going for the middle ground; and then we will use the Raleigh USA range to put the brand's aspirations clearly at the top end.

I admit we have not always given the support back at base to all our licensees. I am particularly thinking of Israel, where Matzman-Merutz made us the number one selling brand, and we should have done more to support his pleas for help in product and promotion. I want to thank you tonight, Eyal, for holding on so loyally. We certainly never forget you, even if you feel we sometimes ignore you.

I cannot mention Israel without mentioning Iran, where literally our oldest distributor in the world for 93 years, the Tabarrok family, has kept alive the Raleigh name in a market where the world has tried to stop them from doing so – thank you Khosro. We are proud of you.

We have the Del Santo family with us from Argentina. Not only welcome, but let me tell others that Raleighs are manufactured in Argentina and today are the biggest selling brand in that market. You are a valued part of the Raleigh family and it's good to have you with us.

I cannot mention all of you tonight, but, do you know that together, we have put Raleigh and Diamondback back on the map over the last ten years, and are now selling in over 144 countries. Through you we have succeeded in returning double digit growth year on year for the past ten years, and the great news is that we have so much more to do in literally every market.

Tonight is special, with effect from now we not only turn over a new page, but we have all become Dutchmen. Accell has bought Raleigh in its entirety. No one better than the Dutch appreciate the worth of that grande dame of bicycles – Raleigh. To them now the baton is passed in this relay race of life.

We have their top executives with us tonight and while you know them may I formally introduce Rene Takens, the CEO; Jeroen Snijders Blok, Chief Operating Officer; and Hielke Sybesma, Chief Financial Officer.

Gentlemen, with your help and backing, and our know-how in this room, we hope to make you proud of your recent acquisition.

Printed in Great Britain
by Amazon

74457612R00140